Acclaim for this book:

"This book is yet more proof that Jonathan Ames's life is infinitely more interesting than mine. And yes, yours."
—Chip Kidd, author of *The Cheese Monkeys*

"*My Less Than Secret Life* is the kind of book you devour. Jonathan Ames guides the reader on a curvy emotional excursion, from exquisite to filthy to thoughtful to heartbreaking. Without taking a breath. I couldn't put it down."
—Maggie Estep, author of *Diary of an Emotional Idiot.*

And those preceding it:

"Jonathan Ames has always been one of my favorite contemporary writers, both for his limpid and elegant Lost Generation prose style and for his utterly fearless commitment to the most demanding psychosexual comedies."—Rick Moody

"Shy exhibitionist Jonathan Ames has all the qualities it takes to be a great writer: he's fearless, neurotic, worldly, tortured, a unique stylist, excruciatingly honest, slightly creepy, polite (yet attuned to the sham of etiquette), a killer comedian with a healthy dose of self-loathing, tender, and—most important of all—mordantly obsessed with his own penis."—Bret Easton Ellis

"The individual episodes, chapters, rhapsodies—call them what you will—in *What's Not to Love?* are so beguiling, so insouciant, so seemingly breathed onto the page, that it's impossible to miss the fact that the memoir, book, collection as a whole has the formal elegance and perfect wholeness of one of Ames' two extraordinary novels."
—Jonathan Lethem

"Jonathan Ames has displayed an unusual ability to take crack-smoking, balding and Oedipal fixation and whip them up into an elegant, comic meringue . . . His lapidary prose style rapidly seduces the reader into taking his pleasures with him . . . There is also a light beauty to the ephemeral, a beauty Ames conjures up in countless joyous scatological and ejaculatory moments."
—*The New York Times* Book Review

"The self-deprecating Ames is a cheerfully gracious neurotic, which makes laughing at his humor feel easy, uncomplicated and unexpectedly joyful."—*Salon*

Also by Jonathan Ames

I Pass Like Night

The Extra Man

What's Not to Love?

My Less Than Secret Life

A Diary • Fiction • Essays

by

Jonathan Ames

THUNDER'S MOUTH PRESS
NEW YORK

MY LESS THAN SECRET LIFE: A Diary Fiction Essays

© 2002 by Jonathan Ames

Published by
Thunder's Mouth Press
An Imprint of Avalon Publishing Group Incorporated
161 William St., 16th Floor
New York, NY 10038

Library of Congress Control Number: 2002103624

ISBN 1-56025-375-4

9 8 7 6 5 4 3 2

Designed by Paul Paddock

Printed in the United States of America
Distributed by Publishers Group West

for you

The author would like to thank and acknowledge Patrick Bucklew, Ava Gerber, David Leslie, Dan O'Connor, Rosalie Siegel, Russ Smith, John Strausbaugh, and all the editors and publishers of the magazines where my writing has appeared.

Contents

NO LONGER 'THE HERRING WONDER'

PART II: fic'tion, n. Feigning, invention; thing feigned or imagined, invented statement or narrative; literature consisting of such narrative, esp. novels, whence~IST (3) (-shon-) n.; conventionally accepted falsehood. (esp. legal, polite,~). Hence~AL (-shon-) a. [F, f. L fictionem (prec.,-ION)]

PART III: A True Crime Story: The Nista Affair

Nansy Siesel/The New York Times

F.B.I S

Would

Continued from

the government. The
reveal the evidence c
it until the 16-page
partly declassified a
the Justice Departm
One of Mr. Ahmed
is M. Bograd, a staff
American Civil Lib
(Washington, said
showed "just how Iz
the secret evidence
prejudicial it had
Ahmed's case.
  Russell A. Bergerc
man for the Immigr
ralization Service, s
did not discuss "part
still pending before
sa id it would also be i
Comment on evidenc
the F.B.I. A bureau
SePh A. Valiquette, h
The document was
declassified, so it was

The Art of the Fight

It was a match made in heaven for fans of performance art and boxing last night at the Angel Orensanz
Foundation for the Arts on the Lower East Side. In
the light trunks, David Leslie, the Impact Addict,
beat Jonathan Ames, a writer fighting as the Herring
Wonder, in "Box Opera," a P.S. 122 production.

Part I:
The Herring Wonder:
A Diary of Travel,
Boxing, and Some Sex

A Very Brief Introduction

Part I of this book are the columns I wrote for *New York Press* from April of 1999 until February 2000. My column was called "City Slicker" and it was a record of my adventures, humiliations, and musings. Essentially, it was a public diary, which is how I am presenting it here, entitled: "The Herring Wonder: A Diary of Travel, Boxing, and Some Sex."

I began the column in 1997 and I collected the first two years of it in my memoir *What's Not to Love?: The Adventures of a Mildly Perverted Young Writer.* But you needn't have read that book, though I don't discourage it, to get a kick—I hope—out of this "Herring Wonder" phase of my escapades.

I want to let you know that in the pages to come, you'll see that sometimes I make reference to the column, as well as directly address the readers of the column, as I am addressing you now. I did this because it became an odd fact of my life that for almost three years, I was revealing things about myself publicly that I probably shouldn't have even revealed privately, so the act of the writing the column became at times a subject (well, more of an aside) of the column itself.

My hope for this "Herring Wonder" section of *My Less Than Secret Life* is that the immediacy of reading the columns will come across—this feeling of following someone's odd, lonely, and depraved life as they lead it. But also by having them all linked together in a book, I hope that a cumulative effect will occur, that a story will emerge, a story, to quote my own subtitle, of traveling, boxing, and some sex.

Jesus Christ Doesn't Sound Like a Jewish Name
April 27, 1999

I am writing this from Mexico where not much has happened, except for an adventure that involves Catholic schoolgirl outfits and a beautiful lesbian threesome, but before I recount this south-of-the border phenomenon, I want to jot down my final impressions of my recent European jaunt.

The first eleven days of my trip, I was in Heidelberg, Venice, and Florence. In Heidelberg, I successfully performed my one-man show "Oedipussy" to an appreciative English-speaking crowd at the German-American Institute. From there, for touristic reasons, I went to Venice, which drove me mad with its beauty and made me want to be in love, which is always very depressing. The human heart is terribly flawed. We yearn for love and then when we do love we invariably pick someone who won't love us back. I think what we must yearn for then is the depression that precedes love. It's much more popular. So many more people tell me they're depressed than tell me they're in love.

So, handicapped with my own melancholy, I went down to Florence and had a drinking relapse, alcohol being the original Prozac. But alcohol doesn't work very well, probably not as well as Prozac, something about it being a depressant, rather than an antidepressant, and while intoxicated with booze and sadness I almost threw myself into the Arno, the muddy orange river that bisects Florence. This, when I was sober the next day, I perceived to be a bit rash, so I got back on the water wagon, and made a quick exit from Florence and journeyed to the small Tuscan city of Lucca.

Lucca is an absolutely beautiful little town with a perfectly intact several-hundred-year-old wall surrounding it, which at one time was the equivalent of a Star Wars defense, that and the moat. But walls and moats are out of fashion. They're from a simpler time. Violence was more available to everyone; now you need a gun permit or a degree from MIT. Man's brutality has stayed constant, but his methods have become more sophisticated.

The top of the wall, where sentries once patrolled, is wide enough to serve as this elevated park and is excellent for strolling and bicycling and thinking about one's life.

I walked around the entire wall—about three miles—and while I promenaded I took in the surrounding mountains and their white peaks, which one thinks are made of snow but the white is actually marble—Tuscan marble-topped mountains. And as I indicated above, I considered my life, all thirty-five years of it, and came to the usual conclusion: I have no idea what's going on, but I hope I figure things out before it's too late.

During my walk, I met a nice older woman who allowed me to pet and cuddle her dog, who was a small, soft-haired brown little mutt with enchanting eyes. He was named Otto, which didn't strike me as very Italian, but I didn't question his mistress on her choice of *prenom* for the pooch. Otto and I became quick friends. I got down on my hands and knees and put my face into his neck. He in turn kissed my face and ears and then he lay submissively on his back with his paws in the air, indicating to me that I could take him in the missionary position or scratch his belly. Wherever I go, dogs love me and I love them. I can always count on the canine world for affection.

I left Otto, which wasn't easy, and I descended from the ancient wall and penetrated the city, where I visited Lucca's oldest church, which is famous for housing a wooden sculpture of Jesus on the cross. It is called *Il Volto Santo* and is believed to have been made by an artisan who actually witnessed the crucifixion. The sculpture is kept in an ornate vault with windows all around it so that one can peer in and gaze upon the Christian Savior.

I noted to myself that this rendering of Jesus gave him an extremely Semitic nose. In fact, it was so Semitic that it looked eerily like my own Semitic nose. I don't think I have schizophrenia with a dash of Messiah complex, but I couldn't help but note the remarkable resemblance between myself and JC, at least in profile. So I did a little drawing of the *Il Volto Santo* in my journal and added this remark: "He was Jewish and he looks Jewish, but Jesus Christ doesn't sound like a Jewish name, but back then I guess it was."

In the late afternoon, I took a bus to Pisa and saw the leaning tower, which is very amusing to look at. As soon as I saw it, I laughed. It's like a visual tickle—this absurd tower listing to the right. So I took a few photos of people taking pictures of the tower. I did that a lot on my trip, since I was traveling alone and was often quite lonely—I would photograph people photographing one another in front of famous locations. This way I'd get the famous thing but also have people in my pictures, so it wouldn't seem like I had traveled by myself. But for whom I concocted this ruse is a mystery, since I never show my pictures to any one. My mother keeps wonderful albums, but I'm too lazy for things like albums. I put all my photos in an enormous box, thinking that someday I'll make an album of my life. But who would I show such an album to? And who would care? Do I care? And yet there I am, taking pictures of the leaning tower of Pisa, pictures that no one will ever see. I wonder if the people that convince us to take photos are the same ones who get us to smoke cigarettes, pay taxes, and shoot heroin.

Anyway, after about an hour of staring at the tower, I then dragged my bag to the other side of Pisa, where I was to catch an overnight train to Paris. On my way to the station, I passed a young, lovely dark-haired transvestite who was walking in the opposite direction. She was in a red mini-skirt and leather jacket and enormous platform boots. Women and transvestites all over the world, I've noticed, are wearing these shoes with swollen rubber soles. They look like Frankenstein's boots, which doesn't bother me aesthetically, but I am concerned that such shoes are dangerous for the ankle and the health of the female spine.

Anyway, this transvestite intrigued me and since I had time to kill before my train, I decided to tail her, especially since I was reading so many Raymond Chandler novels during my trip. I was kind of pretending half the time that I was a private detective, sort of like Don Quixote deluding himself into thinking he was a knight from reading so many books of chivalry.

Thus, playing Philip Marlowe, I let her have a good

sixty feet on me and I limped after her, my bag weighing me down. And as I followed unnoticed behind her, I was amazed to witness how proudly she marched through the streets while everyone turned and looked and laughed at her. What courage she had! And what carriage! Well, she is a queen—good posture and a strong sense of self is to be expected.

I followed her to a cafe and hid in a nearby doorway. She sat right at the front of the crowded outdoor terrace and sipped her coffee, nobly oblivious to the glances and snickering that she provoked; this was Pisa, after all, transvestites aren't that common yet, unlike in Manhattan, where even the mayors are often cross-dressers. Then she left the cafe and I followed her some more and watched her adjust her lipstick in the reflection of a store window. She had a full rich red mouth. I wished I could kiss her.

Then she started walking again and went through an old Roman arch where young European vagabonds were juggling and playing guitars and begging for coins. They also had some dogs, which made it look to me like a good life. Juggling, communal sex, and dogs—ideal. I was very tempted to meet these dogs and get some free affection, but I didn't want to lose the transvestite.

On her way past the vagabonds, she elegantly dropped some change into an open guitar case—she, whom everyone mocked, was generous and regal—and as I followed a few paces behind, I also dropped some change, wanting to mimic her kindness, thinking it might bring me good luck. Then she disappeared into a building and I wondered what she was doing in there, but there was no way to know and I didn't stake her out. I lashed myself mentally for not trying to talk to her. Maybe we could have had an espresso together. I peered at the building that had swallowed her—what was she up to?—and then I stopped playing private detective and headed back to the station.

It was a thirteen-hour train ride and I shared a tiny sleeping car with four Chinese tourists and a young Indian man. There were three beds on each side of the compartment; they were like protruding shelves, or like bunk beds plus one. For some reason, the young Indian behaved toward me as if he were my porter. He insisted on stowing my bag for me and making my bed as I fumbled with the meager sheet and thin blanket. He had lovely petroleum-black hair, parted right down the middle, which I admired greatly, since the only good middle part I've ever come across is the one F. Scott Fitzgerald has in his author photo.

I thanked this Indian boy for his help, and as we lay in our bunks, he spoke to me at great, somewhat tedious length in his British colonial accent about his uncle, whom he was going to visit in Paris so that he could help him with his store. I endured his monologue as a way to repay him for his help with my bed.

Eventually, he drifted off. I listened to his shallow, innocent breaths, glad that he was done talking so I could nod off myself, but sleep didn't come to me and I was feeling quite flatulent, which was embarrassing. The air in our compartment was very close and I thought my Chinese companions and my young Indian friend would all know that it was the American who was leaking gas. This made me feel some national pride. I didn't want to further my country's reputation for boorish behavior, so I decided to go stand in the corridor and pass wind there and read Joyce's *Ulysses*, which I thought would fatigue me so I could go back and lie down in the compartment. Then I could at least be unconscious while I farted and rudely poisoned my berth-mates.

As I stood in the corridor and read, waiting for Joyce to induce stupefaction, I witnessed a touching scene. We pulled into Genoa and a group of adolescents, obviously on some kind of field trip to Paris, boarded the train. And seeing them off were their peasant-appearing parents— large ancient-looking mothers and stoic drawn-faced fathers smoking cigarettes. The mothers had tears in their eyes, and the young boys and girls when they got in the train hung out the windows and waved and screamed goodbye, as if they were parting forever.

Tears actually welled up in my eyes; the emotions on that platform were as raw as an onion. I could feel the mothers' rip of separation from their children, and as we pulled away, I wanted someone to be sad that *I* was leaving, and so caught up in it all I waved to this one large woman with iron-colored hair, and she reflexively waved back and then she caught herself. There was a questioning looking in her eye—who's this strange man on the train with my child and why is he waving at me? I was worried she would think I was a pedophile so I tried to convey gentleness in my eyes to reassure her, which I hope it did, and then I went into my berth and slept.

In the morning, I was relieved to see that my berth-mates were still alive, that I hadn't murdered them by leaking gas, like a car running its motor in a garage and killing everyone in the house. My young Indian porter was in good spirits, excited to see his uncle, and like a magic trick there were five Chinamen instead of four. Two emerged from one of the bunks, except one of them wasn't a Chinaman but a Chinawoman, with long beautiful hair, grooved like an old record. In the most narrow of cots, a couple had been coupling. Or at least holding on to one another. Incredible. If I had poisoned those two in their sleep, it would have been like a Chinese Romeo and Juliet.

In the breakfast car, I met my own Juliet. She was a blonde Frenchwoman with eerie blue eyes. They were movie-star blue, Paul Newman blue. She and I were the only adults having coffee. The rest of the diners were the excited Italian adolescents from Genoa who had been ripped from their mother's breasts the night before.

I managed, with my poor-to-middling grasp of French, to procure from her a life story. I'll call her Juliet. She was a ballerina who suffered a tendon injury in her ankle, cutting her career short, and now she traveled with a French circus, doing stunts on horses and being cut in half by the magician. She was in her mid-thirties and a single mother of a five-year-old-girl, who was looked after by Juliet's mother while she was on the road with the circus.

It was a little bit of a sad story, but also a courageous story. She was very bright and full of life. When I told her I was a writer she said that her favorite American novelist was Paul Auster. I had heard he was enormously popular in France, sort of the Jerry Lewis of literature. I told her I was also a big fan of Auster's, but my French was too limited to explain to her that he had read my senior thesis at Princeton, a novella that was the basis for my first novel, and that he generously had given me an A.

I did tell her, though, that one time several years ago, I saw Auster walking on Astor Place, which almost sounds like Auster place, a kind of Austerian coincidence, and I approached him. We had never met at Princeton; he was simply the reader for my thesis. He was moving rapidly, like one of his characters who stomp around Manhattan losing their mind, but I caught up to him. "Excuse me for bothering you," I said. "I just wanted to say hello. I'm Jonathan Ames. You read my thesis at Princeton."

"I know who you are," he said omnipotently and mysteriously with his famous dark Jewish eyes taking me in for an instant. We shook hands. "Nice of you to say hello," he said, and then he kept walking.

Juliet liked this story, maybe it seduced her, because she asked me to dinner that night. We parted at the train station and she recommended a hotel near Champs de Mars—the long park by the Eiffel Tower—where I could find a cheap room. She picked me up at eight P.M. that night in her little French mini-car and we had dinner near Invalides. Halfway through the meal, I had exhausted my entire repertoire of French and my brain spasmed and collapsed. I stopped understanding a word she said, but I nodded and raised my eyebrows and faked it.

We went for a walk along the Seine and I was torn with indecision. Should I kiss her? Did she want me to? I usually apply the principle that if I want to kiss, the woman usually wants to kiss . . . but I just wasn't sure. She was very beautiful. A circus performer. A onetime ballerina. So I didn't kiss her. I put my arm through her arm and we strolled. That little bit of contact was very nice.

She drove me back to the hotel and wanted to come up to my room, so I could show her a picture of my son—at dinner she had shown me pictures of her daughter. When I went to get my key at the front desk, we had an embarrassing moment with the ancient manageress of the hotel, who had a horrific, hairy mole right in the middle of her cheek. I hadn't encountered her earlier in the day and that mole was straight out of a Balzac story. As she handed me my key, the woman made a very judgmental remark to Juliet, I didn't fully grasp its meaning, but she was shaming her for accompanying me to my room. It was a small, mom and pop, *mere and pere*, kind of hotel.

So up in the room, I showed Juliet my son's picture—he's a very handsome boy of thirteen with bright red hair—and then she and I embraced. But she was worried about that terrible lady behind the front desk. That woman had tainted everything. Meddler! So after a hug and two quick kisses, we exchanged addresses and she fled. I wouldn't be able to see her again, because she was leaving for Belgium with the circus the next day. I was a little heartbroken, but pleased to have received two quick kisses and to have held her, even briefly.

So the rest of my stay in Paris was quiet and uneventful. I tried to read the Joyce, but it was too much for me, and so I did a lot of email at an Internet cafe near the Luxembourg Gardens. I should have been at a real cafe, Le Dome or La Coupole, but instead I was indulging in my email addiction, surrounded by American college students chewing gum and writing to their friends at U Penn, George Washington, Delaware State. When I lived in Paris in 1984 as an au pair, I'd go to the American Express and get mail once a week. That was much more romantic, like something out of Patricia Highsmith. But now in 1999 in Paris, I was doing email three times a day. I might as well have been in New York. I was writing to the same people I always write to. People whom I never see. What the hell is the point?

I could have had some human contact in Paris, but I chickened out. One grayish, wet morning, as I walked up the avenue near my hotel, I passed an old prostitute. She was wearing white boots that came to her knee and a chic white raincoat over a skirt, and there was a red kerchief around her neck. She was strolling along, making a block last forever, and she was twirling, ever so slightly, her large black umbrella. I would venture to say that she was in her late fifties or early sixties, though the face was well preserved, the legs looked strong, and the mouth was full and sensual and knowing.

I remembered seeing this kind of prostitute in Montparnasse section of Paris back in 1984. These older women used to stand on the corners, looking into the sky, not meeting your eye like most women of the night. They gave the appearance of waiting for someone who should be arriving imminently—they had a certain hauteur. They'd hold on to their purses like bourgeois matrons, and there was usually nothing flashy about their dress, maybe just a bit of leg showing. And they would stand on those corners for hours, like statues, and though I was only twenty in 1984, I knew that a woman stands on a corner like that, night after night, for only one purpose, and so I figured there was some kind of erotic demand in Paris for these older ladies, though they held no appeal for me at that time.

But fifteen years later as I passed the woman in the white boots, I gave her a sweet glance of interest, but I kept moving, not giving her a chance to provide me with any signal. I was a coward. Then I crossed the street and spied on her. I was back in Chandler mode. I admired her—the twirl of the umbrella was so subtle. She was just drifting languorously downstream, and her whole demeanor—the twirl of the umbrella, the boots, the red kerchief—were secret signals. You knew she was going nowhere, unless you asked her to go somewhere.

I went back to my hotel room and lay on my bed and thought of her. I imagined her in there with me. She would undress in the corner with dignity, revealing her old body. Then she'd lie down beside me and I'd climb on top of her and her legs would go around me just like a young girl. It would be nice to make love to someone that old, to have their wisdom seep into you as you made love to them.

Each day after that first sighting, I went back to the same spot at the same time of day, my wallet full of francs, and I would linger, waiting for her to appear. I vowed to myself to be courageous, that life is short and is getting shorter all the time, so do everything, try everything. Proust said you only regret the things you don't do. But she was never there again and I regretted my cowardice that first time I saw her. So I guess Proust is right. Hell, he may have even known her.

So after ten days of doing email and looking for the old woman, I returned to the U.S. and had a long weekend in New Jersey at my parents' house with my son, who in addition to his beautiful red hair is noticeable for being a physical giant. I stand five foot eleven and he's already five foot ten. I wonder what it will be like to have a son who is physically larger than myself. And seeing how mature he is, seeing how he's almost a man, it occurs to me that if he has a child by the time he's twenty-eight, then I might be a grandfather before I'm fifty.

We had a good visit, as usual we laughed a lot—with no one do I laugh the way I do with my son. This trip he was mocking me because I take a fiber supplement, psyllium, but then I let him try some and he saw the results and now understands my addiction to the substance. Even a soon-to-be-teenager appreciates proper bowel functions.

When he emerged from the toilet a few hours after his first dose, I said, "How was it?"

"I never had one so long," he said. "I thought of showing it to you. I think it could have broken a record. I love psyllium."

"Good boy," I said. "Good boy."

After my son went back to his mother in Georgia, I had two weeks to catch up to my life in New York, but now here I am in Mexico. I was invited by Club Med in Cancun to be part of a conference of American writers and journalists discussing the state of American literature. It's an all-expenses paid week and it's gorgeous here. My window looks out onto the azure water and I've spent the last three days snorkeling and waterskiing, and at night there are absurd debates and presentations. The whole thing is mad: American authors on a free jaunt talking about books with French moderators in Mexico. Talk about strange bedfellows. Mexicans, Americans, French. But I don't care, I like strange bedfellows, and the snorkeling is great and many of the women writers seem to have been chosen not only for their literary merit but for their physical beauty.

The first night was quite interesting. I was intimidated by all the famous writers who had been lured down here, and my personality dried up and flaked away like a piece of dandruff, which often happens in the company of people I'd like to impress. I thought of hiding in my room. I was miserable. So I did the only sensible thing. I fell off the wagon again, and my personality, or one of my personalities, emerged. After some tequila and beer, I was now able to talk to one of the famous women writers, though she made an early exit. Then I ended up being befriended by a hard-drinking best-selling author. After countless shots of tequila, he gathered together another hard-drinking writer and a hard-drinking French photographer, and all of us hard drinkers took a taxi into town and went to this bordello.

The girls were lovely and for the peso equivalent of four dollars you could have a lap dance, but to go off to a room with a girl cost about a hundred dollars. And I must say these Mexican girls were beautiful and unusually friendly. They weren't as hardened as American strippers and prostitutes. One girl, who was only wearing a G-string and nothing else, sat on my lap, even though I didn't purchase a lap dance—I had no money, the best-selling author was buying my tequila and beer. But for some reason she took a liking to me, even though I couldn't offer her money, and so I lifted her up, she was very light, and she wrapped her legs around my back and I spun us around to the pounding salsa music and we both laughed. I was like a sailor on leave. Her teeth were sparkling white, her hair long and black, her breasts these little pink swellings, and her ass in my hands a delicious thing.

Later she was in a lesbian show with two other girls. They started out in tartan Catholic schoolgirl dresses, which quickly came off. My girl sat in a chair, another girl kneeled in front of her and put her head between my sweetheart's beautiful legs, and the last one lay on her back beneath the kneeling girl and licked her from that angle. It was three-way cunnilingus. It was very geometric: one sitting, one kneeling, one lying down. Fantastic! And around them on the floor, their tartan dresses were like flower petals. At one point, the kneeling girl's ass was in the air and the shape of it seemed to me to be a thing of perfection.

After this performance ended we left the bordello, and during the long taxi ride home I blacked out or passed out and came to at some roadside grill, where I found myself eating a meat taco, as were my three companions. Through my dim, alcoholic vision, my taco appeared to be mostly gristle—bone and cartilage—and very little meat, but it tasted very good. But then the French photographer spoiled the meal, when he said, "I think we are eating dog meat filled with parasites." His English, though heavily accented, was quite good. How did he know the word "parasite"? But the best-selling author, with alcoholic confidence, said, "We're so loaded with tequila that nothing could survive in our systems." This, to me, seemed like sound reasoning.

The whole next day I spent in bed, ill and destroyed and dissipated and thought I might die—you know, that exaggerated deathbed hangover feeling. But I held on to the vision of that lesbian threesome, particularly that ass in the air, like it was the face of God or something, and this was very healing. Gave me a reason to live.

Maybe for me a woman's buttocks *is* the face of God. This would make perfect sense, since I seem to like to worship the ass—kissing it, prostrating myself before it, praying to it. So am I a monotheist, onanist, or pantheist?

I do hope this spiritual revelation doesn't bring a fatwa or Falwell down on my head. But if it does, so be it. The vision of that divine Mexican rear end got me through my hangover, and by the next day, I was back again on the wagon and was snorkeling, waterskiing, and swimming. I was alive! So thank God for that ass. Or maybe, just thank Ass for that ass.

Restraint of Tongue and Penis
May 11, 1999

For complex New York apartment reasons, I am in a temporary sublet for several weeks. But I almost didn't get this place. The woman whose apartment this is came to my one-man show and had read one of my novels, so naturally she had concerns about letting me sleep in her bed, even if she wasn't going to be in it. During our phone interview for the sublet, she asked, "You won't bring prostitutes or transsexuals to my apartment, will you? I really wouldn't want that."

"Oh, no," I said, "I only go to their apartments, or to cheap hotels that rent rooms by the hour. I'm very discreet that way."

"And you won't go through my underwear?"

"I swear that I will not rifle through your underthings."

The nature of these quite legitimate questions had it looking very grave that I would get the place, but then I told her I'd pay her one hundred dollars more than anyone else. On a much lower scale, I was like Donald Trump trying to buy his way into Palm Beach society. When you have a terrible reputation, a little bit of cash often gets people to change their tune. So the hundred dollars worked, and here I am in my new sublet, and I'm on my best behavior, though my first day in the apartment, feeling resentful and rebellious, I did open the underwear drawer. But then I got concerned that she might have— like James Bond did in a movie—wetted down a stray hair over the opening to the drawer. I looked to see if any such hairs had fallen off. I didn't think so, but I couldn't be sure. So, without even glancing at her panties, I then closed the drawer, like a gentleman, and haven't opened it since.

So this whole sublet problem—the not being trusted— is the kind of thing I must expect. Most men, according to Thoreau, lead lives of quiet desperation, but I, to bring in some money, lead a life of public desperation. Yet it still upsets me to be accused of being someone who might rifle through someone's panty drawer! I'd like to be able to do such a thing and have nobody suspect me. I've lost my privacy!

But it's all my own fault. With what I've written and with what I've said on stage, I've defamed my own character. I should sue myself for libel. I've shown no restraint of tongue and penis. One girl told me that before dating me, she had heard from three different sources that I only slept with boys, that I only slept with prostitutes, and that I only slept with transsexuals.

"Everyone thinks I'm so exclusive," I said. "They should pool their information."

She'd also heard that I was a cross-dresser and a womanizer.

"Did anyone tell you I keep a kosher house? That I have two sets of dishes?" I asked her.

"No," she said.

"Well, if you hear such a thing, know that it's a lie. I'm not kosher! I should be, but I'm not."

Anyway, I was quite upset when the girl reported to me

all these rumors. I was injured, wounded. Who would say such things? How did people know me so well? They couldn't be reading my work that closely. Or reading it at all. I'm not exactly a best-seller. If anything I'm a worst-seller. But there is this column. That's where a lot of these innuendoes get started, at least in this small provincial world of downtown New York, which happens to be my dating pool and subletting pool.

Luckily, though, not everybody considers me a nutcase and a sexual outlaw. The other night, I went to a cocktail party at the offices of a world-famous arts foundation, which has very generously given me a fellowship.

So, like a respectable writer and not a perverted outcast who must resort to bribes for sublets, I was in jacket and tie for the party, which was quite festive and elegant. The other fellowship winners were all there—it was a celebration for us—and at the beginning of the event I was loitering about in one of the smaller foundation offices because it had a fantastic view of all of southern Manhattan (the foundation is near the very top of a Park Avenue high-rise). With me in this office were two of America's leading playwrights—the tall, dark-haired, good-looking Jon Robin Baitz, known to many as Broadway's wunderkind, and the lovely and sexy Eve Ensler, whose work *The Vagina Monologues* is famous for its emotional power, as well as its uniquely feminine worldview. To me, she's the Georgia O'Keeffe of Broadway.

After we had all introduced ourselves, Jon Robin Baitz was good enough to tell me that he was a fan of my column. Since I've never had enough money for theater tickets, I haven't seen any of his plays, so I couldn't repay him the compliment, but I did say, "Thank you. That's very nice of you to tell me."

"You write with such freedom about sex," he said. "I admire that."

"You write about sex? I'd like to read your columns," said Eve Ensler.

"Well, someone I've written about in my columns is a great, great fan of *your* work," I said to her. "And he told me he met you. His name is Harry Chandler. Also known as the Mangina."

I was speaking of my dear friend Harry Chandler, for whom I am the official biographer. He is a wonderfully talented forty-two-year-old sculptor and painter, and about eight months ago, during a period of great inspiration, he invented a prosthetic vagina, actually numerous prosthetic vaginas, all of which are made from plastic-molds of the genitals of some of his female friends as well as hired models. Soon after inventing these vaginas, he began to wear them as a kind of circus act/performance-art piece.

"Oh, my God," said Ms. Ensler. "You know the Mangina!?!"

"Well, yes, he's a good friend and I've written about him extensively."

"The Mangina columns were very good," said Jon Robin, who was growing in my esteem by the second.

"I can't ever forget meeting Harry," said Eve. "I was at this big rape-crisis center fund-raiser talking to Harvey Keitel and Harry approached and said, 'I'm Harry Chandler. I have it with me.' I didn't know what he was referring to. He had called me up a few days before—I just recently unlisted my number—and he spoke to me about this thing, this Mangina. For some reason I didn't hang up on him; I guess because he sounded sweet. But I had completely forgotten the conversation by the time of the fund-raiser. So I had no idea who he was. And then he reaches into his coat pocket, like someone pulling a gun, and he takes out a Mangina. Even Harvey, who's a real tough guy, was frightened. I mean the Mangina does not look like a woman's vagina!"

I could see that she was vividly recollecting with no little discomfort this episode, and then she said, with passion and defiance, "It's not at all realistic! The Mangina is ugly! Unattractive! A woman's vagina is beautiful!"

She may have been quoting from her own play, but I'm not sure. "Well, the Mangina *is* a little monstrous," I said, trying to soothe her, "but when you see him wearing it, it makes sense. You might not know this, but he utilizes his scrotum as labia, which he calls the lotum."

"Yes, the Mangina has to be seen in its proper application," said Jon Robin, standing up for Harry.

"Have *you* seen the Mangina?" she asked him.

"No, but I've read Jonathan's columns, and he paints a very clear picture of the Mangina."

At this point a waiter came into the office with a plate of shrimp hors d'oeuvres. He was a young, handsome, bespectacled black man, and he said, "Are you talking about the Mangina?"

"You know the Mangina?" I said, shocked, though I shouldn't have been, since word of the Mangina has spread far. First there were my columns about Harry and his invention—just as I have made my own desperation public, so have I perpetrated this on my friend. But he's a reformed exhibitionist and likes it when I write about him; in fact, he doesn't really enjoy my work unless I mention him. So inspired by my coverage, Harry then developed a website, with the idea that he could sell his Manginas over the Internet to the growing cross-dressing and prison populations. To help achieve this goal, he then managed to get himself on the Howard Stern radio show *and* television show. The exposure was excellent, but no sales of Manginas have occurred except to one pre-op transsexual waitress at Lucky Cheng's Chinese restaurant on First Avenue, which is famous for its transsexual wait staff, as well as its excellent spring rolls.

"I've seen pictures of the Mangina," said the young waiter. "It's pretty incredible. He's famous. He's an icon in the gay community."

"This is my experience," I said. "Wherever I go, people know the Mangina."

"He's hard to forget," said the waiter and we all took the little shrimp hors d'oeuvres that he offered us and then he left.

"Well, do tell Harry I said hello," said Eve. "He surprised me at the party, but he seems very sweet."

"He is very sweet and he is a huge fan of your work. And I feel the need to say that the Mangina, though it appears misogynistic, is actually an expression of his love for women. A strange love perhaps, but a love nonetheless . . . Also it has something to do with prosthesis. The Mangina is a prosthetic vagina to go along with his prosthetic leg."

"I didn't know he had a prosthetic leg," said Eve.

"Oh, yes. That's essential to understanding the psychology behind the Mangina . . . Once I tried to kick his prosthetic leg, but he kicked me with it first and it hurt. 'Stop that. Both my legs are real,' I said to him."

"Why did you try to kick him?" asked Eve.

"The idea that it *wouldn't* hurt him appealed to me, but of course it was injurious to him emotionally that I would try such a thing."

"One thing is a little bit unclear to me," said Jon Robin.

"Is he the Mangina, or is the Mangina just the name of the prosthesis?"

"Both," I said. "His invention is called the Mangina, and he is called the Mangina. Kind of like the Green Lantern in the comic book world. He has the power of the Green Lantern and he *is* the Green Lantern."

"Have you ever worn the Mangina?" asked Eve.

"No," I said, "that's Harry's domain. Also, I've never fingered the Mangina. And lots of people do finger it. Women say, 'It feels so real, so warm.' They don't realize that they're fingering his excess scrotal sack. They think his lotum is rubber like the rest of the Mangina. But then sometimes they do realize his lotum is his scrotum and still they keep on fingering him. I've seen people really rooting around inside the Mangina. Men and women."

"How come you haven't fingered him?" asked Jon Robin.

"I have an aversion to touching my friend's lotum."

"Really?" he said. "From reading your columns I had you on this pedestal about not being squeamish about anything."

I hate falling off pedestals. It happens all the time. Especially with the women I date, even the ones who come into the relationship loaded with rumors about me. But that's probably *why* I fall off pedestals. I'm not as exciting as all my press. So I said to Jon Robin, wanting him to still admire me, "Oh, I'd finger him no problem. But I've wanted to remain pure when it comes to the Mangina—to simply be its number one promoter and advocate."

At this point we were joined in the office by a fellowship-winning female sculptor and she said, "What are you talking about? What's a Mangina?"

Being someone's official biographer and mouthpiece can be exhausting, but I gave her a quick rundown on the subject, and then got out of that little office to go hobnob. And as I went back into the more crowded rooms, it struck me as mildly absurd that here I was literally on top of Manhattan in a Park Avenue high-rise, in one of the most prestigious philanthropic arts foundations, surrounded by famous writers, artists, composers, scientists, and historians, and I had spent almost the whole cocktail party talking about the Mangina, which, if I look at it, is my life in a nutshell—a nut on top of the world talking about his friend's nuts. So what is to become of me? Will my simultaneous yearning for the high and for the low tear me apart in the middle? Can I—metaphorically speaking—admire the *David* and the Mangina at the same time? Can I be an outsider artist, but make a little insider money? I hope so.

Later that night, I was in bed and before going to sleep I called Harry. "Hi, Mangie. How you doing?"

"I'm in bed. All disassembled. Got the foot off . . . How are you doing?"

"I'm fine. There was a party tonight for the fellowship I won and I met Eve Ensler. She told me how you pulled a Mangina out of your pocket at that rape-crisis fundraiser. She liked you, but was shocked by the Mangina. You didn't tell me that you had pulled one out when you met her."

"I know I was crazed that night," he confessed, his voice a little embarrassed, even with me, his number one fan. "I was like a Mangina gunslinger. I was loaded with Manginas. I really wanted her to see them. *The Vagina Monologues* is so powerful. She might be the only woman in the world who can appreciate the Mangina. But I only had time to show her one, but I had another one in my pocket, *and* I was wearing one. Three Manginas! But she was with Harvey Keitel. He didn't like the Mangina. I've waited on him many times in three different restaurants but he never remembers me. Anyway, I wanted to show her the one I was wearing, but I thought I saw Keitel signal for security, so I got out of there. . . . The whole night was crazy. When I got there I decided at the last second to switch Manginas. I was going to show her the best one, but then I wanted to *wear* the best one. So I went to the bathroom and was dropping Manginas on the floor and the bathroom attendant saw them under the partition and he saw my prosthesis. I don't know what he thought. He said, 'Can I help you?' He must have been completely confused as to what was going on."

"You were like Superman changing," I said. "Still that must have been strange for the attendant to see these rubber organs falling to the floor of the toilet and landing next to a rubber foot."

"Very strange," said Harry.

I thought it was best to move on to another subject, since Harry seemed upset about his failure to connect with his heroine, Eve Ensler. "So what else is going on?" I said. "Give me your headlines."

"I had my testicles waxed," he said.

"Why?"

"It makes them look nice," he said. "I get them waxed, you know, for when I wear the Mangina. My lotum looks better when it's smooth."

"I didn't know this . . . Where'd you get waxed?"

"Took me forever to find this place. It's on First Avenue. I went to five or six places, asking, 'Do you do bikini waxing for men?' They all yell at me wherever I go. They hate me in these nail salons. I really am sick. But then this one woman said she would do it for twenty dollars. We went into the back of her shop. 'Ok, take it off,' she said. She's Korean. So I stripped and she said, 'Time to clean the dungeon.' I just had her wax around the edges, the balls, and the area between the anus and the balls, but sometimes the paper got stuck to the head of my penis."

"I can't believe she said, 'Time to clean the dungeon' . . . Did it hurt when the paper got stuck to the head?"

"Yeah, but it felt good too. I deserve to be punished for being sick. But for twenty dollars, it's incredible. You get all that attention, a woman paying attention to your pubic zone. She asked me if I wanted a pedicure and a manicure, I said no, 'Just bikini waxing.' I'm definitely going back. I got hard-ons. That's why the wax paper got stuck to the head."

"Did she say anything about the hard-ons? Did she grab it and yank it?"

"No she just looked at it. This is my sex life, getting waxed for twenty dollars. But it's not bad. The one other time I did it, at this other place, the woman put a towel over my penis so she wouldn't have to look at it. Then I came back a week later for a touch-up, even though no hair had come back, and they told me to get out."

"You tipped them off that you liked it for more than just the waxing."

"Yeah."

"There are probably gay places where you can get waxed no problem."

"I know, but I like women to do it."

"Do you have a performance coming up with the Mangina that you got waxed for? I'll come see you."

"No performances. I just wanted the attention."

I wanted to tell him that he didn't have to get waxed to get attention, but I didn't know if I could say it with conviction. Ever since he became the Mangina, he's not had a girlfriend, even though he's extremely good looking, blonde, and lean. So I worry about him. It's going to take a very broad-minded woman to love Harry the way he deserves. And I don't know where he'll find her. But where do any of us find the people who will love us? So all I managed to say was, "Oh, Harry."

"It's all right," he said. "Something good will happen to me someday. Maybe even tomorrow."

And with that hopeful thought, we said goodbye, and hung up our phones. My dear friend was disassembled for the night and so was I.

Shades of the Prison-House
May 25, 1999

I went to Boston this past weekend to visit a friend, an old college pal. It was a lovely time, but a quiet time, not much went on—just two friends having a few meals, going for walks along the Charles River, people-watching in Harvard Square coffee shops.

But on the train ride up there and on the train back I had some excitement. It came in the form of two Edward Bunker prison novels, *Animal Factory* and *Little Boy Blue*, and they set me to thinking about men and violence and what kind of guts I have or don't have.

I had never read Bunker before, but I picked up his books because I met him at the writers' conference in Mexico and all I knew of him then was that he had spent most of his life in California jails. I also knew that some influential literary types had helped rescue him from the penal system, primarily the writer William Styron and the former editor of *The Nation* Blair Clark, both of whom are to Bunker what Norman Mailer was to Jack Henry Abbot. But Bunker, unlike Abbot, hasn't been arrested since his release in the seventies; he has used his freedom to write books and screenplays and to act in movies.

(For cinephiles: Dustin Hoffman played Bunker in the 1979 film *Straight Time,* based on Bunker's novel *No Beast So Fierce;* Bunker co-wrote the 1985 thriller *Runaway Train,* and he was Mr. Blue in Quentin Tarantino's 1992 film *Reservoir Dogs.*)

In person, Bunker is gruffly friendly, but he's also somewhat remote and battered, reminding me of an old boxer. He's in his sixties and he has a flat broken nose that prefers the left side of his face. His eyes are light blue, unafraid. His skin is scarred and rugged, and a wet, well-chewed cigar perpetually hangs out of his mouth. He was the youngest convict (at the time in the fifties) to ever be incarcerated at San Quentin and was in some kind of institution from early childhood until his mid-forties. He was once on the FBI's Ten Most Wanted List.

We talked a little down in Mexico, but I didn't pursue him much, feeling embarrassed, since I was unfamiliar with his books. Now after reading his work I wish I had spoken to him more. But what would I have asked him— What was it like to have been in prison most of your life, to have been trapped and beaten since you were a child?

So it's all right that I didn't bother him—which would have been rude and intrusive—because it seems to me that it's all in his novels. On the train up to Boston, with the pretty, sparkling New England coast on the right, I read *Animal Factory,* which is set in San Quentin. It's a story that puts the reader, at least this reader, right into the violent society of prison. And every few pages, I would stop reading and look out the window to the marshes or to the ocean, and I would wonder how I would fare if I was locked up. Could I handle it? Would I fight for my dignity or be turned immediately into a queen?

The prison knives alone would scare me terribly. I hate

sharp things. I'm afraid of papercuts. And so sitting on that train to Boston, it was emasculating to think how miserably I would do in such a world, a world of shivs (homemade knives), a world where the pecking order is determined by one's capacity for brutality. So could I think of myself as manly or masculine, when in such a primal, male, jungle-like environment, I would immediately be crushed?

I then thought of my relations with women. When I make love to them, I enjoy feeling larger, stronger; I enjoy their thrill in being *taken*. Their arms go above their heads and I push down on their wrists—they want me to—and I feel masculine and powerful. But how masculine am I if in the most masculine of universes, the prison yard, I couldn't make it for a second? So as I sat on the train, all my lovemaking seemed like a sham to me. All the women had been fooled.

But then I tried to rally my image of myself as a man. I thought of the few fights I've been in. In Paris, in 1984, in a bar brawl, I had my nose broken and my lip split open by a superior fighter. When I was alone afterward, I cried, and ever since then I've avoided fights as best I could. Life itself often feels meaningless, but violence seems even more meaningless. I play a fair amount of pickup basketball and I always walk away from confrontations. One time though, a few years ago in Saratoga Springs, I didn't. I was playing five-on-five with my friend Vivian and a bunch of local youths. Vivian is an excellent player; she's very tall and can more than hold her own with men. She can also trash-talk with anybody, and after the game she gave it to this young black man. He had been trash-talking all game, coming after me mostly—I was older, white, and skinny; the only other white player was Vivian. I was covering him and he dunked on me once, very rare in a pickup game, but he didn't cover me too closely, didn't want to show that respect, so I scored quite a few points and then I stole the ball from him at the end and scored the winning basket, though he fouled me hard as I went to the hoop. Everyone started dispersing, no one could believe, even my teammates, what I had pulled off. There was an odd quiet. Vivian went to the water fountain at the side of the court and so did the young man. To rub the loss in his face, but also to stick up for me, since he had abused me all game, Vivian said to him, "Nice game, *chump*."

He went into a fury and they started a name-calling argument. She knew all the street slurs from playing basketball in her Bed-Stuy neighborhood back in Brooklyn. She said something about him being nappy-haired and he was calling her a bitch several different ways. I didn't step in, knowing that Vivian would be angry at me, but then he called her "ugly cunt."

That seemed too much to me. So I said, "Why don't you shut the fuck up." I was about five yards from him. He had been holding himself back, wanting to hit Vivian, but the cardinal rule of not hitting a woman had kept him at bay, but now he had a target and he sprinted at me with his fist raised like a hatchet. His friends, some of whom had been my teammates, also came racing over. Eight of them surrounded me.

"Say that again," he said, his fist still raised. He was a very powerful young kid, muscular, a great athlete, about eighteen.

"I don't want to be hit," I said calmly. I thought of his fist crashing into my head, me falling to the concrete. I had books I wanted to write. My honesty surprised him, but still he cocked his fist back further. I didn't raise my hands. "Did you tell me to shut the fuck up?" he asked.

"I don't want to be hit," I repeated, but I said it strongly, not like a coward.

"Get the fuck out of here," he said.

Vivian and I walked away from the court. He called after us, "You ugly cunt and white eyebrow freak." He was referring, rather astutely I thought, to my albino-like eyebrows. Vivian and I got in my car and I was shaking with adrenaline, but we laughed—"white eyebrow freak" was funny to both of us.

So I don't know what would happen to me in prison. I am not without a little bit of mad courage, but would I just give up? Be raped and murdered without a fight? Bunker's books are like Holocaust memoirs. Somehow his characters, like concentration camp survivors, are able to hold on, kept alive by the most meager glimmer of *hope*. Would I have such resources?

It occurs to me that the idea of prison has had a peculiar hold on me for some time. As a child one of my favorite games with my friends was to play "escape from jail." We'd sweep the little patio in front of my house, then all of a sudden we'd take our brooms and attack imaginary guards. Then we'd unlock the front gate to my yard and we'd go sprinting to the woods that surrounded my house. It was exhilarating. We were escaping. We were free.

Years later, when my father felt he couldn't afford my Princeton education, I decided to join ROTC at the end of my freshman year. I did this because I had romantic notions of the military, primarily from the movie *The Great Escape*. I loved the Steve McQueen character: he was handsome and he wore a leather jacket and he knew how to ride a motorcycle. He was in a German prisoner-of-war camp and he was always breaking out, but then getting caught, and so the guards would put him in solitary confinement. He'd do his time by throwing a baseball against his cell wall and catching it in his mitt. That's what I would do—I loved baseball. So I was eighteen and I joined ROTC because I needed the money, but I was also thinking that I'd be like Steve McQueen. I signed a contract that gave the army the next fifteen years of my life: three years at Princeton as a cadet, four years on active duty, and eight years of being in reserves.

The first time I put on a uniform my sophomore year, I broke into a cold sweat and almost vomited. I had made a terrible mistake. Twice a week, I had to be in uniform for special ROTC classes and drills. Sometimes we went away on the weekends for more extensive training. I couldn't march, I couldn't read a compass, I couldn't shine my shoes, I couldn't break down a rifle. Being in the army was not about leather jackets and motorcycles and being a hero like Steve McQueen.

Midway through my junior year, I became terribly frightened. That coming summer I was to spend six weeks at officer-training boot camp at Fort Bragg. I knew I couldn't cut it. During one of our preparatory weekends at West Point, to get us ready for boot camp, we played war games, and one night we were being taught the tactics of an ambush by a Green Beret, a Vietnam vet, and I remember thinking to myself, "I'm spending my college years learning how to kill people."

I knew I had to get out of the military. The only thing to do was to became a Conscientious Objector. There was no other way out of my contract. But becoming a Conscientious Objector is not easy; it's like going on trial. I was assigned a prosecutor. Over the course of a several-month-long process, I had to prove my sincerity—that since joining the army I had had a change of heart and was now morally and ethically opposed to being a soldier, to warfare, and that on a battlefield I would not be able to kill. If I did not prove this I would be charged with violating my Army contract, defrauding the government (they were paying for my very expensive education), and I would be placed in military jail. I had joined the army because Steve McQueen was handsome and heroic in prison and now I faced the possibility of going to prison myself. Maybe it was wish fulfillment.

But I won my case and I told the government that I would pay them back the money they had spent on my Princeton tuition, which I was able to do over time. My only souvenir from the experience is my name tag, AMES. My son has questioned me many times why I didn't stay in the army; he has the movie notions that I once had. I've tried to explain to him my stance and as he gets older he seems to understand.

If I had stayed in the military, I might have gone to the Gulf War. Most of my ROTC friends served over there. So I didn't go to Kuwait and I didn't go to military prison. Maybe I have something of an Eddie Bunker character in me—I'm an escape artist.

As I read Bunker's books this past weekend, an odd thing happened—I began to feel like I was in prison. I felt infused with the paranoia of that world. On the train and then on the streets of Boston and New York, I trusted no one around me. Violence seemed imminent. I had to be clever and wary at all times. I longed for freedom, even as I am free. I felt like I had done something wrong and was going to be punished.

So the metaphor of prison existence seemed to highlight and bring to the fore my natural responses to my life:

I feel inherently guilty and criminal, I am wary and distrustful of other people, and I don't feel *free*.

But does anyone? There's this passage from Wordsworth's "Ode: Intimations of Immortality" that I've always loved, maybe because it makes me feel less alone with the idea of self-created prisons:

> Heaven lies about us in our infancy!
> Shades of the prison-house begin to close
> Upon the growing Boy

The Curse of the Fried Plantain
June 8, 1999

My friend Grubin, a muddled and brilliant photographer, called
me the other day in a moment of need.

"Jonathan." His voice was weak and hushed. "I would
like your advice."

I knew that some kind of confession was about to occur.
Whenever my friends call and sound like Grubin, they're
worried they have a venereal disease. And I am the one
person whom they feel they can turn to and not be judged.

It is flattering to be trusted, but unflattering to be considered a lay expert on genital infections. But it is my own
fault, my struggles in this area are well documented, and
so I've been consulted on rashes and bugs and burning
sensations, most of which prove to be false alarms. I hear
their symptoms, I make my diagnoses, and then what I
advocate to all my friends for diseases and paranoia of diseases is vigilant safe sex. I can't imagine sex any other
way. I don't even like to come on myself anymore.

So I said to Grubin, a large bear of a man, in my most
kind and soothing tones, "I'll try to help you. What's
going on?"

"This afternoon I was at Mi Chinita," he said, referring

to our favorite Spanish restaurant on Eighth Avenue, "and I was sitting in the back fuming. Three commissions have fallen through in the last few days. I can hardly pay the rent. After I ate, I got up to pay my bill. As I walked to the register, thinking of my troubles, this dim-looking character was using his hands to eat fried plantains. I watched him put one in his mouth. His fingers were black with dirt. I don't want to see that kind of thing. But those plantains looked good, and when I walked past him I shot my big paw down to his plate and grabbed one with my own dirty fingers. It was only when it was halfway to my mouth and I saw him staring at me that I realized what I had done. But I ate the thing, threw five dollars on the counter, and staggered out of there ashamed."

"What did the guy do?" I asked.

"Nothing. He was too shocked . . . So I want to know—do you think I'm cracking up? Need therapy? I told Greta about the plantain and she wants me to see a psychiatrist. I thought you would be a good person to ask."

For once it wasn't venereal maladies—this time I was being consulted because of my experiences with mental problems. But this is good, I thought, my suffering enables me to help others.

I was immediately against the idea of Grubin getting shrunk. Greta, his longtime girlfriend, keeps Grubin under pretty tight screws, and I saw this as one more way she was trying to control him. I had to fight her.

"You're not cracking up," I said. "We all have these kinds of thoughts—like grabbing someone's plantain. Normally we keep them bubbling under the surface. But every now and then one of these things—compulsions—leaks out and we act on it, like an unexpected twitch or shudder. Because of all your stress and financial problems, your guard was down and a compulsion shot out. I have lots of them. I always want to grab a policeman's revolver, but I don't. So you're perfectly fine. You don't need therapy. You just need some commissions."

Grubin was heartened. He called out to Greta and said, "Ames doesn't think I need therapy. He's an Ivy leaguer."

"So what?" I heard her say.

"Fight her, man, fight her," I whispered, and we rang off.

I had helped Grubin, but *I* became undone. As the result of our conversation, I was suddenly aware of how many socially inappropriate things I want to do to other people. Just as the poets and the painters of the nineteenth century depicted the mist over the River Thames and thus revealed it for the world to see (according to Oscar Wilde), I had revealed my own mad impulses to myself and they were driving me nuts. I gave them a name, Grubins, and I divided them into three categories: men, women, and dogs.

Toward men I have hostile thoughts. When I pass one on the street, I mutter in my mind to him, "Watch out!" And if I'm sitting in a restaurant and a man walks toward me I want to strike him in the stomach. It is something about being eye level with the abdomen.

Toward women, I have sexist impulses. If from a distance I see an attractive woman, I say to the locker room in my mind, "What have we got here?" And then when she comes alongside me, I say to her in my mind, "Hey, baby." And then when she passes me, I want to smack her rear. This compulsion is particularly strong if I have a newspaper, then I really want to give those beautiful butts a good swat.

And toward dogs, I have unbridled affection. I want to

get down on my knees and wrestle with them and rub my face in their necks. If there's more than one dog present, I say to them in my mind, "Hi, guys." And whenever I pass a dog and it's not appropriate for me to cuddle with him or her, which is just about all the time in New York, I make secret eye contact and whelp silently. I must have been a canine in a previous life, and also as a boy I was molested by my uncle's sheep dog, Oliver. I was six years old and he pinned me down and rubbed his wet, pink uncircumcised (even though he was a Jewish dog) cock between my thighs—I was wearing shorts. So I may be drawn to dogs as a way to recreate that moment, which is often the case with victims of sexual molestation. But if the molestation is pleasurable—I liked having Oliver on top of me, except for the wetness of his dog-cock—then is it wrong to want to recreate it?

Having named the Grubins, it has become difficult to repress them. Two days ago I was on a crowded F train around six o'clock, but I had a seat. A chubby Wall-streeter was standing in front of me. He had thinning red hair and looked like an ex–college rugby player gone to seed. His raincoated abdomen was at my eye level. I resisted the urge to punch his stomach, but then when I stood up for my stop, Broadway-Lafayette, I sneered at him, "Watch out!" A Grubin had leaked. The Wall Streeter was also trying to get off the train and he said, "What did you say?" We stumbled onto the platform.

"Nothing."

I could see his eyes hide a certain rage. He was longing for the old college scrum. I didn't give it to him. He turned his back to me and headed out. I should have given him more lag time because as we climbed the stairs he was right in front of me and his ass was in my face.

Near the top of the stairs, I was a little out of breath and my nostrils were dilated and the ex–rugby player at this precise moment farted right through his raincoat and straight into my brain. It had to be on purpose. It was something I had dreaded on subway stairs for years. The odor was Proustian. It smelled like a childhood salami sandwich. I lost vision. I stumbled backward into a pretty, large-bosomed black high school girl. She pushed me over the last step and onto the main concourse.

"Watch out!" she said to me. For her it wasn't a Grubin, just a normal phrase of self-defense.

My nostrils were scalded and I looked for the rugby player, but he was gone. I should have punched him when I had the chance. I raced outside and breathed as much fresh air as I could. I wondered if you could get the flu or TB from a fart.

After such an experience, I needed beauty. I started walking to Cafc Gitanc on Mott Street, where I often go to look at the city's loveliest young girls. Before I got there, I came across an unusual couple: a yellow Labrador and a rock-and-roll girl who had a shaved head and lip earrings; the dog's coiffure, thankfully, was normal and he had no piercings.

"Can I pet your dog?" I asked, which was another leaking Grubin. In New York, I almost never solicit affection from a stranger's dog. In the provinces, dogs are quite friendly, but in the city they're slightly mad from being cramped up all the time. Also, in New York people don't like to share their dogs, and the dogs pick up on this. I once saw a friend of mine have his chin eaten by a fancy Chow that he bent down to pet. We had to rush him to St. Vincent's and he's had trouble shaving ever since.

"All right," said the girl, clearly annoyed. She didn't

want to let me pet him, but I guess she saw how earnest and needy I was.

So I knelt down and rubbed my face in his neck. My whole agitated being was soothed. He responded to my caresses and put his tongue in my ear. It was wet and invigorating. I felt guilty about the taste of wax in his mouth, but I gave him the other ear. Then the rocker girl dragged her dog away.

This was a good Grubin, I thought, and so with freshly cleaned ear canals, I strolled happily to Gitane and when I opened the door to the cafe a tall brunette approached. I held the door for her and she smiled at me—she liked my gentlemanly ways. As she passed me through the door, I was able to restrain from patting her rear, but I said, "What have we got here?"

Her disdain was immediate. "Are you nuts?" she asked, and she went in and I let the door close. I stared through the window. I was cut off from life, from beauty. But I didn't dare go in. Who knew what I might pull.

I walked home quickly and kept my eyes on the sidewalk. I can't go out anymore, I thought. I'm liable to punch a man's stomach or swat a woman's ass. I'll be beaten, arrested. A dog will kill me. I'll suicidally attempt to snuggle with some chained-up pit bull. I thought of Grubin. It was all his fault. Why did he tell me about that damn plantain? He had passed me his neurosis. Why couldn't he just have a simple venereal disease like the rest of my friends? At least those weren't contagious over the phone.

I Should Sue Myself for Libel
June 22, 1999

Last night, I gave a reading at the Princeton Club. The event was held in an intimate lounge and about twenty-five people were in attendance. It was mostly a handsome older crowd, with a few younger Princeton alumni thrown in. After I read the opening two pages of my most recent novel, which, naturally, featured a scene with sexual content, I apologized for having uttered the word "erection" in such a hallowed establishment and in return I received polite laughter from the well-mannered audience.

I then continued reading for another twenty minutes or so and when I was done I opened things up for questions. An elegantly dressed, silver-haired gentleman in the back of the room immediately and eagerly raised his hand. I called on him and his voice boomed out with great joy: "I don't really have a question. I just want to say that you're a milestone! You're the first openly gay writer ever to give a reading at the Princeton Club. There should be some kind of plaque. I'm honored to be here when you're here. I applaud you!"

"How do you know he's gay?" asked a dignified, Brahminesque matron, who was sitting in the row in front of him, and who felt, and rightly so, that the man was somewhat out of line.

"Yes, how do you know?" asked a bald, intelligent-looking man on the other side of the room.

"You can't separate the writer from his work," said the silver-haired man. "Mr. Ames has obviously written from his experience." What experience he was referring to is unclear since I hadn't read a specific homosexual love scene. I did read a scene where my young protagonist puts on a brassiere, and then three scenes of dialogue dealing with F. Scott Fitzgerald, the possible homosexuality of the Duke of Windsor, and, yes, the homosexual love affair between Danny Kaye and Laurence Olivier, but nothing that would clearly indicate that I was writing about *my* homosexual experience.

"I disagree," said the bald man to the silver-haired man. "For a writer the imagination is key."

"I'm not trying to start an argument," said silver-hair, rather aggressively, implying that he was quite capable of starting one. This was bad. I was causing a fight to break out at the Princeton Club. And I had a new lovely girlfriend in the audience who had just heard me described as an openly gay man. I had to take charge of the situation.

"I'm glad to be a milestone," I said loudly, commanding the attention back to myself at the podium. "But I should say, though, that my sexuality is a profound mystery, mostly to myself . . . But let me share with you a brief anecdote. A few months ago, I met with several people at a publishing house—editors, marketing people, that sort of thing. They were thinking of buying a book of mine, but wanted to check me out. One of the editors said to me, "You have a very strong gay following. What do you think of that?" Now I don't know what the intention of that question was, but I gave them my standard reply, which is: "I seem to have a great appeal to all sexualities, which is very good for sales." "

The audience laughed and order was restored; if the man wanted to think I was gay that was perfectly fine, and for the rest of the audience I had made a confusing enough statement for them to project whatever sexuality they wanted onto me. I then fielded simpler questions and comments, and afterward I sat at a little table and signed books. Everyone was quite gracious and complimentary, but I was distracted by a conversation going on between silver-hair and the bald man, who said, "I still maintain that writers rely on imagination."

"Bullshit," said silver-hair. "Writers write their life stories. Somebody said to Evelyn Waugh's wife, 'Your husband has such imagination.' And she said, 'No, he's just a good editor.' Meaning that he left out the boring events of his life and wrote about the interesting ones."

Silver-hair then approached my little author's table. "I hope I haven't outed you, young man."

I smiled limply. My lovely girlfriend, who was still in her seat, glancing at *The New Yorker* to pass the time, cocked her head to listen, as did the dozen or so remaining attendees of the reading. "Don't worry," I said. "In, out, upside down, it's all the same to me." And what else could I do? Say to him, "No, I'm not gay," and humiliate him in front of everyone?

"Well, you certainly made history here tonight," he said. "On top of everything else, no one before you has ever said 'erection' at the Princeton Club."

"No one's ever had an erection at the Princeton Club," piped in the bald man.

"That's not true," said silver-hair rather mischievously, and I could only imagine how he's carried on in the locker room by the squash courts. Then he left, and I signed a few more books and my duty was done.

My lovely girlfriend and I left the Princeton Club and walked down Fifth Avenue. The sky was a deep, beautiful evening blue. My arm was around her. I thanked her for coming to the reading, and then said, "How did you feel hearing me be described as 'openly gay'?"

"I just felt that you handled it beautifully," she said. "Good for you for not protesting . . . To me, you're beyond labels."

It was an endearing thing for her to say and I squeezed her tight. "Yes, it seems to be my mission in life," I said, "to be the standard-bearer for a new, as of yet unlabeled sexuality. What I need to do is come up with a classification for those people who do not conveniently fall into the heterosexual, homosexual, lesbian, transsexual, or bisexual categories. You'd think that would be enough, but obviously it's not. This new category, you know, is like the most powerful political party—the undecideds . . . I should run for mayor on a sexual platform . . . I wonder if any politician has pursued the pervert vote? Maybe pansexual would be good title for my sexual-political party. Though people might confuse that with Peter Pan fetishists, of which there are a number."

"Really?"

"Oh, yes . . . Who knows, someone might even tell you that I'm a Peter Pan fetishist." She laughed, but I was serious, and I thought now was a good time, with the Princeton Club experience so fresh, to brace her for any rumors she might hear about me. "I should tell you that if you happen to mention to anyone that we're dating, they may report to you the most outlandish things about me. Most of which are true. I've come to realize that I'm the source of all my bad gossip. I should sue myself for libel."

"You wrote that in one of your columns," she said.

I was caught stealing one of my own lines. Very embarrassing. "Well, I should sue myself for libel *and* plagiarism."

"Jonathan, I like you for the way you treat me. I don't care what other people say about you. I don't care what you say about you."

I couldn't ask for anything more and I took hold of her and kissed her. She was beautiful.

We strolled all the way down Fifth Avenue. My arm was around her the whole time, she felt so good against me, and we were happy. We went to her place. There we decided to try something neither of us had ever done. Ear coning. I had always thought it was called ear candling, but her package of wax candles designed to cleanse the ear came with a set of instructions entitled, "Ear Coning."

So I've always wanted to ear cone. I like any process that cleans me out. I am all for fasting, colonics, and nose picking. A few months ago, I bought something called a netti pot, which allows one to transfer salt water from one nostril to the next, which helps to clear the sinuses. I did it for a week or so and then lost interest and reverted back to my old method of sinus clearing—frequent nose-picking, a nervous habit I've indulged in since childhood. And, for me, it's a dangerous habit, since I once caused a hemorrhage in my right nostril when I was fifteen and had to be rushed to the hospital for an emergency cauterization. I may be the only person in the world to have almost killed himself by nose picking. And yet to this day, twenty years later, I still pick. It's like smoking. You know you should quit, but you can't. And like smoking it has to do with the hands. Keeping the hands occupied.

Anyway, my lovely girlfriend and I got into bed with our ear candles and a bowl of water. After carefully reading the instructions, I coned her first. She lay on her right side and I lit the twelve-inch candle. It was hollow, with openings at both ends, and was made from a thick, somewhat slow-burning, waxy paper. Once it was aflame, I placed the non-burning end of the candle in her left ear. The concept is that the smoke from the far end of the candle will draw the wax out of the ear canal. As the candle burned down, she was visibly moved and pleased. There was a look of wonderment and delight on her face. "This is like smoking opium through your ear. I hear this crackling sound," she said.

After the candle burned down two inches I removed it and cut off the ash and put it back in her ear. After another two inches burned off, I wanted to cut the ash again, but she didn't want me to remove the candle. "It feels too good," she said.

"You better let me cut the ash," I said. "I don't want to burn down your apartment. People will say we were smoking in bed and think poorly of us. You know how people always look down on people who smoke in bed and set fires. And we're not even smokers!"

She let me remove the candle; I clipped the ash and then put the candle back in. I let her use up another two inches of the candle and then doused it in the water—we needed to save the second half for her other ear. After having put out the flame, I looked inside the hollow candle and saw this caramel-colored globule of her earwax.

"It worked!" I proclaimed. With a chopstick I knocked her earwax out of the candle and into the bowl of water. I then coned her other ear and removed another globule of earwax. She then coned me. It was quite sensual and a lovely act of trust to allow someone to put a burning candle in your head. I, too, heard the crackling and felt a certain, calm peace as my earwax was sucked out of me. Like hers, mine was also caramel colored, which was nice to have in common. When it was all done, we both felt as if our hearing was greatly improved and we lay in her bed. Her back was to me and I kissed her bare neck and shoulders. I held her close to me. She fit very well in my arms. She wanted to try out her new ear canals. "Whisper something," she said.

"You're beautiful. I adore you," I said, and then I kissed and licked her ear and it had an interesting taste. "Smoked ear," I said to her. "As a Jew, you know, I love smoked foods." She then kissed my ears and then I kissed her ears some more and so it went and what happened next I will leave to the reader's vivid imagination.

Jew England
July 6, 1999

I'm on an island twelve miles off the coast of Maine. It's morning. Overcast. Cool. Out my window, I can see the see the island's small yacht club—the numerous sailboats and the gray, old docks, alive in their subtle treading of water, resting on the chest of the tide, like my girlfriend laying her head on my breast as I breathe. But so much for tender thoughts: how easily distracted is a man: a young girl on the docks just tossed her dark ponytail in a fetching way. My male eye takes her in. Evaluates. Salivates. She smiles. Beautiful. A comely, budding figure. She and several other young girls and boys seem to be involved in some kind of sailing class, getting their boats ready, following instructions, putting on orange life preservers.

The yacht club has one main, brown-shingled building and on top, furling and unfurling, is the American flag, like a bed sheet, like a sail sheet. So there's a good breeze and it's low tide. I can see through the clear, lapping water to the bottom, a bottom littered with thousands of mussels. Another girl, a towhead, bends over in her khaki shorts. I like that. Farther out I see a red sailboat. It looks rather noble with its red belly. Through my window comes the smell of the ocean and the smell of gasoline from the motorboats. The odors of harbors everywhere. Romantic smells. The dark ponytailed girl is out in her boat. Setting off. She turns her head quickly to the right and left, trying to catch the wind. Back and forth goes the ponytail. In the far distance, I can see the dark green and light green pine trees of another island. There are hundreds of islands off the coast of Maine. I didn't know this before. The class sails off to the right, out of my view. Goodbye, sweet sailor. Pubescent breasts bound in orange vest. Now an old, large schooner goes proudly by, its prow, like a regal chin, tilted a little upward.

So I'm deep in the heart of New England. A Jew out of water. It took me a few days to get here. I'll start from the beginning.

My girlfriend and I rented a car. I was behind the wheel first and we got caught in a downpour as we escaped the horrible greenhouse of New York. Later, I asked my girlfriend, looking for a compliment, what she thought of my driving and she told me that I drove carefully, but too slowly. I found this to be emasculating. I have always taken pride in my driving. Drove a taxi for two years. Have driven across the U.S. twice. "The roads were wet," I said to her, fighting to get my balls back. I had been trained how to operate a car by my father, who had survived driving eighty thousand miles a year for thirty years as a traveling salesman and never had an accident. Driving for him was like a military operation: constant awareness of the enemy—other drivers, even those far ahead—and deep respect for weather conditions. But my girlfriend didn't acquiesce, the wet road argument didn't appease her. In her mind, I was a slow driver. I had to stay calm and know that my manliness is not so fragile. I restrained from telling her that I have numerous points for speeding violations.

Anyway, our first stop was a small town on the seacoast north of Boston. Updike country. In fact, we drove through Updike's town, Beverly Farms, and passed his driveway, which my girlfriend pointed out. I peered down the leafy lane. Only saw a PRIVATE PROPERTY sign. The house was set too far back. It was interesting to think that Updike was back there somewhere, writing his poems, his reviews, his books. This enormous WASP intellect tirelessly commenting on everything, and keeping pace with his female counterpart Oates and his Jewish counterpart Roth.

So what would it be like to have a brain like Updike's? The sheer volume of his work is astounding, and that's all I can really comment on, since I've read but a smattering of his criticism and only one his books, *The Centaur,* which I liked very much, though I did read it years ago, and as I change personalities every two years or so I'm not sure if my current self would like the book, but my old self did, and I will trust my former self's judgment, which I happen to have shared with Updike himself. About two years ago, in Brooklyn Heights, on a cool fall night, I saw Updike pushing a baby carriage, which held, I presumed, his grandchild. He was accompanied by his wife, and I followed this icon of American literature into a gourmet deli on Montague Street. I thought I should talk to him, which is something I do whenever I chance across a famous writer on the street: I make brazen, yet banal approaches, saying something light and meaningless about the author's work—I can never come up with anything resembling an intelligent remark—and I have done this to Allen Ginsberg, Paul Auster, Dominick Dunne, and Richard Ford. An unusual collection that.

Anyway, I followed Updike into the shop and his wife took charge of the carriage and Updike was studying a freezer filled with cheeses. He was tall, gray-haired, wearing preppy clothes—corduroy pants, a sweater, a Patagonia jacket—and was sporting his famous profile. I sidled up next to him and said, "Sorry to bother you . . . but I just wanted to let you know that I loved *The Centaur*."

I knew this was a somewhat risky thing to say as *The Centaur* was one of his first books, published in the very early sixties, before even the start of the Rabbit series, and so there was the chance perhaps that he would think I was dismissing his last nearly forty years of output. But Updike smiled kindly at me, he knew I was being sincere, and he said, "I think I remember writing that one." And we both chuckled and then he continued along the freezer of cheeses. There was nothing more for us to discuss, so I said, "Well, so long," and he gave me a nice little nod of his head and I got out of there, leaving him to his shopping. It's not quite what Nicholson Baker, who famously admires U, might have done in the same circumstance, but it wasn't bad—I can always say that I've met Updike.

So we drove through Beverly Farms and a few towns over we came to our friends' large and beautiful ocean-front home. We took a late freezing swim, followed by a glorious, hot outdoor shower, and then we got dressed for dinner. As I combed my hair in the bathroom and kept it close to my scalp by rubbing in my special French brilliantine gel, I noticed that a disastrous haircut I received in May had finally begun to grow in. My fringe at the front of my head, which I comb back (which I must point out is not the universally despised *comb-over* but a *comb-back*, though I will say that the comb-over is unfairly criticized; I know numerous older men who look perfectly attractive with comb-overs, in particular this one Italian waiter in midtown who combs over one strand and I think he wouldn't be himself without that strand; so I now publicly take on a new role: defender of the comb-over!), is now almost long enough again to cover the bald spot in the middle of my head. But what is really nice is that the thin hair at the back of the head is also almost reaching the bald spot. So by utilizing a fringe-comb-back and a Julius Caesar–comb-forward, I nearly have complete coverage, which is quite a recovery from the scalping the barber gave me in May. I specifically told him at that time not to cut my fringe, but he misunderstood me and cut the thing in half, leaving me with a horribly exposed bald spot. But, as I've said, the fringe is healing, i.e., growing, and so I went down to dinner that night in Massachusetts feeling very good about myself.

It was a pleasant meal of the ubiquitous salmon, and my girlfriend and I played footsie under the long table, straining, like ballet dancers, to reach each other's calves. After coffee and dessert, I went and stood outside with my host on the large back porch and we took in the lights of the gigantic, hotel-sized mansion glittering down the beach a ways. "The money is so old around here," he said, "that it's disintegrating."

"That's a good line," I said. "I might have to use that."

We spent the whole next day and night in Massachusetts, and then the following day, we got back in the car and drove a few hours to an exclusive Maine beach community, a bit north of George Bush's Kennebunkport. We stayed with relatives of my girlfriend and that night we went to a very fancy dinner party in an elegant home. It was right above a great tumble of those famous Maine, Winslow Homerish coastline rocks, and the view of the

Atlantic was glorious and uncluttered. And the people were straight out of Cheever central casting. The women were all handsome and tall and light-haired and tan. The men were thickset, strong chinned, and glittered-eyed with drink, and they were like a military outfit: each one was in a fresh, deep, dark blue blazer. But no ties. It was a laid-back summer Saturday night dinner on the Fourth of July weekend. I too was in blue blazer, but not a sharp, pressed one like my fellow men. Mine was a crumpled, but attractive Agnes B. linen blazer that a French friend of mine pulled some strings to get at a great discount. So I was sort of all right in the blazer department, but my shoes were a bit of an embarrassment. All the men were in delicate Italian-looking loafers with no socks. I was in my cumbersome, better-suited for winter, hobnail-looking-and-needing-polish Clarks. But the shoes, like my unshaved chin (the only one in the house), weren't a complete disaster: I could afford to be eccentric in the shoe and shaving department: I was a writer—practically an artist—in their midst, not one of them, but welcome.

We had drinks in a blustery wind on the outer deck, and then for dinner the party was divided into two tables, and my girlfriend and I were put at different tables, as all couples were separated this way. I was seated between two very nice women, who quizzed me quite a lot about my writing. I gave them the titles of my books and added, "They're each just out in paperback, should you want to pick them up." The hostess overheard this and she said she'd buy both tomorrow, and I rather regretted this, thinking that she would be horrified, should she read the books, that I had been let into her house and generously fed and welcomed. But I consoled myself with the hope that by the next day she'd probably forget. The women next to me questioned me further about my writing and I told them that I pen a newspaper column.

"About what?" asked the woman to my left.

"My adventures, things I do," I said. "For example, last week I wrote about—and I don't mean to disturb your dinners—ear candling, also called ear coning, which I tried. It's where you put a candle in your ear and it helps to clean the ear out." I didn't want to say the word wax, not wanting to be too disgusting.

"Are you pulling my leg?" asked the woman to my right.

"No. I'm not joking. It's an ancient ear-cleansing process," I said, adding the ancient part to lend the activity some dignity.

"I can't believe we're talking about this here in Maine," she said, and she laughed happily. I was making her feel naughty. She was enjoying my society.

Then somehow it came up in our conversation that the rest of Maine does not like the community where we were. "Why?" I asked.

"Because it's private," said the woman on my right, "and has this reputation of being this place where are all the greedy Philadelphians and New Yorkers came years ago and took the most beautiful spot for themselves and didn't let anyone else in. Which used to be true. Like a New York co-op board . . . My husband is Jewish and twenty years ago he never used to come to the parties."

"Someone once told me," I said, "that this part of Maine is often called Philadelphia-on-the-rocks."

The ladies liked that line, and privately I thought to myself how all my adult life I find myself at the epicenters of WASP culture. Princeton, Philadelphia, Palm Beach, New Port, and the Upper East Side are all places where I've been and have mingled with those whose families are listed in the Social Register. And in these circles, I'm often mistaken with my white eyebrows and mildly English appearance for a Bostonian Ames—a Brahminesque clan—when the fact of the matter is that Ames was the actual name of my Jewish-Czechoslovakian-Kafkaesque forbears.

So having studied these people, America's WASPs, like an anthropologist, I can safely say, that similar to the comb-over, they have an undeserved, unfair reputation. They are clannish, value their families, and enjoy certain activities and rituals—in other words they are like most groupings or tribes of people, neither better nor worse. And like gay men—another tribe—they seem to have a real talent for finding some of America's most beautiful spots. And at one time, perhaps, they erected barriers around themselves, but slowly these barriers are crumbling and others, like myself, are gaining access, which, in my opinion, is neither good nor bad. It's simply the nature of things. People stake a claim and eventually others follow, no matter what.

And here I am now—having left that Maine community the next day after the dinner party—on an island whose highest point, interestingly enough, is called Ames Nob. So I guess I was meant to come here. The place has been waiting for me. It has my name.

The Tenderloin
July 20, 1999

I'm in San Francisco holed up in a hotel room drinking cold coffee. I'm in the Tenderloin District. Don't know why it's named that. Probably used to be where they did the meat-packing. But regardless, it's a good name for this part of town. The loin part and the tender part. This is where all the whores are. Women. Men. Queens.

I was cruising around here last night, soaking up the atmosphere. I felt like I was in America. Or old America. People are allowed to fall apart here out in the open. And if they want to pursue vice, then they can pursue it, though with some supervision, some threat of arrest, so there's not total chaos—I did see one cop car last night. And it all makes me realize how antiseptic Manhattan has become. How can New York not have a red-light district? Where's it gone? I think Times Square has moved to the back pages of the *Press* and the *Voice,* and to the Internet, which is the biggest whorehouse ever. But it's not live. One needs to be able to walk through or drive through a red-light district. It's like Paris cafe culture. You can always drink coffee at home, but it's more fun to drink coffee around other people. Same thing with sin. It's better to be with other sinners, it's less lonely and there's more opportunity.

Anyway, I came out of my hotel last night around twelve-thirty and was walking up this street called Eddy. I had taken off my tie, which I had been wearing earlier, and I drew my collar of my coat around my neck so I'd look a little less muggable (a taxi driver told me you can get mugged in the Tenderloin) and at first I didn't see anything. And then my eyes adjusted. Night vision so to speak. I realized there were women in the shadows of doorways, and men in tight jeans in alleys. There was a staticky streetlight glow and a cool breeze. It's like fall, here in San Francisco. And the buildings, in this part of town, are only a few stories high—you can see the sky and so you don't feel tiny and diminished. The buildings are also crumbling and need painting, which gave me the feeling of being in an old city, a Western-frontier city, and it was nice to remember that America is not all New York spit and polish and money and phony-looking Plaza Hotel brass.

I made a left up a hilly street called Hyde. I was walking on the outside of the parked cars, almost in the middle of the road, so nobody could jump me, and on the other side of the street, coming the opposite way down the sidewalk, were two not-very-dolled-up prostitutes. They were wearing jeans and tight little coats. Nothing about them was gaudy in the way you'd expect, but their leisurely walk told you why they were out there. I made that special kind of eye contact with one of them. Her face was unusual, striking. High cheekbones, a fierce jaw, a long, thin red mouth, and kinky curly blonde hair. And her skin, in the light, was some weird kind of translucent, diluted white, like underneath it was some original coat of paint, color unknown. But it was there somehow, as if that top layer of white hadn't been painted on thick enough. So I held her eye and she sidled across the street to me.

"What are you doing tonight?" she asked sweetly, gently. She was humble. Shy even. Now that we were up close she didn't quite look at me straight. She was worried I wouldn't want her. Her jacket was open and she was wearing a tank top and I could see that on the exposed flesh of her belly there were light brown discolorations and green bruises, and on her face there were small thin scars. She had been on the street a long time. She was probably in her late thirties, and she didn't necessarily look older than that, except she *was* old, the way young people look old when they are dying.

"I'm just walking around tonight. Looking," I said. I thought of my girlfriend back in New York.

"You have a room?" she asked.

"Yeah, at the Phoenix."

"That's a nice hotel. Nicer than the others around here . . . Why don't we go back to your room and have a lovely time and in the morning go to Reno and get married." She laughed. A nice laugh. A laugh at herself. But that's probably why she's still out there—the one-in-a-million chance that some man might yet save her.

"I don't think I want to go back to my room, but thank you for offering," I said, wanting to be polite. I started strolling. She walked alongside me.

"Where are you from?" I asked. "I hear a bit of an accent."

"Australia," she said. "I'm half Aborigine, half white." She was quick to tell me that. I guess people were always wondering what she was, and so she got that information out there as soon as possible rather than wait for the question. "Where are you from?" she asked.

"New York."

"What are you doing here in San Fran? You're a businessman?"

"No, I'm a writer. Also, I perform, I do storytelling. That's what I came here for. I did some storytelling at a club tonight."

"I tell stories," she said, kind of excited, asserting herself, sensing an angle. "Why don't we go to your room and I'll tell you dream stories and you tell me stories from New York. I've never been there."

"Dream stories. I like the way that sounds," I said.

"So what do you say? Why don't we go back to your room? It doesn't have to be a big sex thing. I'll tell you my dream stories and I'll give you a nice massage." She said massage like a real Brit colonial, with an emphasis on the first syllable. I looked at her closely. Her nose was wide and interesting looking. I could really see the Aborigine in her. And her mixed blood explained her odd skin, skin I had never really seen before. But I didn't want to be alone with her in my room. She was sweet and I wanted to help her somehow, but to see her body would be to know too well the agony of what she's been through.

"I don't want to waste your time," I said. "I really don't think I want to go back to my room. But if you want to walk with me, I'd like the company and I'll give you twenty dollars for that, if you don't mind." I had called her over with my eyes just wanting to talk to her for a moment—I like to talk to people when I'm out having adventures—but I felt bad to have led her on, to have given her some hope of making money, so I was glad to try to hire her as my guide, companion.

"You'll pay me just to walk with you?" she asked.

"Yes," I said.

"Are all gentleman from New York like you? I heard men from New York will say fuck you if you ask them the time."

"No. There are no gentlemen like me in New York," I boasted. "I am completely and hopelessly unique." And I laughed and so did she.

So we walked and I felt safe with her. We passed a number of small packs of homeless addicts and drunkards, all of whom looked pretty feeble, but they might have tried something on me just because of their sheer greater numbers, but because I was with her, a fellow street person, there was little chance anybody would try to hurt me.

I got a bit of her life story. Not much. But a glimpse. She came here in 1985 and right away started working the streets. Her husband was her pimp. They were married seven years.

"He didn't mind you being out here?"

"No. He saw it as a business and so did I. When I first came out here it was good. All the girls were in furs and heels. You could meet a businessman and he would give you one hundred and a fifty-dollar tip. Now it's all changed. There's not as much money, so the girls aren't the same. No more furs. And AIDS scared people away too . . . Now it's hard to get by. A lot of the girls are on drugs. That makes it real tough to keep your head above water."

"Are you on drugs?"

"I smoke my weed, but I'm not on drugs . . . Well, to be honest I'm on methadone. Three years."

"What happened to your husband?"

"He went to jail. He's still in there."

"Why?"

"Some kind of fraud . . . But I don't miss him, really. He

didn't beat me, but I wasn't in love with him. I loved him, but I wasn't *in* love."

We kept walking. The whole neighborhood was filled with SRO hotels with locked gates for entrances. We passed other whores. There was this one old blonde whore, she was maybe forty, but she looked fifty, and her face, tanned and leathery, was mad, stricken. She was wearing a loud, flower-print dress and white heels. She was kind of like that old prostitute I had seen in Paris. I wondered if she would get any business. She looked clean but insane.

"Do you want to stop being out here?" I asked my friend.

"I'd like to. My sister is always writing me, telling me to come back. But I guess I'm one of those people who has to be on their last leg and limb before they'll go home."

And thinking about her saying that, it's hard to imagine that she won't die here, that she'll never make it back to Australia.

"I've never met an Aborigine before," I said.

"I'm not a full Aborigine. I'm not really even half. My father was half . . . There are a lot of people like me in Australia. A lot of people with black blood. That's why my hair is kinky . . . And my face is kind of like a boy's cause it's bony, which I get from my father. Sometimes people mock me, say I'm a queen. Other people say it makes me pretty. I don't know how I feel about it. If I look like a pretty boy it could be a compliment. A lot of the queens out here are beautiful. More beautiful than the real girls."

"There are queens around here? I've written a lot about queens."

"They have the next street. That's their corridor. You want to go there?"

"All right," I said.

We went to the queens' street and it was good to see them again, especially since in cleaned up New York they are nowhere to be found. We passed two large buxom black queens and their flowery scent was strong. Queens often lay it on thick.

"You can really smell their perfume," I said, when they were out of earshot.

"Oh, yeah," said my friend, laughing, "that's true."

Then we came upon a drag bar called Motherlode. "That's where they all hang out," she said. "If you go in there you might find something more to write about queens."

I decided to go in the place, but my friend didn't feel comfortable coming with me; she didn't want the queens to think she was trying to compete with them in their bar, so it was time for me to pay her and I gave her the twenty and the few extra singles I had. "Be careful in there," she said. Then she thanked me and kissed me on the cheek goodbye and walked away, and that was it.

I went inside the bar and sat in the shadows. It was a narrow thin place and near the entrance was a small elevated stage with a big mirror behind it. A few queens were up on the stage and I watched them dance by themselves. They faced the mirror and while they danced they adjusted their hair, their breasts, their lipstick. I always like to watch queens. It's like theater.

After half an hour, I left the bar and headed for my hotel. A few blocks from the queens' street, I saw three real girls, young blondes with long thin legs. Two of them were peroxide blondes, one of them was natural. They were all quite beautiful. Quite young. Not one of them more than twenty. Where had they come from? They were on heels like stilts. Their dresses were short. They teetered and clicked down the road. They were all leg and white-blonde hair. I passed by them. Stared at them. They were like slivers of light, wavering. Beautiful filaments. Young girls. I kept going.

I scanned the streets for my friend, my guide, but didn't spot her, but if I were to be here tonight, which I won't be, I'm sure I'd see her again.

A Live Death
August 3, 1999

Yesterday, I saw a dead man for the first time. It was ten-thirty in the morning. I was walking back to my building and at the corner there was a firetruck, an EMS van, and a police car. A half dozen people were standing by one of the windows of the Exquisite Cleaners on First Avenue. I joined them and being taller than the woman in front of me I was able to look in. An EMS worker was pumping on the chest of a black man lying on the floor. His liquidy, light brown belly was rolling from the pounding on his chest.

"What's happened?" I said to the crowd in front of me.

A man without turning said, "He's dead. A heart attack." We all stared through the window. There were about a dozen technicians surrounding the fallen body. I watched a squatting rescuer tear the paper off a needle. He was wearing rubber gloves. The needle was put in the man's neck. The technician who was pumping the man's chest was watching a blue monitor with a silver-white line going across.

"Flat line," said a woman.

The man's legs were crossed peacefully at the ankles, as if he had decided to stretch out and relax. He was wearing brown pants and simple white leather shoes that had been repolished many times. The soles were made of thin rubber. He had been wearing those shoes for years. He had bent down that morning to put them on, then came to the cleaners. The top of his hair was spotted with gray. He must have been in his late fifties or early sixties. His face was turned to the side. He looked calm. He was sleeping.

I walked across the street to my building. I didn't want to be disrespectful, to stare at the man. I went inside, pushed the button for the elevator. Then I thought, You're a writer. Go back out there. You need to know about life. It was my rationale for morbid curiosity. I went back outside and rejoined the crowd. We looked through the window like a TV. We were watching a live death.

The line on the monitor was jagged. They were still pumping his chest. "What's happening?" I asked. "Is he coming back?"

"No," said the man who had answered me earlier.

"But the line," I said, and then I added to the man on the floor, "Come on. Come on."

"They have him on artificial respiration," said the knowledgeable man. "Every time they pump his chest it sends blood through his heart and the line goes up. But when they stop the line goes flat."

"Are you a doctor?" I asked.

"No, an engineer," said the man. He stared intently through the window. I had yet to see his face, only the back of his head, the collar of his shirt.

I watched the dead man's stomach shake. His right hand was up by his shoulder, it was curled in a fist like a sleeping child's hand. Who was he? Would he be embarrassed to have everyone working on him? They were pounding on his chest so hard. And all the rescuers had solemn, professional looks on their face, a mix of concern and detachment. I wondered if they had crossed his legs on purpose. Something to do with circulation. It seemed such an odd pose. I asked the knowledgeable man, "Did they cross his legs? Does that do something?"

"No," he said, puzzled. He thought it was a strange question. I watched the line on the monitor with the technician who watched it. They wouldn't stop working on him. Up and down on his chest. "Please come back," I said in my mind. I stepped away from the crowd. A short, red-haired policeman with a pinned-up ponytail was reporting to his sergeant, who was tall and had decorations on his chest. I didn't know that police were allowed to have ponytails. I heard him say to his superior, "The wife's work number was on him. But we'll let them call from the hospital."

The decorated policeman nodded that this was a good course of action. I went to the other window, where no one was looking in. You couldn't see anything from this window except for the old tailor who was behind the store's counter, sitting down at his little worktable. He was Middle Eastern, ancient, yellow-olive skin, long nose, incredible hands, fingers. He was working on a pair of black trousers, tearing out a seam. Had he watched them try to save the man for a while and then went back to work? The other employee or owner of the store—the tailor's son?—was also behind the counter and he was dragging a bag of laundry to add to a pile of bags. He tossed it on top. The numerous EMS workers stood with their backs to the counter. The tailor studied the pants. He picked up an enormous pair of black scissors. I had never seen such big scissors. I went back to the other window. The engineer had left.

They picked up the man and put him on a plastic, orange stretcher. They kept pumping his chest the whole time. I went and stood near the door. A lot of people were milling about. The ponytailed policeman told us all to back away. I looked at a clipboard he was holding. A form was filled out. At the top was a name, which I assumed was the dead man's name. I could make out the first part, Dennis.

They had trouble getting him out the door. Someone should be here to say a prayer, I thought. I wished that a Hasidic Jew would come by. A Hassid would know what to do, how to honor the dead. The man was pulled through the door. I started to say the Sh'ma; it was the only thing that came to my mind; it was the only Hebrew I could remember. I'm most likely an agnostic and I said the words not knowing their meaning. But then his body was right alongside me and I stopped praying. I was too busy gawking. No window between us. My first dead body. His chest was naked, bare. His skin was sallow. One of his eyes was partially open. I could see the white. He was gone, empty. It didn't look like he was sleeping now. His legs were uncrossed. His shoes were old. He was over. The technician kept pumping his chest, hoping for a miracle. They put him in the ambulance. People dispersed.

I looked inside the store. The counterman was sweeping up the bandages and wrappers that the EMS had left behind. He was sweeping them into a big dust pan. There was no blood, but I could see from his face that he was loath to touch anything. And there was a large piece of maroon fabric on the floor and he swept that into the dustpan. I couldn't tell if it was the man's shirt. Had it been ripped open and left on the floor and now looked like a piece of fabric? Maybe his wife would want his shirt.

She'd want everything of his. I wanted to tell the man to save it for the wife. But what if it was a piece of fabric? I was afraid to say anything. Maybe I would seem irrational. And this man and the tailor had seemed so callous, throwing a bag of laundry, working on a seam, but what else could they do? Gawk like the rest of us? Still, I was scared of them, scared to appear like an oversensitive fool. And what if the counterman gave it to me? You bring it to the wife. I was frightened myself to touch the shirt. To be that close to a dead man, to hold it and imagine him wearing it that morning, not knowing he would die. I watched the counterman empty the dustpan into a garbage bag.

So I rationalized: the EMS workers had been so attentive, they wouldn't leave his shirt behind, it must be a piece of fabric.

I walked over to my building. I went to my apartment and sat down on my bed. I thought, The wife would want the shirt, I'm a coward. I imagined her getting the phone call from the hospital. I remembered to pray again. This will make up a little for the shirt, I thought. I sent a prayer to follow after him in the ambulance. But I still was a coward. I should have asked for the shirt.

Later I went back outside. I walked past Exquisite Cleaners. A few customers were inside. They were standing where the man's body had been. The floor was all cleaned up. The tailor was behind the counter sewing. The counterman took his customers' clothes. I wanted to tell the people, A man died in there today, you should stay away, he should be honored. But that's only what I thought. I didn't say anything. I knew I was overreacting. It was my first dead body.

Into Thin Hair
August 17, 1999

*My mind is all fragmented, so I think this will be a fragmented
entry. I'm feeling this way because I've been moving around so
much. In the last six weeks I've been in Massachusetts, Maine, California, New Jersey, West Virginia, and Pennsylvania. And my
lovely girlfriend, who is out of town and has been for the whole
summer, told me that when you travel—and she was quoting some
ancient culture's maxim, but I don't remember the culture—that
your soul doesn't get places as quickly as your body, that it goes at
the speed of a camel. The meaning I've taken from this is that when
I come back to New York from my various excursions my body is
here, but my soul is still elsewhere, in transit.*

Last night, Sunday night, I got back from a weekend-
long family wedding in Pennsylvania, and when I entered
my chambers, because my soul was on some slow-moving
camel, I was overcome by this wild panic and anxiety. It
was exactly what I felt when I got here the previous
Sunday night coming back from West Virginia, where I
had been for a writers' conference. Both times when I got
home, I frantically opened mail that had accumulated,
paced around, put on the computer to check email, ran
the water to clear the lead, opened the windows . . . But it

was like I was headless, and I was burning up with the adrenaline that had propelled me home.

So last night I quickly did the above-mentioned tasks, but when they were finished I didn't know what to do with myself. The idea of being with a friend didn't seem like an answer—I was feeling too crazed for company. And I can't drink, but if I could imbibe like a normal human being it would have been a good time to go to a bar, but I can't drink—dammit—so what I ended up doing in a crazed fury was going through my pile of recycled papers, coming up with a *Voice* and turning to the back pages, which are like a porno magazine, and more photo-rich, I have to say, than my own *New York Press*'s back pages. I then studied the numerous ads, was intrigued as always by the sheer volume of prostitution available—what's this say about the demand?—and absorbed all the images in my retina and transmitted them to the sex center in my brain, where yet another connection was made to the nerve endings of the fingers of my right hand, which by this time had the old phallus in its grip. This one ad in particular was quite provocative. It featured a busty, smiling girl with a 718 number, and I was thinking how nice it is to squeeze a woman's breasts when she's beneath you and you're in the heat of copulation—Your bosom is delicious! We're making love! And you like it and I like it! Life! *L'chaim*!—and all the while I kept abusing myself manually, and this lasted about eighty-six seconds, ending with my production of a horrid orgasm.

I say horrid, thinking about it in retrospect, because if you do anything too much it feels like that T. S. Eliot sentiment in the Prufrock poem where your life is measured out miserably in coffee spoons, or the other similar sentiment in the poem, where you're like claws scuttling across an ocean floor—Death! Death! It's all a sad, pathetic march to death—coffee spoons, claws, and, in my case, years of habitual self-release.

So after the burbling of the semen and the immediate dissolution of the pleasurable thoughts of the 718 area-code breasts there was my dejected walk, like claws, across the apartment floor to a towel to clean up my recessed, defeated white-capped cock. But I must admit that my orgasm was medicinal. Right after I cleaned myself up for the nine millionth time in my life, I suddenly realized I was deeply and profoundly fatigued. The getting-home-adrenaline had had me thinking I could run to the top of the Empire State Building, but all I really needed to do was just eat something and go to sleep.

So readers—and this is valuable advice during the vacation-heavy month of August—when you come back from a trip, put down your bags and immediately climb on the bed and get your hand on your penis or clit, depending on what you have, and go to work. That's my recommendation. The masturbation calms you down until the rest of you—your soul—arrives. In fact, I may have to masturbate right now. It's like taking an aspirin every four hours.

Some more thoughts on masturbating. What lasts longer than a cock? Maybe a cast-iron frying pan and a good New England chair, but definitely not an airplane, a car, or a boat. They all break down. But a cock, you can really put miles on the thing. All the times I've flown the flag from my sunken state to my full powers (I'm a grower, not a shower), well, the distance, if you add up the inches, must be remarkable. It could be the length of the Jersey Shore, which I think is one of the largest beachfronts in the United States. I'm proud of this, since I was raised in New

Jersey and spent my summer vacations, like Philip Roth (trying to draw some meager parallel between myself and the great man), at the Jersey Shore. But little did I know as a boy, digging holes in the sand and riding waves, that my cock, with cumulative erections, would someday be as long as the beach where I was playing.

Last night when I really needed to sleep I woke up at three A.M. All summer long I've been troubled with poor sleep, and Dr. Bronner, who sells that good soap I use, castile soap, writes on the side of his soap bottles that the two keys to health are sleep and cleanliness (i.e., using his soap), and I happen to agree with him about sleep, so I worry that my health is deteriorating.

Anyway, I woke up at three A.M. anxious about the title for my new book, which is a comic autobiography based on my columns. For months I've been struggling with what to call the thing. Most of the chapters of the book, which could be a good source for titles, just don't work with a mainstream press and the hope of attracting *some* mainstream readers. For example, the book can not be called: "I Shit My Pants in the South of France" or "Bald, Impotent, and Depressed" or "Enemas: A Love Story" or "The Lord of the Genitals" or "An Erection Is a Felony."

So last night, at three A.M., anxious about this problem, I jotted down four possible titles, which sort of capture my life story and which were inspired by current nonfiction best-sellers: "The Perfect Nervous Wreck," "Into Thin Hair," "Tuesdays with Mangina," and "Jonathan's Asses."

All these are quite apt, but I don't want my title to be a play on words with best-sellers that could easily be forgotten, and so after writing those down, not thinking that I had hit upon what I needed, I then read a bit of the latest Eddie Bunker book I'm enthralled by, *No Beast So Fierce*. Now there's a good title. I finally did fall asleep around five A.M., only to have a nightmare that I was back on my high school fencing team and had let the squad down because I had lost my helmet and could only fence with *my* helmet, the meaning of which, I think, has to do with feelings of unworthiness, disappointing people, and losing my mind, all of which are feelings I experience quite often. Anyway, the title problem has been solved. When I went for coffee this morning, I was reading the sports section and saw a phrase in an article on the young Spanish golfer Sergio Garcia that works perfectly for my book. The sportswriter was complimenting every aspect of Garcia's game and then wrote, "So when it comes to young Sergio Garcia, what's not to love?" Eureka, as they say. When I came home, I called all the necessary people: editor, literary agent, and mother. They all agreed that "What's Not to Love?" is a good title. So maybe tonight, I'll sleep.

My eighty-seven-year-old great-aunt Pearl, during the five-hour car rides to and from Pennsylvania, did not stop talking the whole time. It was a constant litany of complaints, criticism, fearful predictions, and a few stories from her past, which was the only part that was enjoyable. And I love her dearly and if I think for a moment of her not being in my life the thought is too horrible, but her constant chatter *was* a bit maddening. It made me think of that Flannery O'Connor story, "A Good Man Is Hard to Find," where a serial killer—the Misfit—slaughters a family because of a grandmother who wouldn't shut up, and the Misfit says of the grandmother, "She would of been a good woman . . . if it had been somebody there to shoot her every minute of her life.' "

But my great-aunt did come up with some good lines yesterday. Speaking of the twenty-year-old daughter of a distant cousin of ours, a good kid who at the moment is struggling with college, she said, "You never know with children. You're better off going to the track. You'll have better luck with the horses than how your own kids will turn out."

And then out of the blue, while I was behind the wheel and my parents were asleep and my son was staring out the window with boredom, she said, "I wish there was a machine you could go into that would make everything perfect. If I went into the machine, I'd like to have my breast back." She lost her right breast to cancer twelve years ago. "I went to a specialist you know," she always brings up this specialist, "and I asked him for a fake breast. They take it from your rear end now. That's how they make breasts. But he said he wouldn't touch me for three million dollars, told me that my skin is too old and thin. He had a breast on the wall that was dripping. I pointed it out to him. He said that it was saline solution and he thanked me for pointing out the drip . . . You know they can build up a man's penis. The same way, fat from your rear, or the salt water, I guess. I've known a few men in my life who could have used that."

My thirteen-year-old son, who is very patient and good with his great-great-aunt, started to laugh at her talking of building up penises. And then I said, "Or you can just have them insert a hot dog into the penis and it has two functions: it makes your penis bigger and if you ever get hungry then you can just take out the hot dog and eat it.

Like emergency food." So my great-aunt Pearl laughed and my son laughed and my parents still slept.

I have to say that being with my son was very good. I was depressed before he arrived. No real reason, just depressed and down. But then I picked him up at the airport and right away we were joking around and laughing and I wasn't depressed anymore. Having someone else to think about is a good thing. I'm full of advice today: children are good for depression and masturbation is good for your nerves after a trip.

A friend of mine called a few minutes ago; he's something of a West Coast vegetarian guru, so whenever he talks to me I feel hopeless and suicidal. Today he was telling me about the importance of amino acids. He said, "You know, for a man, the amino acid glycine is very important, especially if you have sex a lot, because there's a lot of glycine in semen." This caught my attention. I try to compensate for my considerable loss of semen by eating fish. I once read that seafood restores one's ability to get erections. I picked up this valuable information while glimpsing briefly at some Eastern-Tantric book, but it's ridiculous how I operate my life on a hodgepodge of ideas from esoteric sources that I don't study closely.

"Do fish have a lot of glycine?" I asked. "I try to eat a lot of fish."

"Well, all sources of protein have glycine. But they say you should hardly eat fish. Small children should never have it, and adults maybe once a week. Fish is loaded with mercury, and mercury stays in your system forever and really messes with your neurological functions. Sardines aren't bad. They're small and have little fat, so they don't carry much mercury. Myself, as you know, I try to eat very low on the food chain, less poisons."

"Oh, God," I said, *the world.*" Which was my way of saying that I can't take the environmental hell we've created. So then me and my friend both sighed wearily, and I made a mental note to get a tin of sardines to balance out the masturbation I indulged in last night, plus the self-abuse I engaged in a few paragraphs ago, which I wasn't going to mention. Like Hemingway, I was going to leave some things unsaid and have them filter through the work, let the reader feel it that way, but then my friend called with this glycine-semen report and so I've brought it up.

This morning after my coffee, I went to the post office to pick up some package that couldn't fit in my box. Turned out to be a large envelope with two London magazine reviews of my novel, *The Extra Man*, which has just come out in England. I read them, they were pretty good, and then I went to get something to eat at the Greek diner on the northeast corner of Fifth and Second, which used to be on the northwest corner, but recently moved over because of lease problems. Anyway, I sat in the window and a few tables over was Quentin Crisp, the renowned writer and performer, who famously always eats lunch in this diner. In one of my English reviews there was a reference to Crisp and I thought this might amuse him, so when I finished my meal, and he finished his eggs and toast and was just staring out the window, I approached him. I began with apologies for intruding, but then explained to him how I had just received this review in the mail that mentions him. He was sweetly intrigued and asked me to join him. He then read the review with a magnifying lens that he took out of his coat pocket. I watched him read and he was looking rather splendid: his signature black cowboy hat, green eye shadow, long ancient nose, and green ascot at the throat. I think he's over ninety years old.

We ended up having a pleasant twenty-minute conversation, and Mr. Crisp is so eloquent I don't want to mangle our discourse, but here are some snippets of what I remember of our talk.

"I like to sit in this window," he said. "It's a way of being in life, but not *in* life."

"When the restaurant was across the street, I often saw you in the window," I said.

"Yes," he said, "like a Dutch prostitute."

"I've always wanted to go to Amsterdam because of the prostitutes. I almost went this year when I was in Europe, but I was afraid I would get in trouble. So I went to Italy and got in trouble there."

"You know they say that New York is not America, London is not England, Paris is not France, but Amsterdam is most definitely not Holland. Holland is just this flat place of broken windmills and tulips, and then Amsterdam is this city awash with sin, which is very interesting."

Another snippet: "I had a book come out in England," he said. "They told me if it did well, they would publish it over here. Well, it was doing all right, but then I caused a *scandal*. This journalist called me up and asked me about this gay gene they discovered and how if they could detect it in the fetus should a mother have the right to have the child aborted and I said yes. What else would I say? Well, I got these calls, 'How could you say such a nasty thing?' And they wrote that I said it for the publicity, to help my book get published in America. But I say things because I mean them, and they didn't understand that I would say yes because it would save the homosexuals from this terrible, terrible life."

Another snippet: "People have hobbies," he said. "They put galleons in bottles. 'Why?' I ask them. 'To kill time,' they say. Well, I don't want to kill time. I don't want it dead, I want it alive . . . I'm trying to do less and less so as not to kill time. I like to do nothing. Whenever I have to do something, I ask myself one question. And the question is: 'Can I get out of it?' If the answer is yes, then I get out of it. That's how I live my life now. Much better."

Mr. Crisp seems to have figured out a lot of things, and I wanted to ask him questions about my life, like asking a fortune-teller, but I didn't want to be rude. Many people must turn to him this way. So I thanked him for talking to me and I came home.

Tomorrow, I go away again for two weeks. I'll have to leave a note for my soul where to find me. It must still be on some camel in Pennsylvania.

The Orgy
August 31, 1999

I was sitting in my apartment, feeling a bit depressed. Well, maybe more then a bit. Of late, I've been in a terrible state of despair. A few days ago my relationship with my beautiful girlfriend came to an end. I went to see her on Martha's Vineyard and it's over. We are still very fond of one another, but it wasn't meant to be. And I feel like I have failed—why couldn't I have loved better? How could I lose her? What is wrong with me? I don't know who I am, what I am, where I am, or what I should do. I'm like that Gaugin painting where he scribbled in French, along the edges of the canvas, similar ponderings.

I don't think I have been this existentially morbid in some time, perhaps not since my undergraduate days. I remember when I was a sophomore, under the influence of reading a lot of Beckett, I wrote a depressing story called "The Ticket." It was about a man who gets hit by a train—a train that he had been waiting a very long time for, a train that was going to take him where he *needed* to go—and after he's hit by the train (a gross betrayal, really), he lies on the tracks, dying, and thinks, "Everything hurts, and yet I feel nothing."

I haven't recalled that line for some time, but I think

it's apt for my current state of being. I'm in so much pain that my heart has shut down. I'm in agony yet numb.

I don't even have enough enthusiasm to concoct one of my suicide fantasies, which really are Tom Sawyerish reveries, because I usually focus not so much on the actual way of killing myself, but on the funeral service that follows and the hoped-for sad headline in the *Press*—"Ames Dead." And all of this fantasizing—when I engage in it during normal periods of acute depression—is rather life-affirming and healthy, I think, because I must be imagining, when I picture the memorial and the headline, that people love me, care about me, which must be a way for my psyche to generate a sense that life is worth living. And I'm not alone in thinking that suicidal ideation can be positive: Nietzche wrote something about how thoughts of suicide can help one fall asleep, at least that's my memory of my brief skimming of the work of Mr. Nietzche, though I do hope he wrote that before the syphilis had gotten to his mind.

Anyway, I was sitting here, late yesterday afternoon, doing nothing, just sitting in my chair, not really feeling anything except for occasional lashes of self-loathing, and then the phone rang. When the phone stops ringing, then you're really done for. But it was ringing. Somebody out there was thinking of me. It was my friend Gene.

"Jonathan, there's an orgy tonight," he said. "I can't go. I have to entertain clients from LA"—Gene's in the entertainment business—"but the girl who's running it said I could invite people. The only thing is you have to come with a woman. No single men are allowed, and it's sixty dollars to get in for the two of you. She does let in single girls for thirty dollars."

"Men are always discriminated against in this way . . .

Oh, well, it's understandable with the way men are prone to stand in corners and masturbate, which is never very attractive . . . But I don't know if I can come up with anybody," I said.

"You must have some chippy who'll go with you."

"Well, I'll try to think of some one."

Gene then gave me the West Village address of the orgy, told me I had to arrive between eleven and midnight and that I was to bring my own towel, though condoms would be provided. Then he said, "Tell Mangie about it. Invite him." He was referring, of course, to our mutual friend, Harry.

"Ok, I'll call Mangie. And thanks for letting me know about this. I've never been to an orgy."

"No problem," he said. "I knew you'd be interested."

People are very generous with me, always proposing odd adventures for me to go on—they know I have to find things to write about. And I was grateful to Gene for calling me. An orgy seemed like a fine antidote to despair.

I called Harry. "Mangie, there's an orgy tonight. Gene told me about it. But we need to bring two women. Otherwise we can't get in. Do you want to go?"

"Sure. I'll bring my Mangina."

"More importantly we need to bring women. Can you think of two who will go with us?" I figured there was a good chance that Harry would know ladies who would be inclined for such an escapade. As a painter he knows numerous freethinking models who have posed naked for him, and also for several years he was the resident artist at the Blue Angel strip club—his Blue Angel period—and became the friend of many in the burlesque profession; thus, between artist models and strippers there were bound to be two women to accompany us to the orgy.

"I'll make a few calls," he said. "But you have to try too."

"I know one woman who might go. You know, my friend Vivian. I'll give her a call. Let's check back with each other in a little while."

I called Vivian, who is such a dear friend that I get away with grabbing her rear and putting my face in her neck and telling her I love her, which is true, and so I invited her to come with me to the orgy. "We can just sit on a couch and watch," I said, and she would have done it she said, but she has a new boyfriend, whom I hadn't heard about, *and* she was having a dinner party at eight, which she invited me to. I said I'd be there, and my evening seemed to be unfolding nicely: dinner party, then orgy— if Harry got hold of two females. But I was feeling hopeful of this, and my overall despair seemed to be lessening at the prospect of such a full night. A little while later, I called Harry. "Any luck?"

"I've left several messages, but no one's called me back."

"But do you think somebody will want to do it?"

"I think so."

"Well, Vivian can't do it—she's having a dinner party, which I'm going to go to, in Brooklyn. Do you want to come? I can call her and ask her."

"No, I'll stay here and wait by the phone. I want to go to this thing."

"That's the spirit, Mangie. I'll call you from Vivian's at ten and see if you've come up with anything. We have to be at the orgy between eleven and midnight, so I figure we should get there at eleven thirty. Also, you need to bring a towel."

"I don't have a towel."

"What do you mean you don't have a towel?"

"I varnished my floor and used all my towels."
"So what do you dry off with when you take a shower?"
"T-shirts."
"Well, do you have a sheet you could bring?"
"No."
"Why don't you have sheets?"
"I do have one sheet, but it's red. I don't think it would be good to walk around an orgy in a red sheet."
"You're right . . . I'll bring the towels. I own two. A green one and a white one."
"Are they clean?"
"No. But don't give me a hard time—at least I have towels! I'll call you from Brooklyn at ten."
At the dinner party, which was a charming backyard buffet, my despair about my lost girlfriend returned and so I lay in a hammock, unable to make social chitchat, but the food was very good. At ten, I called Harry.
"Nobody's called back," he said. "Nobody wants to go with us to the orgy."
"We have to go to this thing. How many times in life is one invited to an orgy? Listen, we'll just show up. You'll bring the Mangina. We'll say that you're a woman, or a woman-substitute. Maybe the girl who is throwing this thing will have heard of you and will want the Mangina at her orgy."
Harry agreed to this and we made plans to meet at his place after I picked up the towels. I said goodbye to Vivian and the others gathered, and one of them said, "Jonathan, don't leave yet, it's early."
"I'm sorry," I sniffed, "but I have to go to an orgy." Everyone thought I was joking, and with that I made my exit. I cabbed it back to Manhattan, put two towels in my backpack, and then went over to Harry's. He was

busy playing with his television, which he's rigged up to give him access to the Internet. He showed me that he is advertising on eBay. Many of his cutouts, paintings, Manginas, Wenises (prosthetic molds of his penis that women can wear), and Semen-Hats (these fantastic odd plastic helmets he's made) are all catalogued, priced, and photographed, and he's only been on eBay one week and has received hundreds of hits, though no sales. But he told me that if the Internet doesn't bring in money, he's still hoping to make some cash by touring and marketing the Mangina at prisons.

"You'll get raped," I said. "Forget prisons, stick with this eBay. How does one find you on it?"

"You just have to type in Harry slash Chandler."

I looked at the screen and saw that his name was spelled Harry-Chandler. "That's a dash, not a slash," I said. "A hyphen."

"Oh, no, I've been telling everyone slash."

In addition to his artwork, Harry showed me a photo of himself he's posted, it's sort of a calling card to his site, and beneath his quasi-naked image, I read what he wrote: "Crazy New York Visual and Performance Artist . . . Lately I've been performing a kind of stand-up tragedy routine."

"Oh, my God, Harry. That's the most brilliant thing of all time—*stand-up tragedy*! You're a stand-up tragedian on one leg. You may have created a whole new genre of performance."

"What can I say? This whole Mangina thing is building, gaining momentum. And this technology really helps. I can download images and send them anywhere. I downloaded a picture of me fingering my Mangina and I emailed it to my father. But then I thought—What am

I doing? Why am I sending pictures of my scrotum to my father? 'Look dad, I'm a woman!' I must really be losing it. He wrote me back. Said I didn't have to send him any more images like that."

"I can understand," I said. "You really do want his approval . . . Well, we better get going to the orgy." So we put his Mangina and the Wenis—in case some girl wanted to wear a prosthetic penis—in my backpack and headed to the West Village.

The building was a small, three story walk-up. We both felt nervous, but I buzzed the appropriate buzzer and we waited in the vestibule. A very beautiful girl with dark eyes and wearing a black slip came down the stairs. She opened the vestibule door and looked at us suspiciously.

"We're here for the *party*," I said. "Gene sent us."

"You need girls." She was a tough young woman, running a tight ship. "Didn't he tell you? Where are your girls?"

I quickly went in to Fuller brush–salesman mode. "Have you heard of the Mangina?"

"No. What are you talking about?"

"My friend here, Harry, has invented a prosthetic vagina that he wears. So he'll come in with me as a woman, my date. He's quite famous. He was on the Howard Stern show with his Mangina."

"Really? That's cool," she said. She was obviously a Stern fan.

I pulled the Mangina out of my backpack and showed it to her. She stepped back, a little shocked, but not completely repulsed. "You were on Stern promoting *that*?" she said, addressing Harry.

"Yes and because I'm an amputee." Harry pointed to his left leg. He was wearing shorts and on his left knee was a big, black knee pad, and below the pad you could just see his pink fiberglass shin. "When I take off my prosthesis, my stump is very phallic."

"Yeah, Howard Stern's TV show often begins with a clip of Harry stroking his stump."

"Oh, my God, that's so cool," she said.

"So can we come in? Harry will be my girl."

"Are you guys gay?"

We looked at each other. "Not really," I said. "But we can pretend. I'll hold his hand."

"I can't let you guys in. You need girls. That's the rules."

"Even if I wear the Mangina?" Harry asked.

"No, you can't wear that. People will be disturbed . . . Listen, get two girls and come back."

"What if we just get one girl? Can we both get in with one girl?" I asked.

She looked us over. "All right, you guys are cute. So come back with a girl! And if you don't find one, I'm having another party on September eighteenth. You guys should be able to get two girls by then."

"How many people are up there now?" I asked.

"Five hot couples."

We left the vestibule, and Harry checked his answering machine, but there were no messages from the women he had called. We sat on a stoop across the street from the orgy.

"Let's stake the place out," I said. "If any single girls show up, we'll run over to them and ask them to be our dates so we can get in."

"This is a typical Mangina moment. Sitting outside an orgy, not allowed in," said Harry, but he wasn't genuinely depressed, he was using his fake-depressed voice.

"It's like this Thomas Mann story," I said. "*Tonio Kruger*. It's about a boy who stares in the window at dances, but can't go in because he's too afraid."

We sat on the stoop and it was actually quite pleasant. We were on an active Village street and it was fun to watch the stream of passersby—a parade of tourists and pretty girls. Pretty girls whom we both thought of asking to come with us to the orgy, but we knew the suggestion would be ludicrous. But I've always just liked sitting and watching people. Especially girls. Wondering where they're going. Insanely hoping that one of them will look at me and like me and ask me to kiss her. Something like that.

So we studied the door to the orgy, but no one showed up.

"Know what I've been thinking lately, Harry?" I said. "I think human beings don't realize the full extent of the misery they're in all the time. Granted, I only have myself as an example, but I don't have *any peace*. Always underneath everything there is anxiety. Maybe for a few moments when I read the baseball box scores in the morning do I have peace. Or if I'm in the ocean. Or a few times making love. But really I have no peace. Look at this city. All the buildings, taxis, groceries . . . bars! It's all a mad distraction to the pain of being alive. Every religion is about pain. Buddhism says, 'Life is suffering.' Christianity has Jesus on the cross, the Jews are always wandering in the dessert losing their minds, Muslims are so sexually agonized that their women have to walk around in bedspreads with breathing holes, pagans torture their bodies in weird ways . . . I do like sitting here, though. This is peaceful. So I guess I should be grateful for this sliver."

"That's why I make art," said Harry. "Human beings need art. And now my life *is* art. I've combined the two by wearing the Mangina . . . Pseudo-dot-com, this website, had a three-day party and they had me walk around wearing the Mangina. They had performers on different floors, but they wanted me to just cruise around, to be an ambient presence. And all these bridge and tunnel kids would gather around me and look at the Mangina and finger it. This one girl, a cheerleader type, said, 'Is that your nut sack hanging out?' I said, 'I prefer to call it the Lotum.' I don't know. I felt peace just walking around that party . . . Then I'd come home each night and take the Mangina off and take my foot off and be alone. But I keep going. I'm sort of like a retired person these days."

I had this image of Harry as a kind of St. Francis. Instead of birds gathering on his shoulders, I saw young people clustered around him, unafraid, looking at and fingering his Mangina.

We sat outside the orgy for an hour. Then we gave up. When we shook hands goodbye, to walk home our separate ways, I said, "Maybe we'll get in on the eighteenth."

"We'll be organized this time," he said. "We're bound to find two girls. That's something to look forward to. It's always helpful to have something to look forward to."

So I walked to the East Village and along the way I came across an old bum sleeping on a futon. The futon was on fire in the corner. I woke the man up and we put out the fire by pulling out the burning cotton. I joked with him, "Didn't your mother tell you not to smoke in bed?"

"Yeah, I was smoking in bed." He was laughing. "Almost burned myself up! Thanks for helping me out."

When I got home, I realized I had the Mangina and the Wenis in my bag—and I finally broke down. For a whole year, I have resisted putting on the Mangina, but alone with it in my apartment, seeking some kind of spiritual comfort, I put the thing on. But it didn't fit me right. I couldn't pull out my scrotum through the special hole to create the Lotum. It was kind of like King Arthur and the sword—

only one man can pull it out of the stone! Only one man can pull his scrotum out of that hole! Only one man can be King! Only one man can correctly wear the Mangina!

Nevertheless, I went to the mirror and looked at myself in the too-small Mangina and I laughed. It felt good to laugh.

Then I took the Mangina off and hid it my underwear drawer. But I didn't like having it in my apartment. Harry hasn't had a girl in a year since he started wearing that thing. Would the curse of the Mangina fall on my house?

I lay in my bed and tried to sleep, but I could feel the Mangina in my chest of drawers, like it had a life of its own, like it was something out of Edgar Allan Poe. I had a tell-tale Mangina in my house. The thing wanted to get out. There was also the Wenis! I had a mold of my friend's cock in my underwear drawer! What was my life coming to?

I thought of putting both items on the fire escape until the morning, but I worried that a rat might eat them or some bird would fly off with them, and that was an interesting vision—the Mangina and the Wenis being whisked across the sky in the mouth of some fierce bird. What if somebody on the street looked up and saw that, like that bum on his burning bed. He'd think it was the DTs.

I figured, too, that the curse would really descend on me if I lost the Mangina, so I left it and its counterpart in the drawer. But then I wondered if I was already cursed. I had lost my girlfriend and my heart was crushed. I took hold of my pillow, like it was her, and I held on. It was going to be a long night. It was going to be a long life.

The Vanilla Thrilla
September 14, 1999

On November 10, 1999, my health and even my life will be in serious danger. I have somehow managed to get myself corralled into a real live boxing match with someone who has no regard at all for physical safety; in fact, he is someone with a bit of a death wish. And it's not good to be involved with people with death wishes. When they close their eyes and make their wish and blow out their candle, so to speak, and you happen to be standing nearby, then you too might get snuffed out. All this is a metaphor for the brutal fact that I am getting into the ring with a mild psychopath. He's also a friend. At least he was. So without further ado, ladies and gentleman, let me introduce, David "The Impact Addict" Leslie.

I met Leslie in February of 1997 at the Den of Cin performance space beneath Two Boots Pizza on Avenue A. After the show I had attended was over, people were milling about, and I overheard Leslie—a medium-height, barrel-chested man with thinning hair, a sweet smile, a peacockish posture, and a vibratto of physical vitality—talking to a friend of his about boxing. Leslie had produced the show I had just seen and I knew that he was a retired performance artist, that he was something of a legend in the East Village, but I didn't know why exactly. I managed to join his conversation—he and his friend were discussing a big fight that was coming up—and as we talked it became clear to me that Leslie was a huge boxing fan and then it came up that he had dabbled in the sport himself. I then said, rather offhandedly, "Maybe you and I could box sometime," and then I had an expansive idea. "We could even make it a performance—two artists fighting. People would come to that."

That was about all I said. And I meant it, though I was more looking for someone to spar with, to fool around with, than actually fight. I just wanted to play around with the sport—I've always had an interest in boxing. I grew up watching the fights on TV before the expensive advent of pay-per-view, and I got to see—at least these were the fighters who made the biggest impression on me—Ali, Frazier, Foreman, Norton, Spinks (Leon), Holmes, Leonard, Duran, Benitez, Hagler, Antuofermo, and Hearns. And I feel lucky that I caught a lot of the Ali fights in the seventies and then the ones in the early eighties where he was like Willie Mays at the end of his career when he was playing for the Mets—slow and old, no longer beautiful to watch, a humbled man not knowing yet he's been humbled. But still there was the feeling of seeing something great, of something magisterial, even if it was in decay.

In addition to watching boxing as a kid, I fantasized back then about being a boxer. When I was around nine years old, I had a set of boxing gloves, and when my friend Stuart Ginsberg would come over, I'd give him the right-hand glove—wanting to give him some advantage since I was a grade ahead of him and a bit stronger—and we'd fight. But he was very timid and would cower in the corner of my room as I pounded him with my left. One time, though, he poked out a punch and caught me in the nose and I began to bleed. But this was not an unusual occurrence for me. I was something of a nasal hemophiliac as a child. I had a weak vessel in my left nostril from having been beaten at the age of five by a violent, retarded ten-year-old boy, who was later institutionalized; the boy, while sitting on my chest, had broken my nose, causing the weak vessel, which I made worse over the years with frequent nose picking. To this day I still bleed rather easily and freely from the nose because I haven't been able to quit putting my finger in it, and also I live in New York with steam radiators that dry out my nostrils, making them vulnerable in the winter months.

Anyway, when Stuart Ginsberg drew blood, I loved it. I spread it all over my face and said to him, "Now I'm a real fighter!" And I pummeled him more. I hope I'll be that brave on November 10.

So my epic battles with Ginsberg were my only experiences as a pugilist, until 1992, when I moved to Manhattan and decided to experience boxing firsthand. I was hoping it was something I could write about; it had been three years since my first novel came out and I was desperate for material. So I joined the Kingsway Boxing Gym on Fortieth Street and Eighth Avenue, looking for stories. For about three weeks, maybe two or three times a week, I went and trained in the evening. I shadow-boxed in front of the mirrors with young black and Latino men. Then after my training, I'd walk three blocks and go to Sally's—this transsexual bar—on Forty-third Street, where other young black and Latino men (well, men at one time) stared in mirrors, but in a very different way, for very different reasons. Eventually, I dropped the boxing, and took the lazy route and just went to Sally's. And what you do is what you write about. I wrote about Sally's, and not about Kingsway.

So boxing dropped out of my life, except for a brief fight with a man in the St. Mark's Hotel in 1996. A man I met on a phone-sex line who had a fetish for boxing. I was addicted to phone-sex at that time and was game for just about anything, so I met this man and we went at it—head gear and gloves, the works. All in a small hotel room. He was a fellow writer. A fellow nut. The winner was supposed to get a blowjob. This was a good motivation not to *lose*. I knocked him out. And I didn't ask for a blowjob. The victory was sweet enough. Also, he had a mustache and the idea of oral coitus with him was unappealing to me.

My one other fight was the one in 1984 in a Paris disco when I was severely beaten about the head, and in particular had my nose smashed. The fight was over a woman. I lost. But my opponent didn't get the girl either; she fled the scene. I wonder if the fellow was that institutionalized boy from long ago and without my knowing it he had sought asylum in France, but recognizing me, he felt the need to pummel me yet again. Anyway, my record is 2–1. Ginsberg and the fetishist in the hotel being my two victories.

Now back to 1997. After meeting Leslie that first time, we became friends. I learned that in the eighties he was known as "The Impact Addict." MTV called him the "Evil Knievel of the performance art world." His resume included jumping, in 1988, off the roof of the six-story-high Performance Space 122, while dressed as Maria von Trapp, and landing on some kind of platform that he plunged through, suffering but minor injuries; fighting in 1987 the then young heavyweight contender Riddick Bowe during the duration of a Staten Island Ferry crossing; and in 1986 attempting to fly a rocket over a mountain of watermelons on a Soho street, but the rocket exploded and he was pulled from the flaming wreckage.

The man had put his life on the line for art. He had cracked ribs. Dislocated shoulders. Defied odds. Made the nightly news. Then at the age of thirty-one, in his prime, he retired. He became a casting director and a producer of downtown events.

A few months after we met, he produced a show for me at Den of Cin in June of '97. I told stories and then challenged audience members to come onstage and arm-wrestle me, as a sort of homage to Andy Kaufman. I beat three men in a row and then Leslie took me on. I had been weakened by my three previous battles, but I pinned Leslie as well. And his arm was twice the size of mine, but I've always been lithely muscular, deceptively strong.

Our friendship grew; often I went to his house to watch fights on pay-per-view. Then in January of 1999, he called me up and said he was going to call me again the next day and wanted a cameraman to film me taking his call. "Why?" I asked.

"Can't tell you," he said, "just let the guy in and I'll call you."

I agreed. Figured it was some kind of joke.

The next day the cameraman arrived—the photographer and filmmaker Richard Sandler, whose documentary *The Gods of Times Square* is a classic. So Sandler got set up and then the phone rang. It was Leslie. "Jonathan," he said, "remember when you challenged me to fight you a year ago?"

"What are you talking about?" I said.

"A year ago at Den of Cin, you said you wanted to fight me."

"Oh, yeah, but that was *two* years ago. It was hardly a challenge."

"I don't care when it was. To me it was a challenge. And I'm calling to let you know I accept your challenge."

"You've been stewing about this for two years?"

"I'm sick of you telling that story about beating that guy in a hotel. Sick of you prancing around acting like you're a fighter . . . So do you accept? You'll fight me?"

My manhood was on the line. My reputation for being a risk-taker was on the line. I was on the phone line, *and* I was on camera. I'm a ham. It was something of a setup. "Yes," I said. "I accept."

"All right, we're on, fucker. This is going to be a real fight. I don't do things halfway. I'm coming out of an eleven-year retirement as a performance artist to kick your ass."

"Oh," I shot back. Trying to make it a firm, "Oh." But it needed something more. "Just remember what I did to you in arm wrestling," I then added, hoping to take the wind out of his sails—I could practically smell his testosterone through the receiver.

"Fuck pussy arm wrestling. This is the real thing, and you're going down."

Then he hung up. The horror of what I had just agreed to dawned on me. I hung up the phone. Sandler came in for a close-up. I decided to rise to the occasion. Even though it was January—and I'm notoriously depressed during this month—I suddenly went into a manic tirade, bouncing around my apartment, throwing punches, imagining myself pummeling Leslie as if he were Stuart Ginsberg, and all the while Sandler was following me about, the camera on me, and then I shouted into his instrument, "I'm going to be the reincarnation of a Lower East Side

Jewish boxer! I'm going to train by eating herring. And I'll eat herring right before the fight and have terrible herring breath and keep Leslie away with my fierce breath and my fierce jab. I'll be known as 'The Herring Wonder!' I'll float like a butterfly and stink like a herring!"

It was a moment of true inspiration and so my fight name was born—"The Herring Wonder."

It took a few months to get everything set up, but now the fight is on for November 10 at the Angel Orensanz Foundation, a theater and art gallery, which in its first life was a nineteenth-century synagogue. So this strange theater, with its profound Jewish roots, is the perfect setting for me to unleash my Yiddish wrath. It's a four-round fight, we'll be wearing fourteen-ounce gloves as well as headgear (I may have a yarmulke under mine), and before our "main event" there will be three unusual undercard bouts. To announce the rounds of our fight there will be card girls, and, naturally, the Mangina will be one of them. The whole thing is called, "A Box Opera." David, who is producing this spectacle, wanted to call it "Rock'em Sock'em Opera," but I suggested "Box Opera," with its double implication of boxing and box office. So that's what we're going with. But an alternative title, since we're both white, could be "The Vanilla Thrilla."

Leslie, in addition to being white, is forty-two years old, stands five feet ten inches, and weighs 178 pounds. I'm thirty-five, five eleven, and weigh 152. If this was a gay phone-sex line I'd give my hair color and my penis size, but this is a sports article. I'm younger than Leslie, but he has a lot more fight experience, having dabbled in the sport for the last twenty years—he even had a few amateur bouts in Texas, where he went to college. But I'm hoping that he'll be a bit slow, since he has been known to wear himself out as a passionate denizen of the New York nightlife, whereas I have not smoked crack cocaine since 1994. But I do bleed easily from the nose. I'm not sure who has the advantage based on the above facts.

Anyway, I've been training for one week now. I've been extremely fortunate in that I've enlisted one of the best trainers in New York, Harry Keitt. I met him when I went to a screening of the beautiful boxing documentary *On the Ropes* (since nominated for an Academy Award). Harry is one of the main characters of the film, if not the star, and I asked him after the screening if he would train me. He said yes. And so the last week has been the most intense physical experience of my life. I've recently moved to Brooklyn, and for the first few days of my training, I rode my bike to the Bed-Stuy Boxing Center on Marcus-Garvey Boulevard, where Harry began to teach me how to fight.

"Your head is the meat and your hands are the bread," he said the first day. "Keep your head between your hands. Like a sandwich."

"Head between the hands. Like a sandwich," I repeated.

"Keep your hands up and you'll be all right."

The first four days I was at Bed-Stuy, but now for the last two days, I've been training with him at Gleason's Gym under the Manhattan Bridge, which will probably be our headquarters for the rest of my "training camp." I don't want to reveal the secrets of my rigorous training—Leslie will read this, he's a devotee of my column—but I hope to be ready to dismember come November.

Two days ago to help promote the fight, Leslie and I did a talk show at Performance Space 122 (PS 122, for short) called "The Lucy Show," which beats the drum for the theater's upcoming events. PS 122 is helping to throw the fight, and will stage a press conference and weigh-in on September 28. I should mention that in addition to PS 122's assistance, we're also being generously sponsored by the *Press* and by pseudo.com, which will do a webcast of the fight; I'm hoping to have the *Press* logo on the back of my robe, and maybe the kosher delicatessen Russ and Daughter's logo as well, since they have the best herring in New York.

So Leslie and I were sitting next to one another on the set of "The Lucy Show," which is set up like a TV talk show with multiple seats for the guests, and is hosted by Lucy Sexton. In response to Ms. Sexton's question about the danger of our event, I made some comments about Leslie not needing a brain for what he does—jumping off buildings, etc.—while I as a writer was putting far more at risk for this fight. To his credit, Leslie took this ribbing about his intelligence good-naturedly. Then after some more questions, Ms. Sexton invited two audience members to participate in a game. We interviewees—there were two other artists, a man and a woman, onstage with me and Leslie; we had been the last to come on—were to be asked about the most exciting place we'd ever had sex, but we could lie if we wanted to. The two audience members were to then declare which artist was telling the truth and which artist was lying and whoever had the most correct answers would win a prize.

So the woman artist said her most exciting place was a back corridor of the Boston Aquarium, the male artist said the basketball court in front of Stuyvesant High School, and then it was my turn, to be followed by David. So Lucy asked me, "Well, Jonathan, where was the most exciting place you ever had sex?"

"Recently," I said, "I was at David Leslie's house and he was trash-talking me, saying how he was going to knock me out and punish me, so I went into his bathroom and masturbated into his shampoo bottle." This brought laughter as well as looks of disgust and shock from the audience.

I then added, "I was also clutching his girlfriend's panties." When I said this, David, as he should have, since I had brought his girlfriend into it, punched me hard in the chest. I then reared back and knocked him off his chair. There's untapped power in my muscles and he went flying and I saw panic and surprise in his eyes. He crashed to the floor, trying to prop himself up with one arm, and I leaped off my chair and shoved him down further and he weakly grabbed at my sport coat, ripping two buttons. The whole thing was Jerry Springeresque, but it was not scripted, we had not planned on fighting, and during the melee, I was vaguely aware of the audience screaming, but I was in some quiet, lovely zone of male aggression. After shoving him, I took hold of this enormous balloon-champagne bottle—an unexplained prop that was on stage with us— and I hit him with it. At this point he rose up, but we were separated by several people. The whole thing was thrilling. My blood was pumping. In our first skirmish, I had scored a victory. I had knocked him down. It may be a vision of things to come. It *will be* a vision of things to come.

My Jewish Cousin, George Ames Plimpton
September 28, 1999

Yesterday morning, I was training for my upcoming fight, as I do each morning of the workweek, and after doing some stretching and some shadowboxing, I climbed into the ring for a sparring session with a pleasant Irish fellow. I landed some good punches; I survived all three rounds; but he most certainly had the upper hand. At least that's how it felt when I was back in my apartment and I was lying on my bed and I couldn't move my neck. My poor stem had been violently snapped from one of the blows I received to the head. I probably have whiplash. Punch-lash. Also, the bridge of my nose was swollen. So I had ice on the neck and on the nose and I was wondering, What the hell have I gotten myself into?

The legend is you don't see the punches you get hit with. This, I am finding, is quite true. And it is a good metaphor for life. We don't see anything coming. We just stumble and muddle forward, getting slammed every now and then with unseen catastrophes, and all the while groping for solace and consolation. But they're so hard to find. I think one's best bet for s. and c. is a warm ass to snuggle up against at night and maybe a sex organ to suck on, like an infant, before you snuggle up against that ass.

I know I experience great consolation when my mouth is between a woman's legs. I think it must be because I'm drinking in her happiness. There's also religion and intoxicants and good restaurants for solace and consolation, but nothing beats hiding under a comforter with someone you adore, holding on to their ass like a life preserver, and waiting for the world and the day to come to an end.

But if you don't have that someone, then things can be a bit dark. Here I am training for a battle, but I've lost my girlfriend. What's the point? A man fights for a woman. Don Quixote dedicated all his insane battles to La Dulcinea. Who will I dedicate my insane battle to? It will have to be for a *someone*, a *you* I don't know yet . . .

That can keep one going, thinking that the person you're going to love is out there alive, doing something, and you just haven't met them yet. So I wonder what *she* is up to right now? Maybe she's drinking a cup of coffee. Maybe she's thinking of me, in the same way I'm thinking of her—where are you? Maybe she's on the toilet. That's all right, she's human. Or maybe she's giving her current boyfriend a blowjob. The bastard! Take your cock out of her mouth! That's the woman I'm going to marry!

I didn't think I was in a morbid mood, but it appears that I am. My mind goes round and round trying to figure things out, but I always come back to the same two things: Loneliness and Death. Life ends before we ever figure anything out, most importantly how not to be lonely. Solitude is fine. But feeling like you have no one to love— abject loneliness—is not all right. I need more time! Life is too short, except during poetry and fiction readings when life feels very long. Maybe that's the key, just sit in readings and achieve immortality. This could explain their popularity, despite their profound boringness. Also, readings are probably good places to meet girls. I think I've come full circle.

At the moment, I'm reading a book my father gave me. A legal thriller. And I'm reading it, even though I have no interest in legal thrillers, because *he* gave it to me. He wanted to share something with me, he thought of me, so I can't ignore this. I'll read the book, like a child taking foul-tasting medicine. It's my way of loving him, respecting him, and this feels more important than ever because I'm frightened of losing him. I'm getting older, but he's really getting older. So each time I open the book I feel like I'm holding on to him. It's my way of saying to the gods—Look I'm reading this best-seller he gave me, and I don't want to read it, but this shows that I love him, so please don't take him away. The whole thing is like being in the ring. I'm afraid of the punches I am unable to see. I know they're coming, I just can't spot them.

But despite my loneliness and profound annoyance with the fact that I have to die and everyone has to die, I do have to say, as I type my way out of morbidity, that my life is quite odd and distracting. Whether it has any meaning or significance is unlikely, but it is definitely amusing. For example, my neck is feeling much better today than it was yesterday, so I'm not regretting too much this mad and loony fight I'm involved in. It's an adventure and I like adventures.

Last night, at Performance Space 122 there was the press conference for the fight. A half hour before the media-session started, I was standing in front of PS 122's building on First Avenue and was with some friends and my wonderful trainer Harry Keitt. I told Harry my neck was stiff, that the Irishman during our sparring session had given me whiplash. So right there on First Avenue, Harry very kindly and unexpectedly massaged my neck and then lifted me up like I was a shirt on a hanger—he's built along the lines of the former champ Larry Holmes—and cracked my whole spine. The benefits were immediate.

A little while later at the press conference, which was open to the public and not just journalists, my opponent David "The Impact Addict" Leslie and I fielded questions from the audience. One astute young man, most likely a reader of my work, asked me, "Jonathan Ames, are you going to give up masturbation while getting ready for this fight?" It was a good question.

"Harry told me that three weeks before the fight, I must give up sex, which obviously includes self-sex," I responded. "This will probably be the most rigorous and demanding aspect of my training. But there are six weeks to the fight so I have three more weeks to make a mess of myself each night before going to sleep. But then three weeks before the fight I will be a pillar of abstention. I promise!"

Brave words!

My answer seemed to satisfy the young man's curiosity and the evening went on with taunts and a weigh-in, which are the usual elements of a fight's press conference, but there were also a few odd twists provided by the presence of the three undercards: First there were the two fierce lesbian gladiators, Shelly Mars and Sarah East Johnson, who are going to wear armor and attack one another with Wiffle-ball-bat swords, and they growled at one another menacingly as if they were loaded up with testosterone, but they were very feminine in their concern about their fighting weights, which they wouldn't disclose; then there was Michael Portnoy, who is famous for jumping in front of Bob Dylan during the Grammys with the words "Soy Bomb" emblazoned on his naked chest, and who, during our press conference, staggered out feebly to the dais, spitting blood into a cup and using a walker—he plans to take on five five-year-olds the night of the fight since he, Portnoy, is twenty-five years old; and, lastly, there was the goofy comedian Zero Boy, who will fight himself in an existential battle.

So last night when I got home from this bizarre press conference, it struck me that I keep getting involved in odd events and performances. What I do for a living—I've come to realize—is behave strangely. And who can complain about a life like that, even if I was complaining about it a few paragraphs ago? My mood is so volatile. Half an hour ago, I was thinking about Death and Loneliness. Now I am thinking pleasantly about my curious adventures as a performer.

Just a few weeks ago I had a particularly good escapade at Joe's Pub on Lafayette Street. I was the host for a night of storytelling put together by this group called The Moth, which has storytelling nights every two weeks or so at different locations—it flits around—though Joe's Pub with its clubby, candlelit atmosphere seems to be The Moth's favorite venue. The theme of the night I was hosting was "icons." So the performers told stories about icons in their lives, and in addition to my hosting duties, I also told a story—about my dear childhood pal Jonathan "Fat" Eder, who for me is an icon of friendship and inspired, nutty behavior.

All in all, there were six storytellers, including myself, and the last performer of the evening happened to be one of New York's—and perhaps the country's—best raconteurs: George Plimpton. To introduce Plimpton, I launched into the following monologue:

"Our next storyteller is George Plimpton, but before I bring him on stage I want to tell you something about him. A few months ago, at a Moth event at the Brooklyn Academy of Music, George was the host and this time he was calling me on stage to tell a story and he said, 'Many people don't know this but my middle name is Ames. George Ames Plimpton. So I think Jonathan Ames is a long-lost cousin. So please welcome my cousin Jonathan Ames.' This surprised me a great deal, but I recovered my wits quickly and when I got on stage I then said, 'What many people don't know is that my middle name is Plimpton. I'm Jonathan Plimpton Ames. And I guess George doesn't use the Ames part of his name because the initials wouldn't look very good on towels—G-A-P, which is not very classy.' Well, that whole little speech got a big round of applause, and then after the show George was hounding me on this issue of our being related. 'So are you of the Boston Ameses?' he asked me. I kept sidestepping the question and trying to move us on to another topics. I didn't want to tell him that I was Jewish, that there was no chance in hell that we were of the same blood, and so I shamefully retreated into Jewish insecurity and secrecy.

"In my defense, I have to say that it was thrilling that he seemed to be taking an interest in me, even if it was only because he thought we might be cousins, which is why I didn't want to disabuse him of his cousin fantasy. You see I've always admired George Plimpton's work. As a young writer and as an ardent sports fan, I put him on a pedestal. He combined both my passions. Here was a writer who got to play pro football and hockey *and* he climbed into the ring with Archie Moore! And what did I write about when I finally became a journalist? Enemas, colonics, and hemorrhoids. My action journalism all took place around my ass! I even self-deprecatingly called myself in one of my *NY Press* articles 'the George Plimpton of the colon.' And now here was the man himself, this icon of American letters, liking me and thinking we were related.

"Well, after that show at BAM, we all went to a party and again George cornered me and inquired as to whether or not I was a Boston Ames. Now for years, I've often masqueraded as a WASP. It's sort of a hobby of mine. A fascination. I comb back my thin blonde hair and put on blazers and khaki pants and infiltrate WASP society. I call it religious cross-dressing. But now I had gone too far. A high priest of the WASP world was ready to take me in as one of his own. And I should have said to him at the party, 'I'm an Austro-Hungarian Empire Jew named Ames. I'm sorry George, but we're not related!' But I was too weak and irrational. It was absurd, but I thought he wouldn't like me if he knew I was Jewish, and so all I said was, 'There are no Boston Ameses in my family.' And shortly after that, having turned my back on my heritage, I left the party. I was acting like Shylock, but with less self-esteem.

"Anyway, I've been thinking about all this, and I realize that George and I might be related after all. The Boston Ameses, I bet, were originally German-speaking, Austro-Hungarian Empire Jews who ended up in England. But then because of religious persecution, they came over with the Puritans on the *Mayflower*. And since they were Jews and most likely rich merchants they could pay to get on the ship. Then once they were on Plymouth Rock, they probably—like the Jews in Spain during the Inquisition—thought it best to hide their Judaism in the New World. And this kind of secrecy or assimilation isn't done out of Jewish self-loathing, but for reasons of survival.

"Anyway, these *Mayflower* Ameses, these Boston Ameses, like the Spanish Jews, kept their secret so well that over time they forgot that they were originally of the Hebrew faith, that they were children of Abraham. And so I believe that of one Boston's oldest families—the Ameses—is actually Jewish. Now George's middle name must come from his mother—in WASP families the middle name is often the mother's maiden name. So George's mother was probably an Ames, which means she was Jewish. And since one's Jewishness is passed on through the mother, George Ames Plimpton is actually a Jew!

"So ladies and gentleman, please welcome my cousin and Jewish-icon, George Ames Plimpton!"

Well, there was general pandemonium at Joe's Pub when I publicly outed George as a Semite. People were howling. If they had yarmulkes they would have tossed them on the stage with joy, which would have made an interesting image. Instead, they merely screamed and laughed, while George gracefully made his way through the crowd and then onto the stage, where he threw a left jab at me because he knows of my upcoming fight. I then retreated to the wings and George stood silently in front of the microphone, collecting himself and bringing the audience to the edges of their chairs. So we waited. And then stooping to the mike from his considerable height, bending at the waist in his WASP-issued blue blazer, he bowed his head and said in his great mid-Atlantic accent, "I've had some introductions in my day, but never one . . . Well, thanks, *cuz.*"

And the audience roared its approval. It was all very pleasing. In one fell swoop, I had reembraced my heritage and had converted George Plimpton back into the Hebrew fold.

President Clinton: My Hero
October 12, 1999

This diary needs a little housecleaning and updating. There's a loose end that needs tying up, and also there is my encounter this summer with President Clinton that I've not yet had the chance to report on.

First off, the loose end that needs tying has to do with the orgy. As some of you may recall, I didn't gain access to the orgy because I brought the Mangina with me instead of a biological woman. But the entry did end with a ray of hope—I reported there would be another orgy on September 18.

Well, the eighteenth came, and sure enough through the perverted channels through which such information is disseminated, I learned the orgy was switching locations— to stay ahead of the vice squad?—from its West Village setting to a Wall Street hotel. I was told the suite number and that entry to the orgy would only take place between 10 and 10:45 P.M. The same rules were in effect as with the first orgy: sixty dollars per couple; single women allowed (for $30); single men *not* allowed; bring your own towel; condoms provided.

I bring all this up because many people—friends,

acquaintances, and strangers—contacted me about the orgy; I received letters (with photos), emails, and phone calls. This orgy issue really seemed to strike a nerve. Quite a few friends teased me—"I know where you'll be on the eighteenth" was a frequently heard remark. And all sorts of people—many of whom I wouldn't suspect of being fans of group sex—were asking me if I could get them into the orgy; if I would write them a letter of recommendation so to speak. These people I stalled. I don't like to be a bad influence. It's bad enough that I have influence over myself.

Then after the eighteenth came and went, everyone was asking: What happened? Did you go to the orgy? Well, I have to report that I let a lot of people down: I did not make the slightest effort to attend this second gathering of group fornication. My new hobby and passion, boxing, which for the moment has replaced my lifelong fascination with all forms of sexual congress, took precedent on the night of the eighteenth—I watched the somewhat disappointing De La Hoya and Trinidad fight. And although the fight lacked excitement, it *was* instructive, since I am currently a student of the sweet science of bruising in preparation for my own boxing match.

I do hope to keep boxing after my big fight, but I will also probably get back to my old studies: the sick science of cruising. And so if there's another orgy planned for late November or December, I'll make a valiant effort to attend, experience, survive, and bear witness. I will then file a full report for all the people who count on me to provide firsthand hand-job accounts of things that most decent people are sane enough not to attempt, though these same decent people are the ones hounding me for the lascivious details. But there's nothing new in that statement. Most people like to keep things at a safe distance, but, nonetheless, they are curious and voyeuristic, especially when it comes to sex. And then there are those of us—I'm referring to myself here—who are nearsighted, so to speak, and need to be right on top of things or on top of someone to fully appreciate them. So it all works out. The sexually sane people need a liaison to the sexually insane. And that's me, that's where I fit in. A man behind the lines. A kind of erotic war correspondent.

Pressing on with my housecleaning: I need to forgo the current events of my humble life and keep dealing with the past and in so doing discuss my August trip to Martha's Vineyard. My vacation there happened to coincide with the President's, and an obvious conclusion can be drawn from our being in the same place at the same time: Libidinous men think alike. And naturally two such similar individuals were destined to cross paths.

When I arrived on the island I was met by my lovely girlfriend at the ferry (this was several days before our sad, yet amicable breakup) and then we drove to the house where we were staying, which was very generously being loaned to us through a friend of a friend. The house was deep in the woods in the quieter, less developed, and more exclusive part of the island. When I saw the place, it reminded me of a cabin I had stayed in fourteen years before when I last visited Martha's Vineyard. At that time, I had lucked into the free use of a cabin for ten days, and during that sojourn I had a very sweet love affair with a beautiful girl who lived nearby.

Now the house I was staying in fourteen years later was not a cabin, but it looked as if it could have been expanded upon. Unfortunately, I was unable to remember the exact address of the cabin, but I knew it was in the same part of the island. But I couldn't easily solve the mystery of my déjà vu because the man who had loaned me the cabin so many summers before had since died and the current owners of the house were not readily available. It was frustrating to feel like I had been there before but that I couldn't prove it.

The following morning after my arrival, I drove to the local general store to get some supplies. As I loaded up the car, I heard someone calling out with excitement, "Jon! Jon! Jon!" I went by "Jon" for most of my life until I tried quitting drinking at the tender age of twenty-two, at which time I asked people to call me by full name. I guess I was seeking a new temperance identity, and since then, whether actively dispsomaniacal or in tippling remission, I have gone by Jonathan. So whoever was beckoning me was someone from my distant past, but because it had been so long since I was called by that shortened version of my name I didn't respond; I thought it must be for someone else. I got in my car and started it up, but then I heard again this insistent plea of "Jon! Jon! Jon!" and sensing that it was for me I got out of the car, and sprinting toward me, like in a dream, was the beautiful girl of fourteen years before. She was running because she thought I was about to drive off, and then when she saw me get out of the car an embarrassed smile came to her face and she slowed to a walk.

She had hardly changed at all. Perhaps the posture was more severe—she was maybe more conscious of her good figure and wanting to maintain it, and there were a few lines around her mouth, but she was remarkably well preserved. She was looking closely at me as well and I was very aware of her gaze toward the bald spot at the front of my head; her eyes went there the way a man's eyes go to a woman's cleavage. Time had been less kind to me than to her; it had stolen my hair. "I'm surprised you recognized me," I said, sheepishly, feeling a bit old and disintegrated.

"I couldn't forget those eyebrows," she said, referring to the albinish lines of hair above my eyes. And I felt flattered: she remembered my eyebrows; once long ago her face had been close to mine. We hesitated a moment and then kissed each other's cheeks in greeting. We were astonished, yet not too astonished to see one another, which seems to be the nature of coincidences: They are too much a part of the way things *are;* they always feel curiously *right.*

Immediately after our embrace, a tall, sturdy good-looking man approached with two young boys. My old flame was very much a wife and mother. I shook hands with her husband and the little boys—"This is Jon"—and then she and I rapidly exchanged information, our headlines from the last fourteen years.

I then told her where I was staying, and being a long-time summer person on the island, she knew the house and informed me that in its previous life, before significant expansion, it *had been* the cabin where I had stayed fourteen years before—the scene of our youthful embraces.

(But did the husband know? Suspect anything? He seemed happy enough to shake my hand; then again my love affair with his wife had been rather youthful and innocent—nothing for him to feel odd about in meeting me so many years later. She and I had never consummated our love in the biblical sense because back then she was in the midst of breaking up with someone and so we had only engaged in hot kisses, like in a Russian novel.)

So she and I were amazed by the coincidence of the cabin, but then there wasn't much more to say. We kissed goodbye, I shook her husband's large hand for the second time, and that was it. I got in the car and felt a little light-headed from seeing her, from being thrown back into the past so unexpectedly—I was crazy about her fourteen years ago. I remember crying because it didn't work out. But the whole thing was deeply pleasing to me—the cabin, running into her—because I live for coincidences. They briefly give to me the illusion or the hope that there's a pattern to my life, and if there's a pattern, then maybe I'm moving toward some kind of destiny where it's *all* explained.

At the moment, of course, there's no explanation for *anything*, but there is the desire to keep recording data. So I'll press on with jotting down the next interesting thing that happened—interesting to me at least—on Martha's Vineyard. A few days after seeing my old heartthrob, my lovely girlfriend and I went to a cocktail party, and Spalding Gray was there, which for me, since he's one of my idols, was very exciting. He was on the island because he was premiering his fantastic new show, *Morning, Noon and Night*, which I had just seen the previous evening.

I perform a fair amount myself, storytelling specifically, and Gray, in my opinion, is the master of this kind of theater. I've seen three different shows of his over the years and each time I've been delighted and amused and captivated. And ever since I first saw him (*Swimming to Cambodia* at Lincoln Center in 1986), I've wanted to find out if he memorizes his pieces or if he just knows his stories extremely well and tells them somewhat differently each show. This is the technique I use and it has its benefits and its drawbacks: There's room for spontaneity and improvisation, but there's often the dreadful feeling that you came up with something the previous performance that was really good but you can't quite recreate it.

Anyway, there he was at this cocktail party and I very much wanted to talk to him, but I was afraid that I would suffer personality withdrawal, which is the usual effect that people I admire have on me. Actually, if I think about it, in almost all social settings my personality disappears. I'm not too bad one on one and occasionally I do well at a dinner party but for the most part if I'm in a large group setting like a cocktail party I bore the hell out of people, I bore the hell out of myself, and this problem of mine, I realize, doesn't bode well should I make it to that next orgy. No one will want to couple with me if I'm psychotically dull.

You see, in person, I come across as depressed, and that's because I *am* depressed. And being depressed makes you shy and scared and boring. But the odd thing is that I'm funny onstage. I'm not bragging when I say that; it's more of a diagnosis, actually. A self-diagnosis. I've come up with a label for my personality disorder: Comic-Depressive. Depressed most of the time; comic on stage. When my friends introduce me to new people they'll often say, "You should see Jonathan perform; he's very funny." And the new person will just look at me and see my morbid face and frightened, glazed eyes and they are always completely unbelieving. I look more apt to commit suicide than make someone laugh.

Anyway, there I was at this party on Martha's Vineyard and my idol Spalding Gray was eating olives and sipping wine. I was acutely aware of his movements around the room and was wondering if I'd have the courage to engage him in conversation and selfishly pose to him this question of memorization that I had been pondering for so many years or if I would just chicken out because I was afraid that my lack of personality would be too humiliating. Then somehow in the choreography of the cocktail party—people escaping from one mindless conversation to move on to the next or better yet to the bar or cheese table—I ended up alongside the object of my admiration.

"I saw your show the other night," I said, showing great courage; I was surprised I didn't stutter or say something nonsensical. "It was very good," I then added. It was a classically dull opening, but not beyond the pale.

"Thank you," he said sincerely, and then he finished a cheese and cracker he was eating.

"I'm sorry to be a nuisance," I then said, plowing bravely forward, "but I do a bit of performing. At PS 122."

I said this knowing full well that he workshops his pieces there. I let this information sink in, and then I sallied forth, "And I sort of do what you do. I had a one-man show there this winter called 'Oedipussy.' "

He laughed. I had purposely said the title of my show so that at least one non-boring thing would come out of my mouth. "Well, anyway," I said, "I've always wondered, if you don't mind me asking, do you memorize your shows or do you tell them differently each performance?"

There. I had gotten it out. And what happened next was great. The answer came: He told me that he *doesn't* memorize his pieces, and we ended up having a brief but very good talk about his technique and I didn't bore him too badly. Eventually, of course, which is the nature of any cocktail party conversation, we ran out of steam and he politely excused himself so that he could make another visitation to the cheese table.

I was thrilled. I hadn't chickened out and had spoken

to the Mickey Mantle of storytelling. I then asked my girl-friend if we could go. I didn't want to risk reencountering Spalding Gray and wreck things by numbing him with a second dose of Ames-dull.

We left the party and I was behind the wheel of our car, guiding us along the dark country roads. Then we came to this four-way intersection, called Beetlebung Corner, and there a motorcycle policeman suddenly pulled in front of us and ordered me to stop. I did so, thinking I had com-mitted some sort of violation. But the policeman simply dismounted his bike and stood in the middle of the road with a large orange flashlight, forbidding me to continue. Then a car from the opposite direction approached and it too was stopped, and the beams of its headlights flooded into our car.

"The Clinton motorcade must be coming," I said to my girlfriend and she agreed, and I was very excited. I love Clinton. Whenever I get into trouble, I think of him and it gives me strength. The problems he makes for himself with his sexual behavior are much worse than mine, but he survives and this gives me courage to face my small (by comparison) crises. I mean, if he can endure an impeach-ment and admit to the whole country that he lied about Monica's blowjobs, then I can certainly face whatever obstacles I erect due to my uncontrollable behavior and erections.

So we sat in our car at Beetlebung Corner and then about a half dozen motorcycle policeman passed us with great drama and flair at about thirty miles an hour. They came from my left, from the third fork of the intersection. Like an English citizen awaiting the Queen, I rolled down my window and without thinking about it just started waving in anticipation.

Clinton then cruised by in a black SUV. He was in the backseat, on the right-hand side, and he looked out his window and he saw me. I was illuminated by the car from the opposite direction and he was also lit up by those headlights. His hair was like silver heat lightning, his glasses were on the tip of his nose, and his head was handsome and enormous. He looked right at me, there was maybe ten feet separating us, and in that brief instant he seemed nice and a little bit lonely in that backseat, like a kid being driven by his parents somewhere. I kept waving and he waved back at me sweetly. And there was no one else he was waving to. My girlfriend sitting beside me was blocked from his view by me and she wasn't waving anyway, and no other cars were stopped on our side of the dark road. He waved at me and only me. Me. Me. Me. Clinton waved at *me*!

Then he was gone. The whole encounter had been maybe three seconds long. But it was like three seconds of very good, high-quality electric shock therapy, which as a depressive was quite beneficial for me. I began to scream hysterically, happily, madly.

"Clinton waved at ME! Looked at ME! Saw ME!" I almost had an epileptic fit. I was banging the steering wheel, jumping in my seat. I could have activated the air bag. "THE MOST FAMOUS AND POWERFUL AND FLAWED MAN IN THE WORLD WAVED AT ME!"

"Okay, okay," said my girlfriend. "It's nice to see you so happy about something."

When we got back home, I called all the Democrats I know and only got answering machines. They must all be prospering because of the Internet and were out eating in fancy restaurants. So I left messages across the country, telling people that I had met my storytelling role model, Spalding Gray, and then had been waved at by my role model for being sexually troubled, the President. My numerous hyperbolic messages were probably very annoying to listen to, but I couldn't help it. I was full of life and energy. The man is a power source, like a waterfall; he energizes those around him. Some in a negative fashion, some in a positive fashion. In my case, positive.

To further illustrate this idea of the President as a source of energy, let me regale you with a conversation I had a few months before Clinton waved at me. A friend of mine, a woman, said to me, rather naively, I think, "I don't understand why Monica Lewinsky would want to just give him blowjobs. How pleasurable could that have been for her?" It occurred to me that my friend was not a fan of fellatio, which is perfectly understandable, especially if you have a fear of choking, that kind of thing, but she was missing the bigger picture, which I attempted to paint for her.

"It is my feeling," I said, "that Monica experienced great pleasure. Sucking on him must have been like having an electric cattle prod in her mouth. Every nerve in her body would be turned on!"

This metaphor of the cattle prod seemed to illuminate the issue for my friend, and, too, it explains why I was so charged up. I didn't have to receive him in my mouth, but just getting a wave sent a few sparks in my direction and the neurotransmitters in my brain snapped to attention and released some much needed serotonin. Also, I should point out that Clinton is an utterly rare and unusual creature. After all, there's only *one* President in the world, and being in close proximity to him is like getting to see a bald eagle or a shark or this dinosaur fish they discovered in the

Indian ocean. Such sightings are thrilling because they almost never happen. At least not to me. I've never seen an eagle or a shark or a dinosaur fish. But I did see the President, and *he saw me.*

The Sacrifice
October 26, 1999

When I moved to Brooklyn about two months ago, my friend
Vivian called me up and asked me if I wanted to attend a live
animal sacrifice at her place.

"Sounds fascinating," I said. "When and what time? I'll
be there with my hair in a braid. Jacket and tie necessary?"

The following evening I rode my bike to Vivian's house
a few neighborhoods away. I was to be the assistant to the
assistant to the Babalao. The Babalao is what a priest is
called in the Ife religion—a religion practiced by the
Yorba, a people indigenous to Nigeria. Certain aspects of
Ife, combined with practices and beliefs taken from
others' religions, including and primarily Christianity,
helps to make up the Vodun religion, which is more com-
monly referred to as Voodoo.

Vivian is a devotee and student of several different religions, including Ife and Vodun. She's always appealing to
various gods to look after her soul, provide good lovers,
and keep an eye on her investments. She needs lots of
gods because she's very busy. She is a sculptor, world traveler, and first-class adventurer. She's been in the middle
of warring soldiers' gunfire on the Amazon, survived a

two-week episode of Malaria in a hut in Nigeria, nearly died of a mysterious fever in a hospital in Bangkok, was tackled and French-kissed by a cannibal in the jungles of the Philippines, and is well liked and feted in the art worlds of London, Berlin, Paris, and Denmark, to name but a few of the cities where her art has been displayed in museums and galleries. In addition to her art career, she's a Brooklyn landlord, possessing several properties, and she's an avid player of the stock market. She's also the most dyslexic person I've ever encountered; she spells my name, "Johnthnan." I love her emails and letters—their beautiful misspellings make them read like poetry or some kind of mad code.

So this past August, she consulted with the Babalao, who was in New York for several weeks, staying in Harlem, and he prescribed for Vivian a sacrifice to help keep her in good standing with the spirit world. And that's where I enter the picture. The sacrifice was to take place on the second Saturday night of September, and I got to Vivian's on time, around eight-thirty, but she wasn't there. I knew she had to go to Harlem to pick up the Babalao and his assistant, which could account for her not being home, perhaps there was traffic. Also, when you travel as much as Vivian does, you're on several different time zones, so punctuality is not one of her strong points, but I wasn't put out—when you know a friend's weakness, it makes you much more tolerant.

Thus, ready for a long wait, I grabbed a *Post* from the corner deli and sat on the stoop of her building. I was prepared to lay siege for as long as two hours, since it's not every day that you get invited to a sacrifice and I knew it was going to happen no matter how late she got back. Most friends I give half an hour grace period for tardiness before giving up, but with Vivian one has to make a much greater allowance. But it's worth it for the things she has exposed me to over the years, the adventures she's taken me on.

While I memorized the baseball box scores and statistics in the paper, which I had already memorized that morning, a beautiful girl, about twenty-three, came out of the laundromat next door and for some odd reason stared right at me. I was instantly smitten. She was of the thin, waifish, small-hipped variety of female who nonetheless are gloriously adorned with medium-to-large succulent breasts. Furthermore, this girl had hair the color of wet sand, her skin was smooth and pale, and her lips were swollen and all too kissable. She wore those bohemian-style pants that come to the hip bones and end tantalizingly just above the pubis. And she was in a small T-shirt, so her braless breasts in all their delectability were stunningly outlined, and, too, since the T-shirt didn't reach the pants, I could see her tender, vulnerable belly. Oh, to kiss that belly! To press my face against it like a beggar.

I insanely wished, as I have millions of times in similar circumstances, that she would immediately and magically fall in love with me so I could then throw her over my shoulder and run to the woodsy, stygian park that was conveniently down the street, and then beneath some tree growing like an erection out of the ground I'd peel away those nothing pants and nothing shirt and behold her in the starlight and the diffuse city light—this perfect beautiful girl—and kiss her and stroke her, be sweet to her . . . she puts her arms over her head, the whole bounty of her body is mine, she wants me to have her; maybe she gets on her knees, proffers herself to me that way, her ass illumined in the night . . .

She looked at me for a lingering, languorous moment then went back into the laundromat. I returned to the baseball box scores—a numbing, safe haven away from the burden of sexual desire.

I was on the stoop about another thirty minutes, having moved on from the sports section to the front of the paper, and then the girl came out again, stood in front of the laundromat and stared at me for the second time. Why? Why did she look at me so? Was she lonely on a Saturday night doing laundry? Could this be an opportunity for a once-in-a-lifetime pickup? I decided to take action. I had a good feeling about this. I made my move.

"Doing laundry on a Saturday night?" I asked.

It may have been the worst pickup line of all time.

And its stupidity was compounded by the fact that I immediately, upon uttering those words, discovered why she was staring at me. She wasn't. She was looking over my shoulder to see if her six-foot-three, handsome dreadlocked Jamaican—at least by appearance—boyfriend was coming to rescue her from the laundromat, which he was, and exactly at the precise moment that I delivered the above line. He heard it and she heard it. He slowed down his stride as he passed me and glared at me. How dare I speak to his girl? said his angry gaze. He then put his arm around her and stared me down some more. I was hardly a threat or a rival—if we were cavemen she would have been his woman by virtue of his superior size—but he was giving me the prolonged hairy eyeball anyway.

"Sorry," I said, and shrugged my shoulders in a gesture of conciliation, having to do something to break the tension, and which was my way of saying to him, "Can you blame me? She's beautiful. You've got a great girl there." He stared at me a few more milliseconds, and the whole thing, to my politically correct sensitized mind, seemed to have some kind of weird racial undercurrent: Here I was a white man in a primarily black neighborhood trying to pick up a white girl who was in a biracial relationship.

Finally, the stare-down ended—I was getting ready to fight or run—and they went inside. I kept reading my paper and wished that Vivian would show up so we could get on with the sacrifice and I could avoid another confrontation with the girl's boyfriend. But Vivian didn't show up and a few minutes later the couple came out of the laundromat and walked past me and the guy stared at me the whole time. I felt like some weird creep who sits on a stoop and tries to pick up girls with terribly bad lines.

So I sat there about another half hour, and then to help pass the time, I went to the deli and bought a banana and a Häagen-Dazs chocolate-covered vanilla ice cream bar. Once I was back in position on the stoop, I began to eat both things simultaneously to create the effect of a banana split, which was something I loved as a child. And then into this happy scene that damn couple returned to collect their laundry—including, I imagined, her sweet panties and bras; I should have gone in there and clutched them to my face when I had the chance—and again the boyfriend stared me down. This was getting ridiculous. So much staring! And I must have looked even more creepy now that I had an half-eaten ice cream bar in one fist and a half-eaten banana in the other. I wished I could explain to them that I was trying to recapture my youth and was also crazy with boredom waiting for a friend who was late for an animal sacrifice that she herself had organized.

They came out of the laundromat with him carrying two large bags and he glared at me one more time for good measure. I had never been stared at so much in my life. At this point, I could have sacrificed Vivian—it was almost ten o'clock and I had nearly been involved in a racial incident with a very attractive couple.

Finally, about fifteen minutes later, Vivian did pull up in her old street-ravaged Chevy and she and the two Yorba men got out. And all was forgiven as soon as I saw her. She smiled at me with happiness and affection—she is like a sister to me—and the way she looked at me made me feel loved; her feelings are not easily hidden or obscured. She has a naive, almost innocent quality at times, which is why I guess she likes adventures, she's still so curious about everything. So I didn't care that I had sat on her stoop for almost two hours and had almost provoked a race riot. Her friendship was more than worth it.

I shook hands with the Babalao and his assistant—they were both dressed in comfortable, brightly colored pajama-like outfits. Vivian was dressed completely in white, including a white handkerchief around her hair. She quickly explained to me that the Babalao had told her to dress this way for reasons of purity. We all went into Vivian's place and then out to her backyard, where the ceremony was to occur.

In dim lighting (she didn't want the neighbors to be able to see to clearly what was happening—sacrifices are most likely illegal), I had to chase around her little backyard this thin white chicken, and I felt like Rocky improving his footwork. Once the chicken was caught, I held on to it and it was soft and nervous and I stroked its head. I knelt near the Babalao, who was chanting quite melodically. He was in a chair and so was Vivian, who sat across from him. The assistant hovered nearby, holding one of Vivian's sharper kitchen knives. At the Babalao's feet, on a plate, was a softball-sized orb made up of cornmeal that Vivian had prepared, and in a cage, at Vivian's feet, was a pigeon. Vivian had bought the chicken and the pigeon at a Brooklyn live-animal market.

At one point the Babalao yanked feathers out of the chicken and pigeon and stuck them in the cornmeal ball and both of them cried out when they were plucked. The Babalao kept up his chanting for quite some time and it was very soothing, but I wondered if I was going to scream when the chicken was killed (Vivian told me, though she hadn't yet explained why, that the pigeon was to be spared).

After about twenty minutes the Babalao stopped praying and told Vivian to hold the chicken to her forehead, which she did. Then the assistant took the chicken from her and quickly cut its neck, severing the head. The Babalao attached the head to the cornmeal orb, and the assistant squeezed the blood from the chicken's neck onto the orb. I didn't scream. Then more prayers were said for a minute or two and then we were done. We cleaned up. Everything was to be thrown away—the chicken was not to be eaten.

Then we all piled into the car and headed for Harlem, and as we careened up the FDR, I felt sort of wonderful, as if I had been meditating or had sat for a little while in a cathedral. Watching that chicken be killed had not been a terrible thing at all, even though for years in a liberal, yoga-influenced way I've been quasi-vegetarian. Vivian had told me that animal sacrifice was meant to show the highest respect for life and was not an uncaring dismissal of the animal's existence. And so while watching that chicken quickly cease to be with a few strokes of the knife, I had a sense of the utter fragility that every living thing shares, that my same-colored blood could flow as easily. Yet this made me felt keenly alive—I felt more aware of the blood in me, the life in me. I felt more grateful for it.

We dropped the men off in Harlem, there were handshakes and hugs all around, and then Vivian and I drove back to Brooklyn. Following the Babalao's instructions, we took the pigeon to an intersection of four corners, where Vivian—after making sure no cars or passersby were coming—took the bird and held it to her forehead and spun in a circle in the middle of the road. After several spins, she let the bird go. It was supposed to fly away, taking Vivian's prayers upward, but sadly, tragically, the poor thing, tired from being caged all day, didn't fly and it came speedily down to earth with a frightening thud. Vivian and I both screamed, thinking that she had killed it. But the clean, elegant, gray bird (it wasn't a dirty pigeon at all), righted itself and waddled off, like a man in a good suit with his hands (its wings) crossed behind his back. It then went onto the sidewalk and just stood there, like it was waiting for a bus.

"Will your prayers work if it didn't fly off?" I asked.

"I don't know. Let's get out of here," she said, afraid that we'd get arrested for abusing the pigeon.

We then quickly walked back to her place and since we were both tired, I didn't come in. We kissed good night and I got on my bike, and feeling very guilty about the bird I thought I should check on it. If it was still on the sidewalk—where some cat could get it—I would try to help it fly. So I cycled over there and as I approached I saw that it was still just standing there, looking rather stunned.

But then when I got nearer, two people walking hand in hand, coming from the other direction, approached the bird. It was the biracial couple! They spotted me immediately. What were they doing out? Why weren't they in bed making love? The boyfriend was taken aback, seeing me on my bike, but he also looked angry. A few hours had passed since our last encounter. He probably thought I was stalking them. The girl looked at me like I was a sex fiend—I had my ridiculous, pointy bike helmet on, which tends to give me a depraved look. And now how could I dismount and attend to the bird with them right there? Some kind of strange confrontation would occur. The boyfriend would misinterpret my getting off the bike. Who would believe I was stopping for a pigeon? I had to make a quick decision: I abandoned the bird and sped, like a maniac, past that good-looking couple.

What must they have thought of me? And what an odd moment it was. The two parts of my evening meeting up at that intersection. I could only hope that maybe the couple would help the bird; I didn't want it to die. It didn't seem fair. It wasn't the one supposed to die. It wasn't chosen for that, though, of course, maybe it was.

The Fight
November 9, 1999

Part 1

Tomorrow night before a sold-out crowd of almost four hundred people, I will enter the ring against David "The Impact Addict" Leslie. For one night at least, I will stop being the writer Jonathan Ames and will become the fighter Jonathan "The Herring Wonder" Ames. Or just Herring, as my friends have come to call me. And true to my word, I ate a lot of herring during this time of training, and will have a small bite of the fish before the fight. This will ensure herring breath in the ring, which will act as a complement to my fierce left jab.

So I am going to write this story of the fight in two parts: The Day Before and The Day After. But will there be a day after? It's not impossible that some grotesque phantom punch will be my undoing, and so in case of a dark outcome I will send in this first part to the *Press* tonight—a lugubrious act, I know—in the eventuality that I am unable to write part two. But to all of that: GOD FORBID! as my mother would say, and mostly I am having positive thoughts. What you think, command all the gurus, is what happens. Thus—I will win! I will persevere! I will not submit!

I do, though, have some reason to be concerned: It's not

terrible, but in preparing for this fight, I've already been mildly disfigured. Last week, during a sparring session, my nose was broken. The upper left nasal cavity, according to my friend, a Fifth Avenue plastic surgeon, was collapsed. This is the fourth time in my life that my nose has been broken, and they were all rather noble occasions, I must say. Noble in that at least I didn't break the nose by walking into a door, that kind of thing.

The first nose-break was the result of a beating I received at age five from a mentally imbalanced ten-year-old whose head was misshapen. I know I often repeat this tale of my beating at the hands of a subnormal, but I can't get it out of my system. This poor creature attacked me from behind as I was playing Spider Man by myself in my own yard, having achieved my costume by pulling my sweater over my head. When he had me on the ground he sat on my chest—he had the most foul peanut butter breath and small, ugly grey teeth—and then he smashed me in the nose. Later, he was incarcerated in some kind of state home.

The second nose injury was during a fencing match in high school—a qualifying tournament for the national Junior Olympics. I was lunging at my opponent and he panicked and put the guard of his saber right into my fencing mask. The mask was crushed and my nose behind the mask was broken. I was sent to the ground, bleeding. A cold compress was put under my lip to stop the flow of blood from the nostrils and for some reason this worked. I then finished the bout and won and qualified for the Junior Olympics as a representative from New Jersey.

The third nose accident took place in Paris, as I've also mentioned numerous times, in a bar fight over a tall, good-looking Danish girl. This was in 1984, during my

Hemingway phase. And this latest nose trauma occurred eight days ago, during my Muhammad Ali phase. I weigh 156 and I was sparring with a 181-pound Irishman. A good fellow and a good fighter. We've tangled quite a few times over the last two months. So eight days ago we had gone two rounds and I was doing well—I tagged him on the chin, causing him to bite his tongue. In the third round, I charged in with my hands down—breaking the cardinal rule of boxing: Hands Up!—and he put a straight right hand into the bridge of my nose. You could hear the bone crack throughout the whole gym and all of Gleason's went quiet, like the silence after a car accident. I screamed, "Oh, fuck, fuck, fuck." It's very painful to have something snap—like a chicken bone—in the center of your face.

I was broken-nosed and brokenhearted—I thought my seven weeks of training had been wasted, destroyed, that the fight would have to be called off. I looked in the mirror, where all the guys practice their jabs. Harry, my trainer, came with me. "It's not too bad," said Harry. The knob of the bridge of my nose (the knob that had formed from all the other breaks over the years) was pushed over to the right; it was rather horrifying to look at. "Harry, it's on the right side of my face!" I said. "It used to be in the middle and now it's way over on the right." "You don't look that different," he said. After all, he's a boxing trainer, and then he told me to go hit the heavy bag, even with my broken nose, so I did, but then my whole face started swelling and I was in bad pain and he told me to call it quits.

But I have healed quickly, I've been taking lots of Arnica, a homeopathic medicine, and the two black eyes that formed after the break have been more than worth it: I've never had women on the street look at me with such come-hither interest. I think the women have responded in a primal, unconscious way to my battered face; I must trigger some ancient buried memory of Early Man—one who is brave and willing to fight and therefore must be a good hunter, a good provider. And if I wasn't trying to be celibate before this battle, I think my broken nose might have found itself in some interesting, sweet places.

So the nose is more or less okay. I saw the doctor yesterday and he has declared my chaste, celibate breathing appendage fit enough to withstand the fight.

"Just try not to get hit there again," he said. "But if you do, it will definitely refracture, and it will hurt like hell, but I can fix it. I had a kick-boxer in here the other day and his nose was pushed over even farther than yours and I have him looking pretty good, so I can repair anything that happens to you. So go box."

I did worry a little that this was his Fifth Avenue ego speaking, but I think I'll be all right. I will be wearing special headgear that has a protective bar right in front of my nose, which despite my honesty in this column about so many of my perverted faults and misdeeds, is growing and growing as if I were Pinocchio.

Anyway, enough about the old proboscis. I want to touch briefly on the regimen that I have endured for the last two months. Each day, I'd wake at seven-thirty and jog to Gleason's Gym; it's about a mile-and-a-half run. I'd then shadowbox in the ring for usually about four rounds (three minutes each) under Harry's watchful eye. Then there's the heavy bag for anywhere from four to six rounds, or Harry would come at me with his pads (these flat mitts that trainers wear) and I'd throw combinations of punches at him, usually for three or four rounds, with one-minute rests in between.

Sometimes I hit a rubber dummy upon whose forehead Harry scribbled "David." Once or twice a week, I'd spar with other fighters, usually after the shadowboxing, and we go anywhere from three to six rounds. And I've played a lot of sports—college fencing-team and high school letters in fencing, track, tennis, and soccer, and years of street basketball—but nothing is more tiring than boxing. There's something about the constant movement, the effort to throw punches, and the frightening immediacy of your opponent, such that it is all incredibly and quickly fatiguing.

Then after all this boxing training, which really works the arms and legs and would last about an hour, I'd do calisthenics, as Harry calls them: forty pull-ups, twenty dips, fifty push-ups, two hundred sit-ups, thirty upside-down push-ups and rolling-neck exercises while standing on my head in the ring, and most importantly, Harry's secret training weapon: I'd take a ten-pound sledgehammer and beat a tire—like the way old-time boxers chopped wood—for thirty, thirty-five minutes. I also often skipped rope, spent time on the Stairmaster, and would roll on this wheel to build my stomach muscles. Then when all this was done, which took about an hour and a half, I'd run a long way home, about three miles. All in all, each day, it was about three hours of exercise.

Once I was home, I'd have a large breakfast, which included my usual dosage of psyllium fiber, but also a glass of juice fortified with a protein powder. Then I'd take my yoga netti pot and with it pour salt water through my nostrils, so that I'd have super unobstructed breathing. And a nice side effect of the netti pot was that for weeks I've had the smell of salt water in my nose and I keep feeling like I'm on a vacation near the ocean and this deceives me into a state of well-being. Then after the nostrils were cleared, I'd take an Epsom-salt bath, after which I'd climb into bed (around one P.M. now) and read a boxing book: either Plimpton's *Shadow Box* or Oates's *On Boxing*, both of which are excellent, but if I couldn't take any more boxing, I'd read and delight in my Wodehouse omnibus, which is very far removed from the world of pugilism. Then after fifteen minutes of reading, I'd nap for an hour. The rest of the day, I'd sort of go about my life, but I would be pretty drained.

So after eight weeks of this hard work, I've gotten stronger and stronger: I've put on pounds of muscle: my biceps have more than doubled in size and I keep showing them off to anybody who will look; it has helped, I think, to sell tickets for the fight.

On the weekends, I didn't train too much. Like a good Jew, I would rest on Saturday, and then on Sunday, I'd go for a long five-mile run, often across the Brooklyn Bridge. And when I'd run across the Bridge, I'd see all the water and I would think how water is more powerful than anything in the world and I would think how I'm going to take all the rivers that surround New York and feel them in me, and then on the night of the fight—tomorrow night!—I'd deliver it all like a flood on David Leslie's chin. And I hope this is what happens. I hope I will enjoy writing part two. I hope I can write part two.

photo: Patricia Sullivan

photo: Nelson Bakerman

November 11, 1999

Part 2

It's the day after. It's 4:10 A.M. I'm alive. I can't sleep. Maybe I'm writing this to show myself my brain still works. Foreman after his fight with Ali in Zaire counted back from one hundred and did other tests to make sure his mind was still working. This is my test because I took a lot of shots to the head tonight. Too many shots.

So I'm going to keep this brief. Strausbaugh, my editor, when I told him I was going to write the column in two parts, suggested that I write more about the fight. But I don't want to write about it too much. I hope somebody else will.

First of all, I lost, and I lost pretty bad. My nose got rebroken in the second round, a hook sliced across the top of the guard of the special headgear and reshattered whatever healing has taken place since the last break nine days ago, and at the moment the nose is all swollen and grotesque and the right nostril is clogged with dried blood. (But this is my own fault; I went into the fight with a broken nose; it just seemed impossible to delay this thing, postpone it. The good news is that the doctor says the septum is in place—after the fight he stuck two rubber-gloved fingers up my nostrils to check; this means, unless the nose looks really horrific, that I have a good chance of avoiding surgery.) My jaw is out of line and I can't close my mouth or chew properly. But a few weeks ago in sparring that happened, so I know after a few days the jaw falls back into place. My neck is a mess. I'm kind of craned over right now typing this. I've been going to the chiropractor for a few weeks. From a punch during sparring, I received a whiplash injury, and it feels like the whiplash is back. And just to complete the medical report, I have scratches on my arms and back from Leslie holding on to me during clinches.

What went wrong? A lot. First of all, my defense was lousy. Eight and a half weeks of training is just not enough time to learn how to block punches, slip punches. So the result is, it seems like I got hit with almost everything he threw. I did land a few myself. I saw that his ribs on the right side turned red and in the third round, I bloodied *his* nose. But overall, his style was unorthodox and clever and it had me confused and he clearly won. In the beginning, he did grab me a lot, which my trainer felt should have resulted in points being taken off, but we didn't have a proper ref—a talented sportswriter in a white shirt and bow tie was in that role—and by the end I was grabbing him, too. One thing Leslie did, though, which I didn't appreciate, was that he taunted me a fair amount. He'd offer his chin or try to wave me toward him. I know he was trying to be a showman, but I think the crowd would have enjoyed the fight without these antics. Still, he was the superior boxer. He's boxed sporadically since his twenties and there was no way I could match his experience. He also had twenty or more pounds on me, and they say a good big man will always beat a good little man, but in this case that doesn't really apply, since this little man wasn't that good.

But he didn't knock me out and I didn't quit, and Leslie had predicted that either he'd knock me out in the third or I'd throw in the towel after the third. So the fight went the distance. Four rounds. And that might not sound like much but getting beaten for twelve minutes felt pretty long and horrible and the last six minutes, the last two rounds, I knew and felt that my nose had been crumpled for the second time in nine days, and it wasn't that easy to breathe through half a nose.

Lying in bed just now, unable to sleep, sort of suffering physically and mentally, I was applying my theory (taken from the Greeks) that almost all of my pain is brought on by my own excesses of character, and so the source of my agony tonight is clearly myself. I accepted this fight. Thought I could handle it. Hubris. Hubris. Hubris.

The hopeful note is that out of the humbling I received, there's a chance for something good to arise. More than one wise person has remarked upon the closeness of the words humiliation and humility, and so after my humiliation, my beating, maybe I'll be in store for the grace that comes with a sense of humility.

Before I end this column, I should comment on the ambience of the evening. The fight was held at the Angel Orensanz Foundation (a nineteenth-century synagogue now used as a venue for the arts) and other than my own personal twelve minutes of pugilistic torture, the evening was spectacular. Leslie did a fantastic job producing this whole mad event and the place looked stunning and the audience was in turn stunned. Right in the middle of this ancient synagogue there was this great big red boxing ring, and hoisted to the ceiling were enormous television screens showing excited audience members being interviewed, and all the while music blared beautifully in the acoustics of the old synagogue. And everywhere you turned there were cameras—which gave the feeling that something exciting was going on. It really was a Box Opera.

And besides the main fight, there great preliminary bouts and entertainment: There was Zero Boy vs. Zero Boy, Michael Portnoy vs. Five Five-Year-Olds, two lesbian gladiators, Shelly Mars and Sarah East Johnston, and in between these fights a scantily clad dance troupe performed. I saw all these people getting ready down in the basement, where I was hiding out, and it was like being in a circus. It was all quite magnificent, especially Portnoy's five-year-olds. One of them was wearing a ballerina's outfit. And of course, Harry Chandler, my dear friend, was running about naked. He looked especially glorious in some kind of penis-hat he's invented, though my trainer Harry upon seeing the other Harry wearing the Mangina, said, "You couldn't pay me enough money to put that thing on! If I was dead they couldn't make me wear that thing!"

So the evening, on the whole, was splendid. I was even given a beautiful robe with a *NY Press* logo on the back and "The Herring Wonder" spelled out, but the most splendid thing for me was how kind people were to me after the fight. Friends and strangers alike congratulated me and told me I did all right, and this was very helpful to me. And I had the feeling that many of the strangers, who spoke to me or made motions of support across the room, were readers of my column; if so, and they're reading this now, I thank them.

Well, it's five-twenty A.M. I guess my brain is all right; I've written for more than an hour. So I think I'll stop and return the ice to my nose and maybe go for a walk on the quiet, dark streets, and then when I get back, I'll be sure to sleep. It will be nice to sleep.

Jonathan *Libre!*
November 23, 1999

Two nights ago, I was on the phone with my mother, and this was a little unusual since both my parents are typically on the line with me. Thus, with the playing field even—one on one, so to speak—I took the opportunity to pass some dangerous information; I casually let it slip to my mom that I'm about to take a trip.

"By the way, I'm going to Cuba next week," I said. "Two friends are in a film festival there. That's why I'm going." I quickly threw in the part about the film festival to make it seem like a worthwhile and acceptable jaunt. To be going there for a reason, for something important-sounding like a film festival, would confuse her, perhaps even thwart the usual frightened response. It worked.

"That's exciting. A film festival in Cuba! When do you leave?"

"December second. I've been wanting to go there ever since seeing *The Buena Vista Social Club.*" My mother and I had both seen and loved the Wim Wenders film.

"It sounds like a great trip . . . Why are they having a film festival?"

"Supposedly Castro is a big film buff."

There was some noise in the background. I heard her say, "Jonathan's going to Cuba." Then she said to me, "Your father wants to talk to you." I sensed the phone being passed like a walkie-talkie in a bunker, being passed from a lieutenant to a captain, and I was the lowly sergeant on the other end of the transmission, up near the front lines, about to be chewed out for insubordination.

"What's this about Cuba?" my father growled.

"I'm going there next week," I said, feigning nonchalance. I'm thirty-five years old, but with my parents, my father in particular, I'm still sixteen and don't have a driver's license. Also, because of my recent boxing match, my father thinks my judgment is faulty and that my instinct for self-preservation has reached an all-time new low. He's not without reason.

"Why go to Cuba?" he demanded angrily, though he was unaware, I think, of his harsh tone.

"Because I *want* to," I said, trying to sound like an adult, but feeling like it was twenty years ago and I was asking permission to go to the Jersey Shore. And I didn't mention the film festival part to him because I wanted to assert my manhood with him; I didn't want to need a film festival to justify my desire for adventure. That was a good excuse to use with my mother, but with my father I have to continually prove that I can't be pushed around. It's the old Oedipal drama being revived again and again and again. It has to be the most popular play of all time.

"But *why* are you going?"

"Because I *want to.* "

We were at a standstill. But my simple desire to go should have been reason enough. After all, I'm a *man*! A man with rights! A man who does what he *wants*! A man who can make plans without asking his parents' permission! Jonathan *Libre*! And I've earned this status—I haven't had to live at home for reasons of financial destitution for four years now, and I haven't asked for a significant loan in at least a year and a half! I've even paid for the last few outrageous phone bills I've run up during my visits home. I've been showing great maturity, though in some ways I can't help but feel that my recent good behavior is simply money in the bank with my parents (to use an apt metaphor) for when I fall on my face again. I can hear myself already: "I haven't asked for a loan for quite some time!"

But let me return to the present, to the Cuba conversation, rather than dwell on the dreary future. "There has to be a reason *why*!" said my father. "You can't just *go*!"

I could have said, 'I can just *go*!' But I decided to placate him, to not escalate this unnecessarily. I was going to have to use the film festival, after all. "Well, some friends," I said, in a soothing tone, "are in a film festival. So it's perfect—I get to be with friends and not travel alone and also there will be plenty of other Americans there."

I mentioned the other Americans, thinking that this would calm down his overprotectiveness. It worked in two ways: There is safety in numbers and also it would make me seem more like a conformist—if lots of other Americans are going to Cuba, then suddenly I'm not such a risk-taker. But his gut was still not liking this trip. So he switched tactics.

"Whose paying for you to go?" he demanded. "The festival?" If I was going for free and if this was somehow related to my career, like my free trip to Germany nine months ago to perform "Oedipussy," then he could understand and maybe accept this Cuba adventure. But if I was paying for myself, then the trip was still not good.

"No one's paying for me," I said defiantly, proudly. "It's coming out of my own pocket." There was silence. The reality of my not backing down—my independence—was getting to him. He asked about the money because he still hasn't gotten over the trauma of bailing me out for years, and it's hard for him to imagine that I can do something extravagant like take a trip.

Also, his joking mantra has always been: "What's yours is mine, and what's mine is mine." So he still feels pain when I spend money as if it were his own money. And spending money is not easy for my father. But this is understandable. He grew up in pretty rough circumstances during the depression in Brooklyn; it shaped his worldview. His bedroom for all of his childhood was in the kitchen, next to the stove. My grandfather was a cabbie, first with horse-driven carriages, and then with cars, and he didn't pull in a lot of money; things were always exceedingly tight.

So it was particularly difficult for my father—not something to make him proud—when the only work I could find from 1990 to 1992 was driving a taxi. Rather than each generation improving on the last, I had slid back. But nowadays, I'm doing better. For the time being anyway, I'm making it as a writer and my father is proud of me, but he senses the precarious nature of my profession and worries about me. And his worry comes out in anger and overprotectiveness, but also generosity. Just a few days ago, he called me up and told me I should get a VCR, that he would pay for it. This was very sweet of him. Being broke for so many years, I've never owned a VCR.

So I thanked my father for this offer and said I would try to shop for one. But this probably won't happen. I've inherited from my father some of his worldview, some of his problems with money. It's nearly impossible for me to spend anything on objects for myself. On travel—yes; on things for my son—yes; on dinners for women—yes; but on objects for myself—no. I always feel like I can do without. That's why every time I do buy an article of clothing, it's a small triumph. About every three years, like some odd lunar cycle, I get a new pair of shoes and stare worshipfully at them for weeks—I can't believe that something so fresh and beautiful has come into the Ames fold, into my life. For years, I had the most ratty collection of underwear, most of which had been purchased for me by my great-aunt when I went away to college in the early eighties. Tarzan had better underwear than me—by the mid-eighties, these things were like dishrags and I wore them for another decade after that. But then in 1996 a girlfriend gave me a pair of boxers from the Gap and they were so wonderful that slowly I relented and have bought for myself, over the last few years, almost a dozen pairs of Gap boxers!

At the start of this underwear renaissance, I was so thrilled by it all—the feeling of esteem that came from buying something nice for myself—that I brought all the shorts (about six at that time) to one of my storytelling performances at the Fez nightclub. With some Benny Goodman music playing, I then threw all the shorts in the air as an act of celebration and exuberance, and I danced underneath the falling Gap boxers like someone at a Maypole celebration.

Anyway, back to the conversation with my father—unable to defeat me, he started to soften on the Cuba expedition. He said, "My friend's daughter and her husband are going to Cuba. I'll find out when they'll be there. Maybe you can meet up with them."

Once my father gives in to the idea of my traveling—

and there's always initial resistance, he's scared that something will happen to me—he then begins to provide me with the names and phone numbers of distant relatives and obscure friends whom I should see and visit. It's some leftover shtetl instinct on his part, this idea that I might have something in common with a fourth cousin. But it's a sweet instinct, and so I feel bad—I never look these people up. It's yet another way I let my father down.

But I played along. "Well, find out when they'll be there and maybe I can rendezvous with them."

"I'll give my friend a call," he said. And then he added, with urgency and foreboding, "You better look into what you do about money there. I hear you have to carry American dollars. No traveler's checks. No credit cards. No bank cards. You better figure all that out. It's probably dangerous to walk around with cash, but that's probably what you have to do."

He was trying to scare me now, but I played it cool. "Don't worry. I'll get all the information . . . It's going to be an fascinating trip. Wait a second. Didn't you go to Cuba, Dad?" I was suddenly recalling a family legend about my father: Before marrying my mom he left Brooklyn to seek his fortune as a salesman in Miami and during this period, I vaguely recalled, he may have taken a trip to Cuba.

"Yes, I went to Cuba. Twice."

Now the advantage was all mine. I'd had ammunition all along. How could he protest me doing something that he had done? "When did you go?"

"Both times in 1952 . . . Maybe you'll run into my old girlfriend Dolores."

I had often heard of Dolores when I was growing up. She was my father's last girlfriend before my mother and my mother would exorcise her jealousy by teasing my father about her. And the way she teased him was to compare *me* to Dolores because Dolores didn't like the way my father ate, thought he made too many sounds, which was an early complaint of mine, an early sign of the Oedipal struggle. I still have a hard time watching my father eat, and supposedly Dolores broke it off with him because of the way he conducts himself when in front of a plate of food.

"Dolores was Cuban?" I asked.

"Jewish Cuban."

"Maybe *I'll* meet a nice Jewish-Cuban girl."

"You couldn't meet a Jewish girl in Israel."

Over the years my parents have lowered and lowered their expectations as to me living out the Jewish-American dream of a respectable career and a marriage to someone within the faith. I *have* provided them with a grandchild, whom they cherish, and so I've brought them a great deal of happiness, and at this point in my life, I think they're really just glad if I'm alive and not in rehab or undergoing a sex change or rejoining the army or going through some other identity crisis. Thus, in some ways, it's become very easy for me to please them, to bring them *naches*—I just have to keep breathing. But, regardless, they would like more *naches*. What parents don't?

"I date plenty of Jewish girls, Dad." I said, protesting his Israel remark. "The relationships may not last long, but it doesn't last long with girls of all religions, but you can't say I don't date Jews. You should be a little encouraged."

"Well, I don't think there are any Jews or nice Jewish girls left in Havana," said my father, "but you better pack condoms. Make a list of things to bring with you. Write down condoms. You might not be able to buy them there because of the embargo. And take Imodium with you. It's probably like Mexico. So write on the list: Condoms and Imodium."

"All right, Dad."

"Just come back in one piece. So make out that list: Condoms and Imodium."

"I got it. You only have to tell me twice. I won't pack anything else. I'll open a black-market pharmacy."

"That's not a bad idea."

"You've got me so nervous now, I'll probably chew a condom for my stomach and taken an Imodium as a birth control pill. Or I'll just wear a scuba diving outfit the whole time, like a body condom."

"Just don't bring back any babies."

"All right, Dad . . . Listen, I gotta go." I didn't have to go, but if I stayed on much longer, I might have thrown in the towel and canceled the trip. He had me equating Cuba with diarrhea, venereal disease, and illegitimate children.

"Goodbye," he said. "Love you."

"Love you," I said, and then we both hung up.

Kooba, *Sí!*
December 23, 1999

The very first prostitute that I met in Cuba had her way with me. I was only in Havana about three hours when the traumatic incident took place. It was around nine o'clock at night and I was wandering around the polished-marble lobby of the hotel Nacional and decided to poke my head out the grand front entrance. There at the bottom of the staircase was a sexy, dark-haired voluptuous woman in a tight red dress. Always with the red dresses. Red must stimulate folly—see bullfighting—the same way that blue is supposed to be soothing. So the red dress and I made eye contact. That special kind of eye contact, like something out of Star Wars. She had the force. Her eyes said, "You will give me money. You will give me money. In exchange, I will give you a dissatisfying, upsetting experience, and you will hate yourself afterward. But I will tell you that your cock is big. You will give me money."

My entire inheritance was just about signed over. I shimmered down the staircase of the hotel toward the woman. A planet drawn to a sun. A lemming to a cliff. A diabetic to a fudge shop.

But then, unexpectedly, I showed great strength of character and sailed past this lovely Cuban. I don't know what came over me. Maybe I was tired from traveling. Regardless, I was feeling virtuous and self-congratulatory, and walked down the long, palm-tree lined drive of the hotel, breathing in the warm breath of the Caribbean air. I was overjoyed to be in Cuba and put the woman out of my mind. I got to the road at the front of the hotel and looking to my right, down a sloping hill, I saw the Atlantic breaking against the wall of the Malacon, the highway that circles Havana. The ocean was blue-gray, not yet fully black with night, and in the sky were purple clouds, holding the last bit of the sun, even at that late hour.

I meditated on this view for a few minutes, enriching my person with its beauty, and then I headed back. When I got to the entrance of the hotel the woman was still there. I had been hoping, as I approached the Nacional, that she would have snagged somebody in the interim, but this was not the case and so I was determined to charge right past her—past her luscious hips and bosom and a buttocks hoisted into the air by spiked heels. Thus, with the will of a priest, I plowed straight ahead. I was like a man of the cloth, but I had the strength of a fullback charging for a touchdown. I was here in Havana for culture, for music, for history, for politics, for the beauty of a lost city, and not here for red dresses at hotel doorsteps! I was going to make it into the Nacional. The goal line was in sight. I was going to win!

She smiled at me. The *force* was strong in her. And weak in me. "Hola," I said, limply. With that smile she had made a touchdown-saving tackle. I was a man of cheesecloth.

"Good evening," she whispered in accented but well-articulated English. She had a sweet face with large brown eyes. She wasn't a girl, she was a woman, probably in her late thirties. She touched my arm. "Are you American?" she asked.

"Sí." Whenever I travel, I speak poorly in the native language and the natives speak beautifully to me in English; it's quite reciprocal that way.

"What's your name?"

"Yonathan." I used 'y' so that she, with her Spanish mind, would understand.

"Jonathan," she said, correcting me.

"Sí," I said, almost ready to give up the fight and just hand over my wallet and my pocket phrase book right then and there. "Como se llama?" I inquired, with an awful accent.

"My name?" she asked, bewildered.

"Yes. Your name."

"Maria."

"It's nice to meet you," I said.

"I am happy to meet you. When you went walking by me, my heart was—" She searched for the word, and unable to find it, she made a thumping motion on her chest. She seemed quite sincere, and it was sweet of her to imply that there was something romantic between us, but I cynically thought that her heart, if it really had pounded, had done so for reasons of mercantile excitement—the anticipation of having spotted an easy mark.

"Thank you for saying that," I said, half playing along and half believing her despite my worldly cynicism.

"Would you like to have a drink together so we could talk more?" she asked.

"Sure," I said, thinking: What the hell, let's have an adventure, I can buy her one drink, it doesn't have to go further than that.

Maria smiled happily and put her arm through mine. In

my company, she could come into the hotel, otherwise Cubans, unless they worked at the Nacional, were not permitted inside. As we ascended the stairs she was all giggly and began to hum that universally well-known chant of "Here comes the bride." This was too much. How much of an easy mark did she think I was?

So with her humming in my ear this matrimonial tune, while affectionately squeezing my manly arm (I was still quite strong a month after the fight), we floated up to the impressive lobby of the Nacional, which is the grandest hotel in Havana. It's an international hotspot, where all the rich South American, European, and American tourists gather. The Nacional is kind of a gigantic Rick's Place of Casablanca: The place is infused with the perfume of intrigue, glamour, sex, and wealth. And booze. Everyone is drinking all the time. The hotel has numerous bars, as well as a large outdoor terrace, where people sit in wicker chairs and talk and drink. And at the edge of this terrace, there is a sloping lawn, which leads to a cliff overlooking the Atlantic and the Malacon. At the end of the lawn there is an old enormous cannon pointing at invaders, pointing at the United States.

Maria, my bride-to-be, led us to one of the inside bars. We took a table by a big glass window overlooking one of the Nacional's two pools. A waiter in black jacket and bow tie glided over to us. Maria ordered a Mojito, which is sort of the national drink of Cuba—it's made of lime juice, several teaspoons of sugar, and a healthy dose of rum— and I ordered one, too.

Normally, I don't drink because I've been classified as dipsomaniacal, but after my boxing match, I suffered some kind of psychological brain injury and went on a strenuous five-week binge, which only recently has been arrested. My sobriety over the past year has unfortunately been like an egg timer: it keeps popping off. I'm worried that I've become a periodic alcoholic, and this is not without consequences. Recently, I emerged from a blackout at a fancy holiday party and found myself in a discussion with the fiction editor of *The New Yorker*. I had never met this gentleman before and if I was sober I would have been polite and terrified in his company. So it was a bit disconcerting to beam back to reality—I had lost about an hour—and to find myself being quite garrulous with a person of such great power (at least in the world of letters), and furthermore to hear myself conveying—it was too late to stop myself, I was still on alcoholic autopilot—an utterly X-rated, lewd, poor-taste tale, which "would make a great story, I'll send it to you!" After I said that, the editor took his leave of me and in his eyes I could see his thoughts, "What a strange, rude drunk."

Well, it's only *The New Yorker*. It's only the one magazine in America that can help a fiction writer actually get well known enough so he can pay the rent with consistency. So no great harm done. And small potatoes compared to the real damage my drinking can do, like not being available, because of incapacitation, for someone, like my son, who might need me.

So I haven't drank today, or yesterday, and I will try not to drink tomorrow. But it is difficult when your worst enemy—cliches don't get to be cliches without good reason—is yourself. I know all my weaknesses and how to exploit them. Well, let's hope for the best, and I'll press on with the telling of this Cuban escapade.

Maria and I had our drinks and we made conversation. She started rubbing my thigh and guided my hand to her thigh. It felt very nice. It was very thighish. Like most thighs it led elsewhere. I ordered two more Mojitos. Then Maria's sister Margaritta joined us. She had somehow snuck into the hotel without an escort. She was a dyed blonde and not as pretty as Maria. She had something of a mustache, but a sweet disposition. I bought her a Mojito and a pack of cigarettes. Maria was on my left and Margaritta was on my right. Maria stroked my thigh and Margaritta fondled my arm. I felt like a 1950s gangster with his two Havana molls. Maria began to make plans for me to come over the next day for lunch and dinner and to meet their mother. I ordered more Mojitos.

Then my two traveling companions, Robert, a brilliant avant-garde filmmaker, and Angelo, a wildly handsome Italian movie star, came into the bar. In a few days, Robert was going to have the international debut of his new film, in which Angelo is the star. Ostensibly that's why we were in Cuba—for cinema, for the ten-day-long Havana Film Festival. My friends waved at me, seemed to show no interest in joining me and the two sisters, and went around the corner to the other end of the bar, out of my sight. Robert was staying in the Nacional, and Angelo and I were going to share an apartment a few miles away. We had the keys to our place, but our bags were still in Robert's room. We planned to take a taxi to our place later in the evening.

I started thinking I should abandon the ladies and join Robert and Angelo. Also, I didn't want to lead Maria on, to get her hopes up for something more. I started telling her I wanted to go be with my friends and she said they should come to us, that maybe one of them would like Margaritta. Right at this moment, two lovely blonde girls entered the bar, looked directly at my table, seemed to scowl, and then headed in the direction of where Robert and Angelo must have been sitting. I figured the scowl was because it was so obvious that I was a gross American entertaining two prostitutes.

The waiter came to my table and I settled our bill. Maria sensed that she was losing me and moved her hand from my thigh to my groin. I responded. She smiled. "Que rico," she said, finally speaking in a little Spanish, though it was directed to her sister, which was even more pleasing—she was praising my protuberance to her sibling. I sensed intuitively that it was praise, and I later learned that *que rico* means "delicious!" I tried to be strong, though, and attempted to remove her hand from my groin, but she only tightened her grip more. I responded more. Couldn't help it. Tightening a grip will do that to man.

Margaritta joined in the fray by turning her body and shielding the rest of the bar's patrons from seeing what was going on. Maria stroked me and whispered into my ear that we should go to her place, that she would feed me all day tomorrow, and if I could give a little something for her "bambina," her baby, that this would be appreciated. I tried to protest, but she was very good with her hand.

Then she pulled my hand further up her thigh and between her legs. She pulled back her skirt. I saw a flash of white panty and black hair along the edges. It was beautiful. It was too much. She gripped me expertly. That flash of secret white panty. Cuba! She put my hand inside her panty. My hand was against her wet sex, her soft hair. She was a beautiful woman. She put my finger inside her. She wanted me to know that she was ready for love, wanted love. You can see a million sunsets and always marvel. Same thing with your finger in a beautiful wet pussy. You marvel. Marveling can express itself in many ways. I happened to explode like a cannon. Like the old cannon on the cliff. My eyelids fluttered. I grunted. Maria was surprised. "Que rico!" she said again. She pulled her hand away. All three of us looked down at my crotch. I was wearing light khaki pants. There was a large visible stain to the right of my zipper. Because of my boxing match, I had become accustomed to abstaining from masturbation and so the resulting explosion had produced a sizable wet spot. Margaritta giggled.

I was flustered, confused, embarrassed. "I better go," I said. I stood up.

"We go to my home now," she said. "I make you dinner. We go to sleep. You will be happy."

"I'm sorry, I can't," I said. "My friends are waiting for me."

She looked at me sadly, then insisted that I write down her phone number, that I call her tomorrow. Margaritta produced a pen and paper. I took the number. Maria stood up, kissed me on the lips, on the cheek. I gave her thirty dollars, enough to live on for several weeks in Havana. But I didn't want to injure her pride, so I said, "For you and Margaritta to take a taxi home." She thanked me sweetly, and kissed me several more times on the face. Margaritta kissed me, too, her mustache brushing against my cheek like a soft caterpillar.

"Goodbye," I said.

Maria kissed me again. Held on to me. Then she said, "Ciao, mi amore," and she let me go.

I wanted to get the key from Robert and go change in his room. I staggered in my sticky shorts and pants to the other side of the bar, only to see that Robert and Angelo were in deep conversation with those two gorgeous blonde girls. I screwed up my courage and approached, drawing my shirt out of my pants to cover the offending stain. I was introduced to the two girls, they were English, "on holiday." They looked at me with odd expressions. I pretended not to notice and I said, "Robert, I've spilled a Mojito on my pants. I need to repair my costume. Can I have the key to your room?"

I was trying to be charming in an uncharming situation. The keys were handed over. I limped off.

I will summarize what happened next: In the room, I changed my clothes and washed my face—it was covered with lipstick, which I hadn't realized. I smelled my finger. It smelled good. Maybe I shouldn't have run away from Maria. Slightly drunk, I returned to the bar. Maria and Margaritta were gone. I joined Robert, Angelo, and the two blondes. Robert, being married, bowed out of the evening early on. Angelo and I drank with the two Brits deep into the night. We paired off, like two couples, and went dancing at a salsa club. Around three A.M., Angelo pulled me aside and conveyed to me some devastating intelligence: The girls knew that earlier in the evening I hadn't spilled a Mojito, though they weren't sure if I had peed in my pants or come, but they knew that something strange had happened, and furthermore, they saw that my face had been covered with lipstick when I came to the table and they thought it poor taste that I had been consorting with prostitutes. My blonde Brit liked me, despite all this, but wasn't going to do more than dance with me, whereas his blonde Brit wanted to come back to the apartment. All this had been communicated to him on the dance floor by his blonde. So, the salsa club closed, and I kissed my blonde goodbye, and then back at the apartment, I listened to Angelo make love all night to his blonde. It was maddening. The girl was a lusty screamer.

Early in the morning, I ran from the apartment, hungover and humiliated. I felt I had destroyed the purity of my trip. I had come in my pants in the hotel bar, missed out on a lovely Brit, drank far too much, and had been kept awake by the sounds of my friend making love. I wandered all around Havana, hating myself. Then I came upon a glorious fifteen-foot-high statue of my hero—Don Quixote. At first I was surprised, but then it made sense, this was a Spanish city, and Don Quixote is to Spain what Tom Sawyer is to America.

The statue was made of metal, now rusted but beautiful, and Don Quixote, with his long, crazy nose, scraggly beard, and sunken cheeks—kind of what Castro looks like now actually, which is rather strange and amazing—was high up on his famed horse, Rocinante, and he was wielding his sword.

I read *Don Quixote*, books I and II (I recommend the Samuel Putnam translation), during the long and horrible winter of '95–96. At that time, I was teaching a dreary composition and grammar class to soldiers in night school at Fort Hamilton, though I was primarily surviving off my credit cards, which when you're broke is like drinking salt water when you're lost at sea. Also, I was in love with a girl who had a boyfriend she wouldn't leave, and a love like that is the same as living off credit cards, like drinking salt water. It kills you. So I was getting it from all angles—the heart and the wallet. What else is there?

Thus, my only solace that winter, as I lay alone in my Brooklyn apartment night after night, was to be with Don Quixote and Sancho Panza. They saved me. They took care of me. So, there in Havana, a few years later, I took incredible strength from seeing my old friend and hero, the Knight of the Mournful Countenance. For someone else it would be like coming across a statue of the Virgin Mary or St. Francis or seeing a burning bush: Don Quixote relieved me of all my self-centered anguish. He had rescued me—a true knight!—yet again. I love him! No one has ever suffered more humiliations than Don Quixote, yet no one has had greater belief in himself and kept fighting on despite it all.

Well, emboldened by this vision of my idol, I stopped feeling sorry for myself instantly, like drinking a magic potion—really, it was remarkable—and I sallied forth into the rest of my trip.

We all like to explore around ruins, to stumble about in places that once were grand, to imagine how people lived, and ruins are always dead places, roped off—I think of sites in Italy, Greece, Israel—but Havana is a *living* ruins. It once was this wealthy city of mansions and hotels and old-world architecture, a European metropolis in the middle of the Caribbean, but now it's falling apart, and yet people still live in the broken streets, the crumbling buildings, and it's all very beautiful. It's like exploring Pompeii with the Pompeians still there, running around in togas. And the decay itself is lovely, gorgeous. More gorgeous than something pristine and whole—an aesthetic of ruin. What makes it even more overwhelming is that the city's comeliness is equaled by its people. Havana is populated by the most radiant men and women, with music playing everywhere, and ancient American cars rumbling by . . . but back to the people—Cuba is the sexiest place in the world. Africa and Spain meet on this small island, and the result is an unusual human beauty and sensuality, and as one woman said to Angelo one night, "All of Havana is fucking right now."

Angelo and Robert left after a few days, after their successful screening, and I happily stayed on, parading around glorious Havana, wearing my light sport coat and thinking I was like Graham Greene, but because I'm Jewish, I called myself Graham Greenberg. I did drink too many Mojitos and Cuba libres, but each morning in my little apartment, a woman would make me breakfasts of eggs, toast, pineapple, guava, and strong coffee, and my hangovers would disappear.

One Friday night, I found a synagogue—there are only two in all of Cuba—and attended services and discovered that there are still lovely Jewish-Cuban girls in Havana. At the end, we all held hands and sang *A'dono Lam*. I could have been in Fair Lawn, New Jersey, or Crown Heights, or Tel Aviv—Adono Lam is universally Jewish. It was wonderful.

Several times, I went to enormous demonstrations for Elian—saw thousands of children in their school uniforms and stood in crowds listening to speeches I didn't understand. The woman who made me breakfast told me that everyone believed the boy should be returned to his father, but that Castro made them attend the demonstrations, that it would be dangerous not to attend—you could lose your job. She also told me that Castro would give these long, long speeches on television, sometimes ten, twelve hours without stopping, and nobody understood how somebody could talk that long—and without going to the bathroom, a great mystery! Everyone was bored by the speeches, she said, and just wanted their soap operas to be put back on. Then she added that he was a great man, but she looked around as she said this, as if she was afraid someone might have heard her blaspheming him to me, an American.

One day I took a taxi to Hemingway's incredible house,

saw his bookshelves, his writing room, and his bathroom, where he wrote on the wall in pencil his weight. There were columns and columns of figures. Then I went to a small fishing village, where I found Gregorio Fuentes, Hemingway's old boat captain, who is the model for the fisherman of *The Old Man and the Sea,* and who is now one hundred and three years old. He was smoking a cigar. I shook his still strong hand. I asked him if Hemingway was strong. "Si . . . fuerte," he said, and he made a fist.

Speaking of fists or fisticuffs, I had quite an ego-gratifying encounter one afternoon. I was coming up the stairs of the Nacional and a young man descending the stairs, an American wearing a white hat and white shoes, said to me, with excitement and admiration, "Are you Jonathan Ames, the fighter?"

I was taken aback. My reputation as a pugilist had made it all the way to Havana. "You saw my fight as 'The Herring Wonder'?" I asked.

"Yes, you were great. The other guy was a jerk. Your style was much better. You were amazing."

"Thank you, that's very kind of you," I said, almost speechless.

"Do you have any fights coming up soon? I'll come see you."

"I'm afraid I've retired. Too dangerous. I have a glass nose."

"That's too bad . . . but you're a great fighter. Well, I have to get on this tourist bus. Goodbye. You're a hero!"

The young man's praise was intoxicating and I floated into the Nacional, feeling like Rocky Marciano, feeling like a champ. I later found out that this perceptive and charming young man is the wildly talented film director

Darren Aronofsky and was at the film festival for a screening of his brilliant movie, π.

So I was in Cuba for ten days and I loved it. Someday I will go back.

To get home, I flew first to Jamaica, where I made an easy connection for New York. When I got off the plane at Kennedy I was quite exhausted and didn't think I could bear the line at customs. In my tired state, I must have looked like a drug addict because I was assaulted by a burly, aggressive drug enforcement agent. He took me off the line and over to a table. My bags were ripped open. My Imodium tablets and all the condoms I had packed, at the behest of my father, were exposed. How embarrassing to have so many condoms left! They looked like a long plastic necklace.

"What were you doing in Jamaica!" demanded the agent. His weight lifter muscles were aching to explode under his blue windbreaker.

I wasn't sure if I was allowed to say that I had been in Cuba. I had heard some crazy rumor that if I acknowledged going to Cuba, I'd receive a ten-thousand-dollar fine. So I started lying about a vacation in Jamaica I never took.

"Just went to the beach every day," I said, and I felt sick. I'm not very good at lying. Exaggerating, yes, but lying, no.

"Where did you stay?"

"Montego Bay."

"In a hotel?"

"Yes, in a hotel."

"What hotel?"

"Montego Bay Hotel."

"What did you do every day?"

"Went to the beach. Swam."

He got tired of this. He put his meaty face right next to mine. "I know you're carrying marijuana. That's why you went to Jamaica. You're acting very guilty and nervous. I can tell you're lying. If you come clean to me now, it will go better for you. Where's the marijuana?"

"There is none."

He squeezed out my bottle of sunblock into a garbage can. It was kind of obscene this wasteful squeezing-out of white lotion. And it took a while, even with his considerable strength and impressive musculature. The lotion was thick and slow-moving because it was SPF 45. I wanted to protest. That's ten-dollar sunblock! But I held my tongue. Ten thousand dollars was a far bigger worry.

After exhausting himself on the sunblock, he ripped open the inner sole of one of my sneakers. Underneath was a strange, brown, gooey rubber. I didn't know that my shoe contained such goo. It was a bit of a revelation.

"Is this the sole of your sneaker?"

"I think so," I said.

"What do you mean, you 'think so'?"

"I've never seen it before." Had I just left an insane police state or returned to one?

He seemed to acknowledge my logic regarding the sneaker; it set him back a moment, but then he pressed on. "You're acting very nervous and guilty," he said. "I know you're lying to me."

I wanted to tell him I'm nervous and guilty for a living—that nerves and guilt are the basis of my entire sad oeuvre. But this guy was well trained—I *was* lying.

"If you don't tell me the truth. If you don't tell me where the pot is RIGHT NOW, we're going to take you to the back and strip-search you, which takes a very long time and you're not going to like it. You'll get in a lot less trouble if you come clean NOW. So you want a strip-search or do you want to tell me the truth?"

I contemplated going through with it. It was the old journalistic impulse taking root—my George Plimpton participatory-journalism gene asserting itself. After all, a prostate massage by a DEA agent would make a very good story. Also, my long-dormant prison-rape fantasy was starting to wake up. But then my guilty Jewish-self came to the fore. To the rescue. What if they did find something up there? If not marijuana, certainly something else incriminating, especially the way I've lived my life.

"I will tell you the truth," I said quickly to the large, weight-lifting agent. "I have been lying to you but not about marijuana. I went to Cuba, but was scared to tell you. Somebody told me that I could be fined ten thousand dollars. So I don't have any marijuana, I swear. I was only in Jamaica for forty-five minutes. I'm a journalist and I was covering the Havana film festival."

"Prove it."

I showed him my laminated festival identification. He threw it into my bag. Then he yelled at me for going to Cuba, that I wasn't allowed go there without a special visa—which is why I had covertly flown from Jamaica, others routes are by way of Mexico or Canada—and then he told me to get out of there.

"No fine?" I asked like an idiot, a good Jewish boy.

He turned his back on me and I packed up my bag and beat it out of there. The guy was good at his job, he could pick out a liar and a nervous person, but he had picked the wrong kind of lying, nervous person. While he was interrogating me, who knows how many marijuana smugglers had snuck through.

I got on the taxi line. The winter air was cold. I was wiped out. Drained. I had been ready for prison and a prison rape, but was set free.

When I got home I put in a tape of a salsa band I had listened to in Havana. I lay on my bed. I was back in America, but pretended I was in Cuba.

Shut the Fuck Up
January 4, 2000

The Bhagavad-Gita says that the "uncontrolled" man has no concentration, no wisdom, no peace, and no happiness. I think this is true. I have none of those qualities; I have lost control of myself. Or rather, I've never had control, but of late it has been worse. So thoughts of suicide—the antithesis of happiness—are frequent. They constantly float in as an answer to my self-created, self-generated torment. My plan is simple: get a hotel room in Brooklyn (a hotel because I don't want to spook my apartment for my landlord, who is also my friend) and take a bath with a plastic bag over my head, like Jerzy Kosinski. I'd leave a note on the locked bathroom door that authorities should be contacted, authorities that won't be mortified by a dead body. But that's as far as the fantasy goes. Suicide—look at the Latin root of the word—is just too horrifically selfish. I can't do that to my parents, to my sister, to my son. And I guess I can't do it to myself. I do want to figure things out.

But what's the right path? How should I live? A few weeks ago, I was walking with my friend Robert in Havana—we were on the boardwalk-like edge of the Malacon, the road that circles the city; the Atlantic was to our right; we were blinking because of the bright sun—

and he is a little bit older than me and seems to enjoy his life, and so I said, "What are we doing? What's the point of everything? I don't know how to live my life."

"We're here to fulfill ourselves," he said, sensing that I needed some basic Existential 101 lecturing. "It's a bad example, but think of the ant; the ant when it's lifting two hundred times its weight, is fulfilling itself. Realizing itself. And that's what we're here to do. We're more complex, obviously, than the ant, so it's harder, but the purpose is the same—to realize ourselves, whatever that means for each person. And to have joy from this."

I had heard this kind of thing before. It's what George Bernard Shaw preached—at least that was my reading of him—and I very much admired Shaw back in college, despite the woodenness of many of his plays. He wrote something about how humans should burn like lightbulbs for as long as they can, and I've often thought of this, tried to rally myself with that notion; and even before college and Shaw, I read *On the Road*, which had a big effect on me, and there was Kerouac saying he liked the people that burned bright like roman candles; and even before I read Kerouac, when I was a junior in high school, I hung a quote from Thoreau over my desk where he said that he went to the woods, to Walden Pond, because he was afraid to die before he had lived.

So I pondered what my friend said. Despite my courting of suicidal thoughts for years (usually in the sunlight-deprived month of January, it should be pointed out), I have tried—influenced by Shaw, Kerouac, Thoreau—to burn bright, to always be curious, which seems to be the path to antlike fulfillment. And, actually, it's not so much that I've tried—I can't really help being driven by a mad curiosity. But at the same time succor always escapes me, probably because I go about my fulfillment like a tottering, openmouthed, single-minded infant looking for the breast; or perhaps because I'm very Christian in a way: I feel flawed, imperfect, deformed—stained with some kind of original sin that can't be cleaned.

So I felt tired when my friend talked of fulfilling the self; I couldn't help but think that you never quite get there, especially when your *self* is this hateful thing. Who wants to fulfill a grotesquerie? Unless fulfilling one's self means learning not to hate one's self.

Robert continued: "And the point is, there is no point. So just try to pleasure yourself, to have fun."

I had read before my trip to Havana about "fun" in Paul Bowles's obituary; it seems that his life philosophy was to try to have "fun." But what a tiny, small word. Fun. So unheroic. So undignified. Is that really the goal of human life? Fun? When I think of fun, I think of playing with a pink balloon. Thus, pleasure is the more adult path. The more adult word. So I do that sometimes: I seek pleasure. I give myself over to Dionysus and Bacchus—I cover all the bases, the Greeks and the Romans—but I get all fucked up, literally and figuratively, and no answers are forthcoming. And then I guiltily regret my drinking because I careen out of control, like a car, and like an out-of-control car I often hurt others, which I don't mean to, which I don't want to. But it's the sin of destruction. It's the stain of my original deformity.

Well, I sense that my editor at about this point in the column is saying, "Ames, shut the fuck up," which is something he often likes to say to me. And the publisher is probably also saying that. My column has to get past both of them before it reaches you, kind and faithful reader, and usually they're very good about not changing *a word,* but I feel that my superiors probably don't like what they've just read in the above paragraphs. But I can't help it; this is what came out of my fingertips onto the keyboard. Unlike most columnists—though not all—I don't concern myself with criticizing the rest of the world; how can I criticize anyone else when I don't know what the hell I'm doing? I don't know where other people get the presumption that they know what they're doing and feel they can criticize, but I assume that their brains are in better shape than mine, and probably the culture, the large collective human organism called society, needs ranters and ravers from all sides and angles to bark at us like sheep dogs, to try to keep us in line, to keep us moving forward in some kind of Darwinian improved way.

But that's not *my* job. I'm supposed to look at myself and make people laugh; not make them think that I'm a sophomoric college sophomore mooning about life and suicide. My editor wants funny stuff or sex stuff or some combination thereof. And I could write something funny *and* sexual in this column, like for example I could write about my friend Harry "The Mangina" Chandler and his latest sexploits, but the *Press* has censored that; every time I try to slip him into a column lately they excise it. They think I've written about my Mangina-wearing, one-legged friend too much. My editor said, "His stump has become your crutch."

But my editor and the publisher don't understand that he's Sancho Panza to my Don Quixote, Neal Cassady to my Kerouac, coffee to my cream . . . he's my Cole Porter ballad, he's the steppes of Russia, he's the pants of a Roxy usher . . . I need him. Because, you see, he's the only person in the world who makes me laugh. Most of the time, I'm so morbidly self-involved that I can't laugh. But my friend Harry, with his gleefully absurd, tragicomic worldview, makes me double over with happiness. But I won't write about him now or ever again. This is the last time, I'm afraid, that he'll be seen in this space. I wonder if these two father figures, editor and publisher, will even let me get away with this small, Manginal/Oedipal rebellion.

But I won't despair. I realize there is one other person who makes me laugh, and that's my son. I just was with him for a week, and I'd like to talk about that a little, but I want to backtrack a moment and briefly touch on some pleasure-seeking I engaged in before my visit with my son.

Starting around the second week of December, I began to hang out at this mad party that Josh Harris, the Internet mogul, as he is called by the popular press, was throwing for twenty or more days, leading up to New Year's Eve. Every night in these two run-down, rented Tribeca buildings (which he transformed by employing numerous carpenters and electricians), he was paying for scores of his friends, plus numerous sycophants and strangers, to debauch themselves. There were feasts every night, with enough wine and food for one hundred people, and the meals were excellent, prepared by very good chefs.

In one of the buildings, there were enormous art installations, as well as rows of bunk-bed sleeping pods so that dozens of revelers could spend twenty-four hours a day at Harris's party; and it was all very communal—there was an open shower area and each pod had a surveillance camera and a TV, so everybody could watch everybody else. In the other building there was a cozy basement lounge with these slanted beds draped in Morrocanish curtains; and in this lounge—named Luvvy's, after Harris's alter ego, a transvestite clown—a free open bar was constantly administering alcoholic medications. So people gathered night after night to drink, smoke pot, grab one another, and see strange performances. It was like the Beat generation meets the Internet. Not the best combination perhaps, but amusing and unusually vital, though there was the sense of great waste; I think the Beat generation culti-vated their madness on a much lower budget, which seems more virtuous, but that's only because I have a poor man's prejudice and snobbery when it comes to money.

So the Internet has created enormous wealth, the way the railroad, oil, and bootleg liquor once created it. And Josh Harris, to me, is like an Internet Gatsby. Why did he throw this enormous bash? Is there an Internet Daisy who once spurned him, whom he was hoping would come by, be drawn in, and he could win her love? He must have spent at least a quarter million dollars while the party lasted, until it was shut down by fire marshals on January 1. He's normal and unassuming on the sur-face, but his outlandish generosity and his willingness to spend money, to pursue his various visions, is enigmatic, Gatsby-like, Howard Hughesian.

About a week before New Year's, I left town to be with my son at my sister's in Los Angeles and I understand that Harris's party picked up steam—there was a wild sex show on the thirty-first, in which my friend, whom I can't discuss, was a principal player, his stump used in a manner not to be found diagrammed in the Karma Sutra, but I don't mind having missed this. Hearing about it is actually quite wonderful, makes it more mythic in a way. Also, I'm squeamish about certain things.

My New Year's Eve, on the other hand, with my son and my sister and her family, was quiet and sweet. And my whole time with my son, as always, was very good. He's nearly fourteen and has grown into this handsome, gentle giant. He's now my height, about five eleven, and he weighs 175 lbs, but he's not a brutish kid. He was very good and patient with my sister's children—a step-daughter who's ten and two twins, a boy and a girl, who aren't quite two.

My son is maturing so quickly that he has a blonde billy-goat beard and before we hooked up in L.A., he said to me over the phone, "I want you to see my beard. I don't want to shave it, but my teachers say I should, so I want your opinion what I should do."

It made me feel good that he wanted to consult me. I feel quite inadequate as a dad, since I only see him about every six to eight weeks (he lives in Georgia), so it pleased me that he thought he could turn to me, even on something simple like his facial hair, though for him it is an important issue. In L.A., after I studied his beard and his wispy red sideburns, we decided that he should shave over the summer because he doesn't want to show up now at school looking radically different, whereas after the long summer break it wouldn't be as noticeable, and also if he didn't like his clean-shaven look he would have some time to grow it back.

Having solved the facial hair issue, he then asked me to work on his stomach. Unfortunately, he's inherited my poor digestion. So he's constipated. All of America is constipated. And one of the things that my son likes about our last few visits is that I often give him a little tablespoon of psyllium fiber in his orange juice and he has glorious experiences on the toilet. But I didn't bring my psyllium to L.A. When I fly with the stuff it always opens up in my bag and my clothing is covered with fiber for months. But he kept asking, "Why didn't you bring the fiber?" Well, it turns out that he's had terrible constipation since our last visit, worse than ever, and he was desperate and in some agony.

So we drove to a good L.A. health food store and I bought him his own canister of psyllium, his very first. I also pumped a bunch of apples and cantaloupes into his system and within twenty-four hours the kid felt good as new. He was rather joyous. And upon seeing his beaming face, I said, "Whose the man when it comes to the stomach?"

"You are!" he said, happily and generously. He then said, "But the problem is you're losing your mind," and he made this comment because he had noted that I seem to be rather forgetful these days, perhaps it's because of my boxing match and all the blows I received to the cranium, plus the alcohol I poured on my brain after the trauma of the fight, further destroying it, but then my son added, "so you're forgetting everything, but when it comes to anal psychology, you're still very good."

When he said "anal psychology" I had a good soul-clearing guffaw. Where did he come up with such a phrase? He really must be my son. So having children is very good for depressives like myself. They make you laugh. They make you not think about yourself, and they give you this sense of purpose, this hope that maybe if you teach them things that they're going to have a better go at it than you did. In fact, I think I'll call him right now down in Georgia and see if he's taking his psyllium. And thinking about him feels good—worrying about his digestion is a much better use of my time than thoughts of Brooklyn hotel rooms.

Booty and the Beast
January 18, 2000

Yesterday, I poisoned myself cooking three eggs. This is not an easy thing to do, but I managed to pull it off.

How did it happen? Well, I put the flame on beneath the frying pan and then got the butter and eggs out of the fridge. This may have been a mistake. The frying pan was too hot. When I put the butter on, it burned. Bubbled. Turned brown. Screamed out in pain.

But I ignored the screams and pressed on. Was too lazy to start over. I cracked three eggs on the side of the pan and dropped their yellow and white selves down into the brown grease. I wished I had organic eggs, but I consoled myself with the thought that the antibiotics in the eggs might be good during flu season.

The eggs immediately turned brown like the butter. A bad sign. But I ignored this sign. I flipped the eggs around a bit with my fork.

I put two pieces of thin German bread into the toaster. I poured a cup of very dark, ink-black coffee, which I had made a few minutes before.

Usually, I do a tablespoon of coffee for every cup of water, but this particular morning I had emptied out the can of Cafe Bustelo because it was nearly finished and I can't bear scraping metal against metal—in this case, the spoon against the bottom of the can. Fingernails on a chalkboard, car keys against aluminum siding, coffee spoons in Cafe Bustelo cans, my father eating—there are certain sounds I simply can not tolerate.

But the problem with my having dumped out the can is that it looked to be about ten tablespoons of coffee and I had only poured into the coffeemaker three cups of water. A ten-to-three ratio is probably not even practiced in Rome or Bogotá, but it seemed like the kind of coffee Philip Marlowe would drink. And I'm always game for playing the hardboiled detective. It helps make my semi-alcoholic bachelorhood feel rough and romantic.

It would have been nice to add a little milk to the cup of petroleum I was calling coffee, but I had sniffed the milk in my fridge and it was bad. I knew it would be rotten, but I sniffed it anyway. Why? Well, human beings often do things when there is no hope. For example, I'm always trying to flag down taxis that have their "occupied" light on. I see the light, register what it means, and yet I still wave at these unavailable taxis. In this way, it's like one's romantic life—we all want the cabs that won't stop for us.

So that milk was several weeks old, like everything else in my refrigerator. But did I throw it away? No. I'll probably sniff it again in two weeks' time, just to torment myself. I have two personalities. Two idiots. The one who sniffs the milk and doesn't throw it away, and the one who sniffs the milk two weeks later.

The inside of my fridge is more like a mortuary or a ring of hell (things dead waiting for the next stage of the afterlife) than an icebox for edible foodstuffs. If you'll indulge me, I'm going to jot down a brief table-of-fridge-contents, as a way, perhaps, to show what kind of person I am (lazy and doesn't take care of himself):

1) Bullion, capers, and an onion, all left by the French girls who used to live in this apartment six months ago.

2) A thickly congealed Paul Newman salad dressing bought during a very brief do-it-your-self-campaign—making salads and such.

3) Hardened organic peanut butter from my son's visit in October.

4) Two small containers of plastic applesauce forced on me by my great-aunt in Queens and taken from her meals-on-wheels package.

5) The aforementioned eggs, butter, milk, and German bread.

6) A container of expired orange juice (to keep the expired milk company).

7) A box of Cuban cigars—Cohibas, Castro's brand—that Angelo, my Italian movie star friend, smuggled back from Havana, and which I plan to give to my dad.

Well, thank you for indulging me. See how this fridge contents compares to your own. And now back to the riveting story: I took a sip of the coffee and the toast popped. I buttered the toast, put it on a plate, and then I took the frying pan and tilted it over the toast. The brown, curdled eggs fell onto the bread. I then sat down at my kitchen table with the *Post* and my breakfast. I went to work with the knife and fork, while I read the gossip, the atrocities, and the sports. This was around ten-thirty A.M.

The next twenty-four hours is a blur of delirium and stomach pain. At first things weren't too bad, though. The caffeine caused mild psychosis and I found myself walking around my apartment and shouting "Motherfucker" a few times, which is interesting, since I'm not much of a curser and find it unattractive when others use vulgarities, but this caffeine-psychosis profanity was brought on, I vaguely recall, by going through my piled-up mail—a pile that has been neglected for two months—and being horrified at finding an invitation to a very nice party I had missed, as well as several enormous phone and credit card bills, all of which should have been paid weeks ago.

I also recall—though it's dreamlike because of the Cafe Bustelo—glancing at the pages of my new book, which had been sent to me by my British publisher for me to proofread. The Brits had computer-scanned the pages from the American publisher, and the scanning had created all sorts of strange typos. A classic, Joycean turn-of-phrase like "I let a fart leak out" had been turned into "I let a fart lead out." I thought of leaving that typo for a moment, as I sort of liked the idea of a fart leading somewhere, but then I changed my mind, thinking that the meaning of the sentence was too botched. And I realized after finding that typo that I was going to have to do more than just skim the pages. I was going to have work hard and reread the whole damn book, *What's Not to Love?*, which is a narrative based on all the columns and articles I've written for the *Press* these last three, happy years.

The book will be in stores here in the States sometime in May, at which point my life will be seriously destroyed. It's one thing to write these self-revealing stories for the *Press*, where they're gone in a week and quickly forgotten, but it's another thing to have them put in a book, a book that will be around for a while and can be read by one's relatives. For example, future relatives like women who could be wives, but who will have nothing to do with me as the evidence mounts—three perverted books now— that I am too strange and damaged to be loved.

Anyway, the poisonous eggs and coffee had me in bed by two P.M., where I more or less stayed for the next twenty hours. The amphetamine-like coffee had over-stimulated me and then I crashed. What happened to me was similar to that game at circuses that tests your strength—I was the weight and the coffee was the hammer and I went flying to the top, rang the bell, shouted "Motherfucker" for about an hour like a Tourette's sufferer, and then came sliding down, back to the bottom and went into a coma. I slept fitfully and with great nausea until about eleven P.M., and then I was up for hours with nauseous insomnia. I hate to vomit and so fought the urge all this time. For a few hours, I tried to read Wodehouse, usually a great pain reliever, and it helped some, but mostly, I lay there tormented, my stomach puckering like the overly fried eggs.

So I was clutching my pillow to my belly around three A.M. and felt quite alone in the world. Being by yourself and being ill can provoke despair, and so I indulged in Tom Sawyerish reveries of my funeral should this stomach ailment have proved fatal. It bothered me, though, that being Jewish, I'd be buried the next day and the service would have to be quickly put together and that many people wouldn't even know about it and would not come, making it a poorly attended performance. But I tried not to focus on this drawback of Jewish burial rites, and I self-ishly imagined lots of weeping, crying, and impassioned, impromptu speeches. It was a way for me, on my faux deathbed, to feel loved. Pathetic, I know.

So what's the moral of the above tale? Well, I see two morals emerging: (1) I shouldn't cook for myself; and (2) I want to be loved. Now there's a perfect solution to both these issues: Go to restaurants. It may seem obvious why this solves number one, but it also solves number two, and that's because restaurants are staffed by waitresses. I've said it before, and I'll say it again: I have a great love for waitresses. No waitress has actually ever loved me back, but that's why I tip well—it's an act of courtship. I have this insane hope that if I leave a 30 percent gratuity that the object of my affection will think that I am a worthy suitor. And when I come across a waitress whom I greatly admire, I swear to myself that I will go to her restaurant for as long as it takes until we are man and wife or at least have a one-night stand.

But I've never followed through on these waitress courtships, except this one time a few years ago. There was this absolutely charming waitress in the East Village who had these translucent blue eyes and who always wore shirts that exposed one of the most beautiful stomachs in the Western world. So inspired by her eyes and belly (not to mention to her very sweet personality and gorgeous face), I made a conscious effort, almost as a performance-art piece, to go to her cafe—a quiet little place—every Monday night for weeks on end (it was my treat to myself after teaching a fiction-writing class on Mondays). The secret rules of my endeavor were that I was to never make a flirtatious remark or go out of my way to have a conversation with her; if she wanted to speak with me that was fine, but I was to take no real action—all I could do was leave a handsome tip and behave like a gentleman. Well, after only four weeks, if she had a moment to herself, she started sitting at my table and would talk to me. I think she admired the way I always read a book with my meal. So a friendship began. She was from Spain and had come to New York to study film. We talked about movies and books.

Week seven, she hugged me goodbye and kissed me on the cheek when I left the cafe. I couldn't believe how well it was going. Week eight, she again hugged and kissed me—when I arrived and when I left! This was the greatest experiment of all time. By week nine, I was preparing to ask her out, but then outside the world of the cafe, I unexpectedly met a wonderful girl and we fell into an immediate serious relationship, and I abandoned the waitress.

Several months into this new relationship, almost as an act of infidelity, I went back to the cafe on a Monday night. My waitress beamed when I came in and my heart broke a little. Maybe I had chosen the wrong girl. And then while I was eating, a young handsome man came into the cafe and my waitress kissed him all over. She had a boyfriend, and this actually soothed my broken heart, because I thought to myself, as if taking a powerful aspirin, "It was not meant to be."

So there are a couple of reasons why I love waitresses. First of all they are often beautiful and men love beauty and are drawn to beauty. It can't be helped. Secondly, waitresses mimic the behavior of my mother—they bring dishes of nourishment to me. My mother was very much a 1950s mother and she served the family all our meals for years, thus creating this early association with love and the placing of a dish of food in front of me. (My mother also cooked the food, but I don't seem to love cooks; perhaps because I never see them.) And thirdly, I love waitresses because of the angle at which I observe them—I stare right into their asses and vulvas, two of my favorite spots, and when they bend over sweetly to warm my coffee, I catch glimpses of breasts, another all-time favorite spot. For example, my wonderful breakfast waitress in Brooklyn says to me all the time, "Do you want a warmer in your coffee, honey?" And she smiles at me when she says this; it's so lovely; and I say yes, and she bends over and I sneak a peek at her kind chest. I only see shadows, but it's enough.

So my breakfast waitress is magnificent, but there is another who is even more so. This other waitress, from whom I can be served both lunch and dinner, is the most beautiful waitress in all the five boroughs of New York City. She's right here in my Brooklyn neighborhood, and she's legendary with the men in this part of town. The restaurant is always packed and I observe my fellow males as they sit there glassy-eyed and in awe.

Recently, I brought my boxing opponent David Leslie to the restaurant for dinner so that he could witness her. I have forgiven him for his boorish behavior in the ring—his taunting and illegal maneuvers—though I'll always bear the mark of that mad event in the middle of my face, with my nose now larger and shifted to the right. But life goes on. So as we walked to the restaurant, I said to him, speaking of the waitress, "She's Jamaican, and I was told by a woman friend of mine, who's currently living in Jamaica and studying Jamaican art for her Ph.D., that the asses of the women in Jamaica are considered to be a national treasure and that a woman's ass has great erotic importance, which I am in complete agreement with, and I'm glad there is a whole culture and country that supports my worldview. My friend also told me something a bit strange. In much the same way that Chinese women used to bind their feet to make them small, Jamaican women do things to build up their rear ends. She told me that she knows Jamaican women who eat chicken feed to build up their butts."

"Chicken feed!" exclaimed Leslie.

"That's what my friend wrote in an email," I said. "Anyway, I don't think this waitress eats chicken feed, but she has the most amazing rear end I've ever seen. It's a booty of astonishing beauty. It should be a Brooklyn landmark, up there with the Cyclone, the Brooklyn Bridge, and Grand Army Plaza. I'm so lucky she's in my neighborhood. Why spend money traveling anywhere when everything I need is right here?"

We were lucky to get a table and Leslie was mesmerized by the waitress. Her rear is truly a marvel. It's like a duplex. It has an extra level to it. Having never seen a buttocks constructed quite along these dimensions, it's nearly impossible to describe. Its beauty is too profound. It's like she has a butt on top of a butt. I think if I saw it in the flesh, I'd have a heart attack even though I'm only thirty-five.

In addition to her amazing gluteus, this waitress also possesses gorgeous, clear café au lait skin, long perfect legs, chiseled features, luminous green eyes, high breasts, and a mole over a full, sensual mouth. She is a wonder of the world who reduces all men to slavering fools, which is very good for her restaurant. Slavering produces hearty appetites.

Leslie was properly stunned. "I thought you were exaggerating," he said. "But you're right. I think she has the greatest ass in the world. Maybe she does eat chicken feed."

"See how it's only men in here? We should do a documentary on her butt. How men come from all over the city to see it, like a weeping Virgin Mary in South America. Maybe her butt has healing powers. I could lead tours."

She came over and brought us our menus and two glasses of water. Hypnotic emerald beams of light shot out of her eyes. If she ran for president of the United States I'd vote for her.

"When we're done eating, ask her to meet you for a drink when she gets off," Leslie said.

"Are you insane? You ask her out."

"This is your neighborhood. You're the one who can do it."

The fellow was delusional. He seems to think I possess the sexual powers of a wizard, which confirms that his desire to fight me was some kind of sublimated homosexual impulse, but I won't go further with this notion. He'll simply want to fight me again and my nose can't take it—one more punch and it will disintegrate. And if I ever then did couple with the waitress, it would be booty and the beast.

"I can't just ask her out!" I said, reprimanding him. "You can't just go up to a beautiful waitress and propose a date. You might as well just say, 'I know nothing about you but I'd like to screw you.' That's insulting. Only a devastatingly handsome man or a famous man or a very rich man or someone with a lot of cocaine can pull off something like that. A quasi-average male like myself has to wear a waitress down. What I'd have to do is come here for months . . . well, in her case, years. It would be like an arranged marriage; she'd get so used to me that maybe she'd fall in love with me. Or come to hate me. But that's not bad odds. Fifty-fifty."

"It's only love or hate?" asked Leslie.

"Love or hate," I said. But then I thought about it some more. "Well, there's also *dislike* and *bored by* and *mildly indifferent to* and *tolerated*. I think I'll aim for tolerated. That's achievable. In the meantime, it's awfully nice just to look and dream and marvel and to have her give me food. There's not much more you can ask for. And in her case, unrequited love is all I'm ever going to get. But that's better than no love."

Leslie listened, but mostly he stared at her. So I joined him. We stared and dreamed and marveled. It was the greatest ass in Brooklyn. It was the greatest ass in the world.

The Long Au Revoir
February 1, 2000

I'm ready now. Had to wait for the coffee. Can't write unless I have coffee. Otherwise I'm too scared. Too tired. Too depressed. Too dead. Just took my second sip. I'm drinking from my lucky "World's Greatest Father" cup. And I need some luck. I'm retiring from the Press. This is my last column. An easy one to screw up.

Should it be cohesive? Should it be funny? Do I tell a story? Do I say goodbye? My hand just grabbed my cock. Like drinking the coffee, I need to do that when I'm writing. I know that other men do this when they're trying to think of things, when they're sitting at a desk feeling pressure. It goes back to being a boy. Holding on to our penises when we were scared, scared most likely of peeing in our pants, so we'd squeeze our penis to keep from pissing. At least that's what I used to do. I remember my mother telling my baby-sitter—I was in the other room, but I could hear this and I was humiliated; I was maybe four years old—"If Jonathan squeezes his penis, it means he needs to go to the bathroom. Please don't let him do this. We're trying to break him of the habit."

How dare my mother tell Mrs. Binney this kind of private information. Mrs. Binney was this big sweet old woman whose house I'd be dropped off at. And I liked going to her house. Her son was grown up but she had saved all his ancient G.I. Joes. There was one who wore an old-fashioned deep-sea diving costume. I still remember his gold helmet with the little glass plate in front. I wanted to steal him, but didn't. I knew even then the difference between right and wrong, though I was made to feel, incorrectly, that holding on to my penis was wrong.

Well, maybe it was wrong. It's certainly not pleasant to see men grabbing their penises on the subway or to see ballplayers adjusting themselves on TV. So at least I do it here where no one can see me. But it would be nice to have one witness—that G.I. Joe. I'd like to have him here with me right now. I still sort of long for him. I'd prop him up on my desk and just stare at him and admire his outfit.

Anyway, what do women grab when they're nervous and sitting at their desks? Do they slip their hands inside their panties? What a distracting thought. Just the word panty is distracting. I love that word; it implies so much. I love how women look in panties, how they're flat in the front. I'm thirty-five, but sometimes it's still this beautiful amazing shock to me that women don't have penises. They just have this lovely little mound of hair and then this tucked away glorious hole. Hole. Wait. Hole sounds vulgar. Is passageway better? Pretty envelope? Georgia O'Keeffe flower? Pussy? Pussy is good. I like the word pussy. Tucked away beautiful pussy. I wish I could put my face in one right now and sing out, "I love you!"

Someone once told me—I think it was a counselor I was seeing—that Freud said that little boys think girls have penises until they find out they don't. Something like that. And when you find this out this somehow alienates you from your mother or from women or causes fear of castration or maybe makes you think that women are other or less than because they're missing something. But it's all muddled in my mind now. I do remember sitting on the steps of the chapel of my university with a friend, and it was spring and all the beautiful girls were out walking around, and I was falling in love with every other young girl, and I said to my friend, with great sincerity, "Can you believe all these girls have vaginas?"

"Stop spreading rumors," he said.

So I'm still amazed by the phenomenon of the penisless female; thus, I must still be, in many ways, a little boy. That's why in the past, on occasions of psychic-emotional disturbance, like my entire late twenties, I occasionally spent time in bars frequented by comely transsexuals. I obviously found it reassuring, in some Freudian sense, to be with girls who have penises. But I've covered this already. There's a chapter in my novel, *The Extra Man*, that attempts to explain this important psychosexual issue; the chapter was called: "A Girl As I Must Have First Imagined Girls."

Well, I just refilled the coffee cup, and I'm feeling slightly tremulous and vaguely nauseous (already had three cups at breakfast, so now I'm on my fifth), and I've just done a word count, 778 words, not including this last sentence, so I've gotten my way through more than a quarter of this final, swan-song column.

(I wonder if any interestingly deranged person will count all the words above to see if this is true; though if I revise, some words might be cut or added; but then I'll adjust the number for those of you who might want to see if my word count is accurate, not that anybody will do this, but I guess I feel like flattering myself to think that somebody might.)

So what else can I tell you? I was watching the Super Bowl yesterday (this sounds like the kind of segue a stand-up comedian would make, do forgive me) and thought it was quite macabre that there was a commercial with a computer-generated vision of Christopher Reeve walking. His face looked beatifically tormented and bizarre, and it was like that original *Star Trek* episode where that pre–Kirk captain is freed mentally and emotionally, though not physically, from his strange computer wheelchair and gets to go into this dreamworld of forever youth and sex with this gorgeous woman in a cave. Like all human beings—or people that ever watched *Star Trek*—I loved that episode. It spoke to all our depths, that somehow we could be freed from the dream of our disintegrating lives and placed in another dream-life where we never disintegrate; though I guess that pre-Kirk captain will eventually die in his wheelchair and so his dream of being young and beautiful will just be shut off; and that's what happens to us when we die: we're just shut off.

Oh, no, I'm onto death. I can't stand it. I can't stand death. The other day I was looking at a picture of a relative I love—and I won't say what relative, because I don't want to create some kind of terrible jinx, anger the gods—and I started thinking how I might look at this picture when the person was dead, if I should outlive them, of which there is a good chance, and how I would long for them, miss them, how I'd feel I hadn't loved them enough while they were alive, and how my heart would tear apart. In fact, it tore apart just looking at the picture the other day and the person, thank God, is still alive. So the key is to love them enough right now. Right now!

Okay, enough of that. If I keep writing in this emotional vein, Oprah might take notice of me, which brings to mind an interesting hoax. What if one of my book jackets was put on a decent, sensitive, humane novel where people don't think girls have penises, and Oprah got hold of this book and read and loved it, but because of the book jacket thought I wrote it. Then she'd have me on the show and I'd become a best-seller, get out of debt, and everybody would think that Oprah had put her stamp of approval on a dipso–sex-maniac. The ripple effect of such a thing could be enormous.

This brings me to the next topic: I'm quitting the column because I can't stand writing about myself anymore. Twenty-eight months I've been doing this, and I'm sure a normal person would have grown tired of such a task long ago, but that's because a normal person doesn't have a narcissistic disorder the way I do. But perhaps I'm no longer narcissistic. I feel that for long enough I've bared my soul and dropped my pants in this biweekly space. I want to go back to baring my soul and dropping my pants in fiction; I want to go back to writing about myself in the guise of a character with a made-up name. Well, so much for my temporary respite from the lash of narcissism.

Speaking of narcissism, I was very glad the other day when I was at the World Wrestling Federation's "Royal Rumble" at Madison Square Garden that this humongous fellow known as Paul "The Big Show" White referred to another wrestler—the best-selling author The Rock—as narcissistic. It should be noted, by the way, that several wrestlers are best-selling authors and if Oprah chose one of their books, the combination of Winfrey and the WWF (we could call it the WWWF) would create the greatest best-seller of all time.

Anyway, I had taken my son to this grappling extravaganza and at first I was secretly wishing he had some other passion besides wrestling, but I was buoyed by the fact that some of the wrestlers' scripted dialogue is sprinkled with good vocabulary, like the word narcissistic, and that my son was getting some positive things, some enriching exposure, out of his love for this strange, theatrical "sport."

We came to be in Madison Square Garden because I had noticed an ad for the "Royal Rumble" back in early December and said to my son I would try to get us tickets. This was lunacy on my part. Why get the kid's hopes up when I'm thoroughly incompetent when it comes to doing something like buying tickets? So for several weeks, true to idiotic form, I pondered how I might go about finding the phone number for Madison Square Garden. Of course, I didn't call information or seek out a phone book. And I was worried that once I did get a number, I would get some kind of phone tape and have to press several buttons, which I would find taxing and enervating, so I kept procrastinating. Meanwhile, my son had actually believed that I might pull the thing off. He loves professional wrestling more than anything else. He watches it three times a week, reads magazines about it, and his wardrobe of T-shirts is mostly of wrestling figures. Then I read somewhere that the "Royal Rumble" had sold out. I felt ashamed I hadn't even made a manly effort. I was going to have to disappoint my son yet again.

Then I remembered that I'm sort of a journalist— perhaps I could get press passes. Not knowing how to do this, I procrastinated some more, and then struck upon a brilliant idea: ask someone for help. I turned to my editor at the *Press*, who is brimming with intelligence—his head seems to protrude in the back, a sure sign of intellect. Responding to my request for assistance, he did the wise thing and enlisted someone else at the *Press* to help me. The appropriate fax was then sent off to the WWF and nothing happened. I waited a week for some kind of response either by fax or phone call or psychic communiqué—but nothing. I then willed myself to make a follow-up phone call—you have to understand that basic life tasks are exceedingly difficult for me; for example I've been living in this apartment for five months and all my books are still on the floor because I don't know where to buy bookshelves or how to build them—and so I left a message at the WWF. No one called me back.

I had to report to my son that things were looking very bleak. He was understanding, but melancholic. Then late on the afternoon of Friday the twenty-first, there was a phone call: two free press tickets would be waiting for me at MSG on the twenty-third, the day of the "Royal Rumble." I went into action. I called Continental. For some reason I'm good at calling Continental—probably because I have their number on a sticker in my wallet—and I secured a ticket for my son first thing Saturday morning. I then called him up down in Florida.

"What are you doing this weekend?" I said. At this point, it was a foregone conclusion in his mind that I had failed to make his dream come true, and, you see, his dream for some time now has been to go to a live WWF event.

"Nothing," he said.

"You don't have any plans?"

"Nope."

"Still taking your psyllium?"

"Yes."

"So you're just taking psyllium this weekend. You're not going to the movies or anything?"

"Nope."

"Well, how about coming up here tomorrow and going to the "Royal Rumble" on Sunday!"

"Oh, my God, are you joking?"

"I'm completely serious."

"Oh, my God! I can't believe it!"

And so it went. The dialogue was straight out of the old Andy Griffith Show, but sometimes life is actually sentimental and corny. And my son, who tends to mask his emotions like his paterfamiliass, or whatever the Latin curse word for me is, was utterly delighted and effusive.

He arrived Saturday morning in Newark, not having slept a wink Friday night because he was too excited. We stayed out in New Jersey at my parents and went sleigh riding and rented movies. It was a good day.

On Sunday, we had a late breakfast and when I was alone in the kitchen with my mother, she said, "You know your son loves you. This morning I started doing a wash and he asked me if it was a cold wash. I said it was. And he said that's good because you were taking a shower and he wanted you to have hot water. There are adults that aren't thoughtful like that. He loves you."

I have to admit, it made me feel good to have my mom tell me this.

In the afternoon, I dragged out photo albums of all the years of my son's visits and we looked at them together. It was wonderful and nostalgic. He's a great big hulk of a kid, the largest in his class, but he's a sweet hulk and it was hard to believe that the little boy in the pictures is now already nearly a man. He's almost fourteen but could pass for eighteen.

Then we went to the Garden that night and the place was packed with 20,000 people. The WWF was very kind and gave us excellent seats and my son was in heaven. And they put on quite a show, these wrestlers, quite a spectacle. For three hours, we watched these great enormous men—some of them quite appealingly freakish and comic—throw each other about and holler at one another for all the world to hear. It was like a gladiatorial circus, and I didn't fully get its appeal, though I certainly wasn't bored. And most important, my son loved it and I was glad to make him so happy, and, too, he seems to have the right attitude toward the whole thing. "It's a cross between a sitcom and a sport," he explained to me.

So the next day, he flew back home quite contented, but also anxious to regale his friends at school. I returned to Brooklyn and a friend of mine lent me an essay about wrestling by the brilliant French philosopher Roland Barthes. Barthes loved wrestling and saw it as a theater of excess, a great cathartic spectacle about "Suffering, Defeat, and Justice." This further reassured me: my son has the same taste as a French genius. I knew the kid was bright, but I didn't know he was that bright. I'm *kvelling* (that's Yiddish for having prideful feelings toward one's child) just thinking about it.

Well, I must start bringing this to a close. What I've done here in the *Press* the last few years is like what Barthes says about wrestling: it's been a spectacle of excess, a journal of my own suffering, defeats, and occasional triumphs. I've happily played the clown, because I am a clown. But it's time to withdraw.

So I thank the *New York Press* for giving me a voice in the city, and I thank you, kind and generous readers, for sticking with me. I hope you have found it entertaining, amusing, and distracting, and should you ever see me in the street do say hello and if you want you can let me know that you liked or loved the column, and you can use as many praiseworthy adjectives as come to mind. And if you're a woman and want to hold me to your chest and let me whimper for a few seconds and maybe let me grab your sweet rear end, I won't protest. And if you're a man and you have an extra ten or twenty bucks you feel like slipping me, I won't say no. Well, I guess that's about all. So as they say in France (it makes for an elegant ending)—Merci and Au Revoir.

Part II:

fic'tion, n. Feigning, invention; thing feigned or imagined, invented statement or narrative; literature consisting of such narrative, esp. novels, whence~IST(3) (-shon-) n.; conventionally accepted falsehood. (esp. legal, polite,~). Hence~AL (-shon-) a. [F, f. L fictionem (prec., -ION)]—The Concise Oxford Dictionary of Current English, edited by H. W. Fowler and F. G. Fowler, based on the Oxford Dictionary, Oxford University Press, Amen House, London E.C. 4, Fourth Edition, 1951

*Note: The following stories all appeared in slightly altered form in *Shout* magazine

A Young Girl

You're not supposed to do ear-candling by yourself. That's what the instructions say. But I had no one to do it with. I'm pretty lonely. But I desperately wanted to get the wax out of my ears. It was nine o'clock in the morning. I wanted to start the day right. So I stood in front of my bathroom mirror and lit the ear-candle. It flamed up pretty good. Then I put the ear-candle in my head. It was about a foot long and had the appearance of a hollow cigar. It was really smoking. The idea is that the flame, the heat, something, sucks the wax out of your ear and up the candle.

When the candle was down to two inches and my earlobe looked like it might catch, I took the thing out and doused it. I put a second candle in my other ear and repeated the process. When I was done, I felt sort of calm. My head was all warmed up.

I brewed some Astralagus tea and went to the computer. I was on this detox kick—tea, earwax removal—because of a drinking binge. But now I was on the wagon again. I'm thirty-seven years old and I've been on and off the wagon for fifteen years. I just can't get it. But that's another story, a real short one, probably be written on my grave: "Couldn't Stay Sober. Never Liked Himself."

Anyway, I was at the computer and hadn't checked email since the night before. I was trying to let it build up. I live off of email like a vampire. I'm a loner who's dying of loneliness. There was only one email. But it was a good one. It read:

"Are you the writer Leon David? I did a search and came up with this address. If you are Leon David, I'm a big fan. I love your books! You write the way I think! If you ever want to do a character study of a college senior (I'm an English major at Columbia), I would love to meet you for coffee, and you could write about me. Only joking! But I would love to meet you.

"Your biggest fan (I hope you don't think I'm a crazy groupie, I just wanted to let you know I love your writing), Hallie."

Every few months a smart girl, who has a nascent, burgeoning libido and goes to an Ivy League school, writes me. I romance her over email and we never meet and after a while it peters out. Still, these correspondences keep me alive. But I decided to play this one differently. I was going to be honest from the start.

"What do you look like?" That's all I typed. Sent the thing off. It was liberating.

Her reply was instantaneous. She was online at the same time. "Is that what you ask all your fans? Well, I'm five foot six, I have brown hair to my shoulders, brown eyes, bee-sting lips, and a cute figure, if I may say so."

The bee-sting line got to me. "I want to meet you."

She instant-messaged me. We were moving fast. "When? :)" she wrote.

"Now."

"Right now?"

"Yes, immediately."

"Where?"

"Your apartment. You live alone?"

"Yes."

"Can I come over?"

"I'm a big fan, but this feels really weird."

"I know. I'm sorry. I'm really weird. I'll put it to you straight. You sound like a sweet girl and I'm really lonely. I want to come over and I want you to be sitting on your couch in a nice dress with no panties. I'll walk in, give you a quick kiss, and then I'll kiss you between the legs and make you feel lovely. That's all we'll do. If you're completely repelled, I understand."

The girl was a natural. A ringer. A once-in-a-lifetime. She instant-messaged me her address. She lived by Columbia. I live in Brooklyn. I told her I'd be there by ten-thirty. She had a class at eleven-thirty. We'd have about an hour together.

I took the subway and tried not to think. There was no way this could work out. I had the *Post* and read it to distract myself. My fingers got dirty from the ink; I hoped the girl wouldn't mind.

I arrived at her building. It was a big Upper West Side prewar monster. I buzzed her buzzer. I waited for the silence. The rejection. Maybe even a policeman. She buzzed me in. I took the elevator. Rang her doorbell. A boyfriend was going to open the door and hit me with a baseball bat.

"The door's open," she said.

I walked in. She was sitting on a futon couch in a slinky black dress. Her apartment was a tiny studio. There was a poster of a Degas ballerina, a plywood bookshelf, a CD player, a cheap rug on the floor, a desk with a computer. On top of the computer were little framed pictures and a purple stuffed animal, maybe a monkey. She was a sweet kid. She had parents somewhere, paying her rent, paying her tuition. My heart broke a little. This was her little home where she tried to figure things out. Make her way. But there was no turning back. I walked over to her.

"Hi," she said, looking up at me, scared.

"Thank you for letting me come over."

"You're welcome."

"You're beautiful."

"I can't believe we're doing this," she said.

I leaned down and kissed her. I hoped my breath was all right. I wondered if I smelled smoky from the ear-candles. Her beautiful lips were yielding. I put my hand between her legs. She was soaking wet. What a girl.

I got down on my knees and started kissing her thighs, her magnificent skin. She lay back. I pushed the dress up. Saw that delicious mound. I pulled her to the edge of the futon and gave her sweet kisses, put the tongue in. Did my best work. I went slow, I went fast, I sucked, I licked, I teased. She tasted good. Smelled good. She came twice in the first fifteen minutes. The futon was low to the ground and I was half-lying on the floor, grinding myself into her rug. At some point, I put her on her belly and went at her from behind. This gorgeous ass was in the air. A thing of beauty. I licked everywhere. She pressed back for more. When she came a fourth time, I came in my pants rubbing against the floor like a dog.

We stopped. She sat up, pulled down her dress. I sat next to her on the couch. Her face was red, sweaty.

"Are you all right?" I asked.

"Yes," she whispered.

"Thank you for being so generous to me," I said.

"I never came so much in my life," she said.

I went to the little kitchenette and fixed us two glasses of water. I sat down again. I held her hand and asked her questions. Where are you from? What are your plans when you graduate? We had a nice little talk. Then she had to get ready for class. She kissed me goodbye at the door.

"You're a beautiful girl," I said. She smiled. "You're sure you're all right?"

"Yes," she said. "I can't believe we did this. But I'm glad." I kissed her one more time.

I walked down Broadway and breathed in her smell, which was all over me. I loved it. And I felt like I was in love. I knew I couldn't be, but my heart was fooled and I let it stay that way. Everybody needs a break once in a while.

Too Far Away, Love

I was sitting at a bar in midtown. I was watching the 1994 Olympics by myself and I was falling in love with the Russian figure-skater Oksana Bauil. Her beauty was too much for me. I was nearly crying. Like most men, I die a little when I see a beautiful woman I'll never be able to have. Also, it was the alcohol, playing with me, but, too, it was the way she moved her arms. Such thin arms—my hands could wrap around them—and she kept putting them over her head. When a woman puts her arms over her head, you'll do anything for her.

Then the competition was over, and Oksana cried when she won the gold medal and I cried with her. I couldn't help it. When a woman cries, I cry. I had to cover my eyes with my hand and pretend to massage my temples, like I had a headache, so that the bartender wouldn't notice my tears. It was embarrassing to cry at a bar.

So I left the bar and it was terribly cold out and I stopped crying. I walked to Lexington Avenue to catch the number 6 subway. At the corner of Lexington and Fiftieth Street there was a prostitute in a long, dark brown fur coat up to her chin and she looked just like Oksana Bauil. I couldn't believe it. She had the same white skin that looks powdered but isn't, the same delicate nose and full red mouth, and the same gold yellow hair.

She was holding her fur coat tight to her neck in her beautiful hands and as I walked past her, even in the cold, I caught a trace of her perfume.

But I didn't stop to talk to this Oksana, I kept on going. I had maybe two hundred dollars to my name. I figured she would cost that or more, and I wasn't surprised to see such a good-looking prostitute—there are a lot of fancy hotels in that part of town, and the UN is nearby, so the few prostitutes that one spots around there are always high class. But this one was more than high class. "She's so beautiful," I thought, and then I stupidly wondered what she was doing out there, why did she have to be a prostitute? I didn't want her to destroy her beauty, to sell it, and I didn't want her to hate men. I didn't want her to hate me. Then I thought how she must be making good money, how that coat looked like the real thing. I walked a block and then I turned around.

I was wearing my black knit hat, which is like a sailor's cap, and I had a red beard from not shaving for a week. My coat was a brown wool coat, secondhand and tattered, and so I looked like a real tough, working-class Irishman, but the truth is I grew up middle class, my blood is Jewish, and I have a college degree. And even though I work, it's always soft, temporary office labor. But that night I looked like a man.

I approached her. I knew what I was doing. I've talked to a lot of prostitutes. I usually act all scared and sensitive with them, I win them over that way, but because of my hat and because I hadn't shaved, I felt tough, and so I played it like I was a tough guy. I was still a little drunk. I said, "How much?"

"What?" she asked.

"How much?"

"You're forward," she said, and she had a hard New York accent, which didn't go with the pristine beauty of her face, the elegance of the yellow gold hair against the fur coat.

"I'm sorry. What do you want me to talk about? The weather?" And I smiled to let her know that I was the kind of tough guy who could crack a joke.

"Are you a cop?"

"I don't think so," I said, still playing the joker.

"Are you?"

"No, I'm not the police," I said, and I raised my hands in supplication.

"Okay, how much can you afford, love? Two hundred?" She called me *love* because I was young, like I was a boy and she was a woman, even though I was a few years older than her. She was maybe twenty-two.

"No, one hundred," I said. I didn't mind giving her half of what I had, and I could tell that she had tried to adjust her price to my coat, that two hundred was low for her. I had been right about what she would ask for, but maybe she'd go for one hundred—it was a cold night, not too much foot traffic.

"Do you have a hotel room?" she asked.

"No, an apartment, we could take a taxi," I said, and I imagined her in my dirty little room taking off her fur coat, how she might not want to put it down anywhere. I'd have to apologize about the mess.

"Where is it?" she asked.

"Ninety-sixth Street."

"Ninety-sixth and what?"

"Ninety-sixth and Second."

She thought about it. "That's too far, love," she said.

She smiled at me. She liked me. She liked how I wasn't afraid to speak straight to her and I figured she thought I was a regular working-class guy, a brother of sorts. I was relieved that she had turned me down. It never works out the way you'd like it to.

"You're very pretty," I said.

"Thanks, love."

I headed back to the subway. It made me feel so good that she had called me *love*. It had sounded so beautiful. It was almost as good as getting to hold her, getting to kiss her neck, getting to smell her perfume up close. I dreamed for a moment how if I was a big success I could save her, I could marry her.

When I was sitting on a bench down in the subway, warm and comfortable, I thought about how much she looked like Oksana Baiul, how strange that was, and I suddenly wished I had offered her more money; she would have come home with me then. How could I have passed her up? For an extra fifty dollars Ninety-sixth Street wouldn't have been too far away.

My Flower

She had some kind of razor wire in her pussy. It was for slicing sperm in half. She was from Sweden. In Sweden they put things like that in women.

But I always wore a condom when we had sex. She didn't want me to, but I made it seem like this was what we did in America. You wore a condom no matter what. It was 1993. Everybody was still scared of AIDS. I was scared. Sometimes I had weird behavior. That's why I was scared. Why did I have to put my life at risk? And worse—why did I have to put other people's lives at risk?

I still do have weird behavior. I wish it would go away. A whole lifetime of weird behavior. Soon I'm going to be old—if I make it—and I'll really feel like a fool. Why couldn't I have figured things out?

I can almost visualize a good life, but I'm like a plane that suddenly has its wing fly off. I'm going along all right, paying the rent, being kind to people, loving people—what more can I ask of myself?—and then I come unhinged. The wings fly off. I crash myself. I kill myself. Or at least I try to. Actually, it might be worse than suicide—I torment myself. It's been going on for a long time. Very tiring.

Back to the Swedish girl. In 1993, I was twenty-nine and still had some handsomeness left, like ink in a pen. So I had the girl. She was stunning. They really know how to make them in Scandinavia. Tall, blonde, skinny but with boobs, a face with cheekbones, gorgeous skin, an ass like the Venus, green eyes, full lips. Good in bed. Would cry into my shoulder so beautifully when we made love—she made sounds like a child fretting with fever.

It was August. Some nice rich people were letting me house-sit for them in the country. It was an old, white farmhouse, alone in the woods, and in the back there was a pool with one of those black bottoms, like the pool had been cut from a stone. It made the water look like the night sky.

The rich people liked me. They supported the arts. They were letting me house-sit so I could write. Write my second novel. I miraculously had published one when I was twenty-four, but now I was broke, and pretty much dried up as a writer. A failure at twenty-nine. But I had these rich benefactors, so I was out of New York for the month of August.

The girl cooked and picked flowers. The word for "flower" in Swedish is *blomma*. I called her "min blomma." My flower. We liked each other.

She was a singer. Had come to New York to study music at Juilliard. She sang when she cooked. But she could also be dark sometimes. She'd drink some wine, not too much, and say things to me like, "You're a very weak person." She had an alcoholic father and that destroyed something inside her. But I didn't mind. I have never been with a woman who didn't have an alcoholic father. I'm alcoholic. I wish I wasn't. But I was sober that summer. Well, that August.

This one afternoon, I was sitting on the screened-in porch. I was at the typewriter. I was old-fashioned, still scared of computers. The girl was sitting in a chair by the pool, half-naked, sunning herself. She had one of those thin cotton skirts on, like a sarong.

I didn't think life could get better. At least on the surface of things. I was a nervous wreck on the inside—a broke failure, who couldn't control himself sometimes—but on the outside I was a novelist at a typewriter and my girlfriend, a topless Swede, was ten yards away. Her breasts were wet. Her nipples were beautiful. Like nothing else in the world.

I typed a sentence. "Her hotel room was dark. The curtains were thick and dirty. She sat on the edge of her bed. She opened her purse for the money."

I took the paper out of the typewriter. For some reason, I thought those sentences were gems. The word "purse." I went out to the girl. I read her the lines. What was I thinking?

"Who's the girl?" asked the girl.

"A prostitute."

"Why do you always write about prostitutes? I didn't like them in your book. Why don't you write about women who aren't prostitutes?"

My first book had been filled with prostitutes, but the girl had stuck with me after she read it. We'd been together about three months.

"I write about prostitutes to show how sick men are, how lost." It wasn't a very good answer. She ignored it. We both didn't want to face the truth, though I must have been trying to tell her. Why else would I read those lines to her?

"I like Marquez," she said. "His writing is musical.

Alive. You see colors. What you read feels flat to me." Her English was very good. They're beautiful in Sweden and well educated.

"You're right," I said.

I limped back to the porch. Marquez. Who could compete with him? I put the paper back in the typewriter, like a writer in the movies, which was fitting. I was make-believe.

The girl came into the porch. "Leon, I'm sorry for what I said."

"You don't have to be," I said.

She undid the skirt. Her beautiful mound. Light brown hair.

She pulled my shorts off. She kneeled down and took me in her mouth.

Then she sat on me. It went in like going into a ripe melon. How'd she get wet so fast? Was she wet from the pool? Wet from thinking she had hurt my feelings? Her breasts were in my face.

"Let me get a condom," I said.

"We don't need it. I want to feel you for once."

She was moving up and down. I wanted to push her off me. We did need a condom. A few days before we had come to the country I had gone on a binge with a friend. He and I ended up in an after-hours club, which was a midtown Chinese restaurant during the day. There were gays, drug addicts, all sorts of hookers. We bought coke from two tranny-hookers and they wanted to give us blowjobs for free in the bathroom. We let them.

But what if I had gotten something from the tranny's mouth? Unlikely. But there was that chance. How could I take that chance with my Swedish girl's life? Even a one-in-a-million chance? You can't do that to somebody else.

But this is the kind of thing I'm talking about. Your wings flying off. You could have a good life, but you don't let yourself.

"Please, let me get a condom."

"No. I want to feel you come in me."

I was weak. She fed me her breast. I sucked on it, like a man, like an infant. I let her ride me. It felt good, though I was dying inside. She started to come. "Slap me," she said. I did. She had an alcoholic father. She came a few more times. I slapped her a few more times. After the slaps, I'd kiss her face where it was red. Sweet kisses.

"You come now," she said.

"No."

She slapped me. I came. It shot up in her. Went for that razor wire. Got all cut up. She felt me come. Kissed me full on the mouth. Breathed her life into me. Then she pulled away. "I love your cock in me," she whispered.

We sat there. I was still inside her. Her cheek was against my face. I could feel her happiness, contentment. I was in another world altogether.

The rest of the summer, I kept thinking I had killed her. It ate at me. But somehow I faked it. Showed her a good time more or less. When we got back to the city, I broke up with her. Couldn't take the fear. I went to a clinic and got tested. I didn't have anything, but I didn't go back to the girl. I had taken a chance with her life once. I might not be so lucky next time.

Good Night, My Dear

I went to a famous, old European city. I read in my guidebook that transvestite prostitutes could be encountered in the woods at the edge of the city. This wasn't mentioned as a recommendation, but, rather, as a warning about an area that could be dangerous at night, and for most readers of the guidebook it would be a warning, but for me it was very helpful, a point of interest.

It was around ten P.M. when I left my hotel. It was early March, so it was cool out, but not freezing. I took the metro and found the woods and felt accomplished as a tourist. There was a long road that bisected the woods and led the way out of the city to the suburbs. A few cars drove by, quick and small with their jaundiced European headlights. Some cars were parked on the road and it was quite dark—there were no streetlights.

Along the edge of the road was a muddy path. I walked along this path and there was one man up ahead of me at some distance. There were only two transvestites standing in the road, and I was disappointed. I thought there would be more. I walked past them—they weren't pretty. The man ahead of me had somehow mysteriously disappeared. I kept walking. Then there was this path that led into the woods. There was moonlight and starlight, enough to see by. I walked in about ten yards. Men were hovering about, moving through the trees, walking down dirt paths as if they had somewhere to go.

Some men stood motionless, hiding by trees in the darkness, but because of the silvery light from the sky, I could see them, their bulk, their shape. The men were playing this tedious game of waiting and looking. I've seen it in woods and parks all over the world. Patience is needed—a man waits by a tree for another man to approach. There are those who wait and those who keep moving, and everyone is furtive and malevolent, unwelcoming, really. Afraid of not being wanted, I guess. And I've never seen anything happen; have never seen a man kneeling in front of another man or standing behind another man. But something must happen; woods like this are always filled—the men wouldn't come if *something* didn't happen.

So I walked around a bit, testing my courage, going deeper into the woods, wanting for once to catch a glimpse of sex, but I saw no coupling. Men sallied forth on their missions, their hunt in these woods, and I thought maybe I would let something happen to me, but I'm never quite sure how to play this game—I'd love to ask someone how it works but no one talks in these woods and I guess it's the kind of thing that you just know how to do. So I'm frightened by this game I don't fully understand, and that night in the woods, my courage failing, I walked back out to the road.

The two transvestites were gone. They were either in the woods or men in cars had stopped for them. The transvestites had been large, with bulky, unfeminine bodies. They had no beauty, no illusion of beauty, but now that they were gone I despaired that I had missed out, that I had come to the woods and would have no solace.

I kept walking on the muddy path. Maybe farther up I would find something. The road was very long. I walked for several minutes. I wished I could go back to my hotel, but I wouldn't let myself. Once a night like this starts, it's very rare that I can turn back. I have to see it through. I *have* to have an adventure. I *have* to hurt myself.

Then my perseverance was rewarded. I saw a light go on and off in a thicket of trees a few yards from the path. I walked toward the light. It was exciting how it went on and off, that someone was there, calling to me, signaling. I kept walking toward the light and then the light went off one last time and I was right next to the person. It was a woman. Not a transvestite. She was in a small fur because of the chilly March air. She had on a blonde wig. I liked her face. She smiled sweetly. She looked to be in her early forties and she was large-breasted. She wore a white skirt, fishnet stockings, and high red boots, good for the mud.

We talked. I knew the language. Her price was very fair: I did the math: only thirty American dollars, and yet a cup of coffee in the ancient city cost nearly four dollars. I've never understood the marketplace. The guidebook should have listed the woods as a spot where a tourist could get a bargain. I took out the necessary currency. She put the flashlight and my money in her purse. I admired her ingenuity, using the light to let men know where she was. She opened my pants and squatted in front of me, balancing nicely in her boots. She put a condom on me and she went about things happily, peacefully, not in a rush. She gave me a few sucks to wet the condom and to arouse me. Two men approached from within the woods to watch; they stood just a few feet away. She took her mouth off me and cursed at them violently and they retreated back into the darkness.

Then she stood up and grabbed hold of a thin white tree, a young tree. She bent over a little and reached behind herself, lifting up her skirt. No panties. Looking over her shoulder, she took hold of me and guided me in. It was lovely, it's always lovely to be in a woman, and she smiled at me, a kind smile, an older woman smiling at a young man who is inside her. Then she turned and faced the tree.

I pushed it in some more. I was pleased not to come right away. I moved it back and forth slowly. I kept one hand on her hip and with the other I stroked her blonde wig, like it was real hair. She pushed back to take me deeper. Then I reached around with both hands, got them under the short fur coat, and squeezed her large, heavy breasts. I liked having them in my hands.

I lay my chest against her back. I held her to me and we fucked. She took quick little breaths, either from the exertion or she may have actually liked it, there's always that chance, that hope, but it was probably the exertion, but at least she wasn't moaning with exaggeration, like most prostitutes. She held on to that tree and kept pushing back for more and I felt almost happy.

We were doing it for a good ten minutes, sometimes I'd just lie against her back and feel good about being in a dark woods and being inside this woman, and I'd kiss her neck beneath the stiff hair of the wig. But I do always like to please the woman I'm with and I knew that what pleases a prostitute is for it to be over sooner rather than later, even though I felt like she was actually enjoying it or at least not finding it horrible, but, still, I thought it would be better to end it, that she would appreciate this, so I came, pushing into her deeply one last time. Then I rested on her back, holding her.

She waited a few seconds, then let go of the tree and I pulled myself out. She took a tissue from her purse and cleaned me up gently. I closed my pants and she said next time we should go to her apartment. Then with both her hands, she held my face, and she looked at me and she laughed happily, her soul wasn't heavy, at least not in that moment, and how can I explain her mirth? Was it because I was young? Then her hands slid off my face, caressing me, and she said, "Good night, my dear."

Her English was beautiful and unexpected. She walked out of the woods and onto the muddy path. I followed her and then went the opposite way, not looking back, remembering that somebody once told me that you jinx things with women if you look back.

I returned the next night to see her. I had been fantasizing all that day about going to her apartment; I pictured it as cluttered and small but warm. A European's apartment! The old world! I'd lie on her bed and she'd be moving about the room, maybe making us something to eat, and maybe I'd spend the night.

Sometimes when I make love I want to tell the woman that I love her. My affection and need and love all feel so strong in my chest that I want to say it, that I want to just break down and give the woman everything, but I always stop myself. But it seems to me that it would be so amazing to tell a woman that you loved her while you were inside her. What would happen? Would I feel free?

And when my chest first lay against the prostitute's back and she held on to that tree, I wanted to say, "I love you." So I went back to the woods the next night, prepared to shower her with money. I wanted to go to her apartment, to be let into her home. And then when we made love, I'd tell her. I'd pay to be with her so I could tell her that I loved her.

I arrived at the woods at exactly the same time of night, but she wasn't there. There were three or four transvestites, but not my woman. I walked up and down the path and hid at the edge of the woods for two hours, hoping to see her light in the trees. But she never came. And I was leaving the next morning, I wouldn't be able to return. It seemed crazy to change my ticket, what if she wasn't here the following night?

Finally, I gave up and talked to a tall, pretty black transvestite. She was from the West Indies and spoke English with a colonial accent. Her price was the same as the woman's the night before. What I wanted was completely different but the cost was uniform, and I thought this was interesting.

The West Indian, regal with good posture, led me for several minutes through the woods to a small abandoned building. It was a concrete square, missing a roof. What had been its purpose in the middle of the woods? And why did she bring me there—to kill me? Rob me? I didn't think so—I trust my intuition when it comes to these things, but it has to fail me someday.

So in the shadow of the building—she must have liked it for its privacy—I gave her the money and then knelt in front of her. She lifted her dress and pulled down her panties and out came her long, elegant black cock. That's always a nice moment when it comes out. The shock of it. She put a condom on and I sucked her while I knelt in the mud. I undid my pants and put my hand on myself. I liked having her in my mouth; it was comforting. A phallic pacifier. But I think it pacifies me because it kills me. Says I'm not a man. Erases me. Must be why I do it. I want to disappear. Give up. Then she said sweetly, "Let me see your bum."

I lifted my coat so she could see it. She bent over some to get a good look and I kept sucking her and touching myself. Then I came on the mud. It was over. Maybe it lasted two minutes. We walked out of the woods together for safety. Then she kissed me on the cheek goodbye. She was kind. I have good luck that way. In the most unkind settings, I meet the kindest people. I go to them to die but they don't really let me. So I only die a little.

I took the metro back to my hotel. It was a long ride, especially after what I had done—it's shameful when you're not homosexual to take another man's penis in your mouth, even if it's the shame I'm after. And, too, I felt very sad because I had touched yet again how desperate I really am, how lonely, how without answers.

I looked down at my knees and saw that my pants were dirty from the mud, but nobody on the train looking at me would think I'd been kneeling in some woods. How could it occur to them? Then I looked in the black window of the metro. It was like a mirror and I recognized my face. These things don't really change you. I wished they did, but they don't.

Womb Shelter

Yesterday, I was watching the girls play tennis.

I was trying to catch glimpses of panties beneath the little skirts.

Meanwhile, bombs were being dropped in Afghanistan. But the girls were still trying. Serving, running, volleying. Bending over. Yeah. Bend over. When I was fifteen I'd be alone in my basement watching Chris Evert on the television, my hands in my pants, waiting for her to bend over.

I also liked Tracy Austin's ass and Evonne Goolagong's. What a name. Goolagong. I think she might have been an Aborigine. You know she had a sweet pussy. A brunette pussy. I wish I could lick it right now. Even if she's fifty. To hell with writing. I'd like to lick Evonne Goolagong's pussy, right now!

Anyway, the girls were playing. Six courts. Twelve girls. End-of-the-day fall light. Very pretty. Clean air. College! Hope! Young people! Flyers on bulletin boards!

Go tennis team! Blonde ponytails. Long legs. Smooth legs. Twelve sweet pusses hidden somewhere in those skirts. Lots of bending over. Bombs dropping.

I was getting this delicious display of young bottom

because I'm Writer-in-Residence for a month at this all-girls college. It's deep in the South. They have me up on a hill in a house, behind some trees, hidden. Like Anthony Perkins in *Psycho*. Down below is the soccer field and the tennis courts.

The tennis match was against Sweet Briar-Fur-Patch College, and I have to say those girls were blonder, richer, classier. You could see it in their strokes. Their sneers. Oh, to have one of them in bed. This thin blonde with a good net game comes to mind. She was wearing glasses! Glasses on a girl can be very sexy.

One time, years ago, late at night on Rue St. Denis in Paris, which is lined with hundreds of whores (it's legal in Paris), I wasn't tempted by any of the women. I enjoyed looking, it was fun, sure, but I was impervious—wasn't going to waste my money, wasn't going to risk getting crabs or who knows what, even with a condom. So I watched the parade of my fellow men. The lonely suckers. There were probably a thousand men marching up and down the street for three hundred hookers. I was in the parade, but I was above it all. A voyeur. A writer observing life!

Then I saw this one wearing glasses. That did it. Had to have her. She was dark-haired and short. A sexy body. Full tits. A pretty face. But it was those cat-shaped black glasses. Oh, those glasses.

So we climb three flights to her horrible room. Low-ceiling. Slanted floor. Walls so thin you could trace a drawing; something like that. The room had seen too much sad fucking. I gave her the money. She told me to undress. I did what she told me. Then she washed my cock with a wet rag. Probably spread diseases on it. Anthrax. Put anthrax on my cock. Wait, this was 1989. That wasn't popular back then.

After the cock cleaning, she undressed. Her body all trussed up in bra and girdle and hoses and clamps and hidden steel beams came melting out. Tits all dead. A cesarean scar and stretch marks on her belly. But I had already paid. She yanked my thing to life and put a condom on it. We lay down. I caught a glimpse of her bush underneath a roll of fat. She took her glasses off, remembering at the last moment, and put them on the little night table. No! I could handle the scar, the fat, the yanking, but I needed those glasses for my hard-on.

But I was too embarrassed to ask. I was young then. Now I know to ask for what I need. Especially when it comes to the hard-on. I deflated, but she grabbed my soft thing and got it in her. She gave a couple of fake moans and kicked her heels in my ass like a jockey. I squeezed a boob and pinched a tired brown nipple. I put my mouth on the nipple and it hardened. This little spark of real life from her, even if involuntary, made me get hard and when I got hard I came. It had lasted sixty seconds. I looked at the glasses on the night table. There's nothing worse than bad sex. Except bad sex that you've paid for. If only she had kept the glasses on.

Anyway, the blonde from Fur Patch College. She had glasses. Thin gold frames. If I had her here in my little house right now on the hill, I'd take her from behind. That tennis-lesson ass would push back for more intuitively. Yes, sweet girl. Push back for it. You sweet beautiful girl. I forgive you your sneer because you're a doll in bed.

Look over your shoulder at me with those glasses. You dear thing. You're wearing glasses but you're on your belly with your gorgeous ass in the air and your puss taking me in. You're a beautiful female animal. We're play-acting at making babies. I love you!

Anyway, these Sweet Briar-Fur-Patch girls were beating my girls pretty handily. Wouldn't you know I end up at a poor man's all-girls college. But what the hell. Better to be here than not to be here. An all-girls college feels like a pretty safe place as we go to war.

I only reported here for duty two days ago. They needed a writer at the last minute. Well, a month ago. But for academia that's the last minute. Somebody recommended me and so they hired me without reading my books. They only read the resume, which looks good: Leon David, Yale '86, three novels. But they should have read the novels before letting me down here. I took the job because it's a one-liner for my friends. "I'm spending a month as writer-in-residence at this all-girls school." Gave everybody a laugh.

But I don't know if it's a laugh. I've masturbated nine times in forty-eight hours. That's way too much at my age, three years shy of forty. I look like I have two black eyes. I'm losing too much semen. All my nutrients are going out my cock. To hell with Afghanistan, I need the government to drop some food on *me*. Drop it on my cock. I'm so horny because I'm Jewish. Jews know their life is in danger all the time, that's why we're so horny. It's distasteful. We're about to get it in the neck again, I'm sure. I think Jews must have alien blood in them. Some alien screwed a sexy Jewess in the dessert five thousand years ago. That's why we're hated. We're part alien. How else do you explain Einstein, Freud, Gershwin, and Lewinsky?

If Lewinsky hadn't been so horny and brainy, she never could have sucked Clinton's cock. Granted, he was a fairly easy target, but still, it took a lot of brains and chutzpah and sex drive to give the President of the United States a blowjob. She's the Einstein of sex. And if he hadn't been dealing with his blow-job impeachment, maybe he could have done something in the Middle East and we wouldn't be going crazy right now, bombing and getting bombed.

Well, it's all too much for me. And now it's lunchtime. I've been writing for two hours, imagining Goolagong's pussy and remembering that French pussy and wanting that Fur Patch girl's pussy. So I'm going to the dining hall, where I'll be surrounded by six hundred real vaginas. Not imaginary. Real. Delicious. Beautiful. All being sat on while the girls eat. Incredible. I'm in a womb shelter. Bring on the bombs.

Part III:
A True Crime Story:
The Nista Affair

The Nista Affair
McSweeney's, 2002

In June of 1987, I graduated from Princeton University. A week after commencement, I sold my senior thesis, a novella, to a New York publishing house. But there were two conditions: I had to expand the book into a full-length novel, and it was due in six months.

In July, a few weeks after selling my book, I found out that I had a fifteen-month-old son. His mother sent a letter with a photograph of him, a baby boy with red hair and blue eyes. I have red hair and blue eyes.

In late October, two chapters of my novel were stolen by a stranger who lured me into something of a trap. The theft occurred on the Upper West Side of Manhattan. I reported the crime to the 24th Precinct.

In November, after not drinking for twelve months and one week, I went on an alcoholic binge and ended up in a psychiatric hospital.

In November, while in the hospital, I discovered who stole my writing.

This story is about how those two chapters were taken from me. I'll start from the beginning.

The novella was twenty thousand words, I had to get it

up to fifty thousand. I was given some money, not a lot, by the publishing house, but I was on top of the world. From Princeton, I moved to New York City. I sublet my cousin's rent-control apartment on the Upper East Side. I set up a writing desk—yellow pads and a typewriter. I had thirty thousand words to go.

That very first week I became scared: I couldn't write.

By the second week, I thought maybe it was the apartment. I learned about a special study room in the public library on Forty-second Street. It was for writers and was in the back of the long reading room. You had to have a key. It was a privilege. I applied and was allowed to use the room. I started going there like going to a job, but the writing didn't improve. The trip to the library would tire me out, and I'd use my privilege only to take naps, my head on the table.

In July I received the letter about my son. His mother was an older woman, a good woman, whom I had slept with once. She and my son lived down South. My plan was to go see her and the baby as soon as I finished the book. I couldn't handle my dream of being a writer and my unexpected fatherhood at the same time. So I was going to tackle the situations as they had arisen, first the book and then my son. I was only twenty-three; it was the best plan I could come up with.

One night in July—though I was half-crazy with fears and anxiety about everything—I went to a party. I was invited by a friend of mine who didn't show up. I didn't know anyone at the party and was going to leave, but the hostess, a woman named Marie, was very nice to me and insisted that I stay. She knew from my absentee friend that I was working on a book. She asked me how it was going, and I told her about the study room at the public library. I lied and said the library was a good place to work. I didn't want to tell her that I was crumbling under the pressure of a professional contract and couldn't write a word. I stayed at the party for two hours. Marie asked me for my number so that she could invite me to her next party.

The following day a woman called me and introduced herself as a friend of Marie's. Her name was Julia, and she apologized for bothering me, but explained that she was a writer and that Marie had told her about the study room in the library. She wanted to know how one could get a key to the room. I told her. She was very grateful. She called me two days later and said she had a key. She said we should meet sometime at the library and go for coffee. She was very funny and flirtatious on the phone. At some point in the conversation, she said, "You know who my father is, right?"

I didn't know who her father was. I hadn't made the connection with her last name. It turned out she was the daughter of an extremely famous writer. I did feel my heart leap a little at my closeness to celebrity, but not too much. I knew his fame, but hadn't read his books. I agreed to meet with her for coffee.

A few days later, I met Julia in front of the library, and the first thing she said to me was, "You look like a Swedish sailor." It was summer, and my hair was very light, almost blonde. She meant the Swedish line as a compliment and I took it as one. She was in her late thirties and she wore a loose-fitting dress—she was heavy. Her face was long and pale. Her dark hair was curly from a permanent. Beneath her large brown eyes were deep purple rings of exhaustion.

We went to a coffee shop and we got along fine. I liked

her. She was funny, and it was good to talk to her. We were both nervous about our writing: I was scared that I wouldn't be able to finish my novel, and she was scared that she would never be able to write hers and escape her father's shadow.

After our coffee together, Julia started calling me frequently, and we developed a phone friendship. We didn't see each other at the library, as she went in the evenings after work.

In August, I began to receive prank phone calls. Someone was calling my answering machine ten to fifteen times a day and hanging up. When I was home the same thing happened. "Star 69" didn't exist at that time, and I called the phone company only to learn that tracing calls was tedious and expensive. I hoped the calls would just stop. Julia told me that the same thing had happened to her a few months before, and she had tried to do the tracing but it didn't work, because the person was calling from pay phones. I endured the constant ringing.

I wasn't sleeping well during this time and often had nightmares. I dreamed one night that the soles of my feet had slit open up like envelopes. When I looked inside my feet, I saw that they were hollow and rimmed with blood. The whole next day, remembering my dream, I could hardly walk. I thought I might be cracking up, but I kept going to the study room, so I could take naps.

One evening in August I became sick. I had food poisoning, some kind of stomach disturbance. Julia wanted to come over and take care of me. I told her that I would be all right, but she begged me to let her nurse me. I assented and she arrived with teas and a giant bottle of Pepto-Bismol and several boxes of antacid tablets. She had stocked up at a pharmacy, gone overboard.

She visited with me for at least two hours. She saw some of my novel on my desk and asked if she could read it. I told her no. I was feeling terrible about my work. She insisted that I let her read something. I kept saying no. She seemed hurt and offended by my refusal.

A few nights later, my stomach problem had cleared up, and she invited me to her place for dinner. She had a nice apartment on the Upper East Side, and she made a good meal. After dinner, we drank coffee. We started talking about our childhoods and she told me a strange story from her high school years. She went to an exclusive all-girls school on Fifth Avenue and, during her freshman year, fell in love—from a school-girl distance—with her music teacher, a handsome Swedish man in his thirties. She found out where he lived and spent her weekends spying on him. With a super-eight camera, she filmed him leaving his building and followed him, or she wouldn't follow him and instead snuck into his building and stole some of his mail. If he did laundry and left the laundromat, she stole an item of his clothing. She did this for all four years of high school, taking his class every semester and never letting the music teacher know she loved him.

Her father eventually found out what was going on and sent her to a psychiatrist. But she didn't stop doing what she wanted. "My father was the one who needed a shrink," she said. At the end of her senior year, she gathered together her movies of the music teacher, the poems and stories and plays she had written about him, the photographs he had inspired, and his mail and clothing she had taken, and she put all of this material in eighteen shopping bags, which was symbolic to her because she was now eighteen.

Julia arranged to meet with the music teacher. She brought the bags to school and lined them up in the gym. She showed him all the bags. "What's this?" he asked. She told him to look in the bags, and he did. She was very excited for him to see all she had done for him, the depth of her adoration and her love. After poking around in a few bags, he said to her, "If you wanted to get laid, why didn't you just ask?"

Julia then stopped telling her story and just looked at me. I pictured very clearly the music teacher standing over eighteen shopping bags. I admired his calm reaction.

"Can you believe he said that to me?" Julia asked, still indignant twenty years later. "I was just a girl. I was in love with him, and he couldn't see that."

I knew she wanted me to take her side, but it was such a strange story. "What did you do?" I asked.

"I just turned around and left him with the bags, and my crush was completely over. It hadn't been about sex. I was so disappointed in him. But what he said was the best thing for me. Worked a lot better than all the therapy. I felt nothing for him instantly."

"Do you think he was angry about the mail?" It was a dumb question, but I loved to get mail and would have been very upset if mine was ever stolen.

"I never heard from him if he was," she said, and she smiled. "I hope he was angry."

"That's some story," I said.

"You can't ever write about it," she said.

"I won't," I said.

The conversation took on a lighter tone and I thought, Well, she was crazy twenty years ago, but now she's normal. We drank more coffee, and she told me she was invited every fall to a party that Woody Allen threw—she had met him through her father, but now was friends with him on her own right—and she suggested I should come with her to the party.

As I was leaving, she asked me at the door if she could kiss me. I wasn't attracted to her. I said, trying to be kind, "I think I'd rather be friends." But then, so as not to reject her completely, I said, foolishly, "We could have a hug goodbye."

So we hugged, and she held me tight. Her breasts were against my chest. I didn't mean to, but I became aroused.

"I thought you just wanted to be friends," she said and went to kiss my mouth. I tried to kiss her on the cheek. Her lips brushed the corner of my mouth. I got out of her arms. I thanked her for dinner and left. It was an uncomfortable moment, but she didn't seem angry.

By the end of August, I was getting nowhere with my novel and thought that it must be New York. I gave up my rent-controlled apartment and moved back to Princeton. My hope was that I could write there, in the quiet. The book was due in three months, but even more importantly, I wanted to finish it so I could go see my son.

In Princeton, I rented a room in a house with two graduate students. I set up a phone line with one of them, listing my name in information. By the second day of phone service the hang-ups started again, five to ten times a day. I felt as if a sick taint had followed me from New York. My housemate kept picking up the phone. I didn't tell her I was the cause of it. I was frightened by the calls and was going to set up the trace this time, but I procrastinated, and then, after a few days, the calls stopped.

In mid-September I received a phone call from Marie, the woman whose party I had gone to in July. She was calling to ask me a favor on behalf of Julia. Marie told me that Julia had a bad relationship with her father and only visited him once a year, usually in September. Marie always went with Julia for these visits to provide support, but this year she couldn't make it, and Julia wanted me to go. For some reason Julia felt too embarrassed to ask me herself and so she had enlisted Marie to make the call. I told Marie that I could do it, and she said Julia would be very happy. I didn't feel good about my motivation, though. I wanted to meet the famous writer.

I hadn't seen Julia since the night she had tried to kiss me, but we had continued our friendship over the phone as if nothing had happened. After speaking to Marie, Julia called a little while later and thanked me for wanting to go with her. "Every year," she said, "it's a difficult trip."

"I'm happy to go with you," I said, "but don't you think you should take a friend you've known longer?"

"I want *you* to come," she said. "I've known you long enough to feel that you're a friend."

The following weekend, I met Julia in New York, and we took the train out to the country. Her father had a beautiful home, and I was put up in a large guest cottage. Next to my bed was an enormous bookshelf with all the foreign translations of his books.

Over the course of the weekend Julia's father treated me like a lost son. On Saturday and Sunday mornings, he made oatmeal for me, a ritual with him. Supposedly he had never made a bowl of oatmeal for anyone else. Julia and his young girlfriend, who was Julia's age, made a big deal about this oatmeal.

He and I went for a bike ride on a path through the woods next to his house, and then we sat in his den and watched a baseball game. We talked about my writing and he said, "Sounds very difficult to turn a novella into a novel. I've never tried to do it. Maybe it isn't supposed to become a larger story."

This frightened me, because I suspected it was true. Then he said, "But you can do it and you have to do it. Don't worry about plot. Just get your character into trouble."

The two nights I was there he had dinner parties with interesting and talented guests. One night there was a famous screenwriter and I regaled the table with the story of a fight I got into in Paris and how my nose was broken. The screenwriter said to the writer, "Where did you get this kid? He has too many stories."

Julia's father beamed, and then he joked, "They're all lies," and he smiled at me. Julia was very quiet.

The day we left, Julia's father gave me several first edition hardbacks of his novels. He gave me all the books he had written in the first person, since I was writing my novel in the first person. "These should help you," he said.

I left him feeling quite good about myself. A famous writer had liked me very much, and I liked him.

On the train back to the city, Julia said to me, "My father had a talk with me this morning. Do you know what he told me?"

"I have no idea," I said. My vanity had me hoping that I would hear some compliment about myself.

"He said to me, 'Why don't you marry someone like Jonathan. He's substantial. You never bring men like him around. That last boyfriend of yours was anorexic.' "

"What did you say?"

"Nothing. He's a horrible and rude man. It's none of his business. And then before we left, he said it again, 'Marry him.' "

"You could have explained to him that we're just friends."

"Why would I tell him that?"

"So that he wouldn't bother you."

"You don't understand my father," she said, and she turned to look out the window, and I let the conversation drop.

It was a long train ride, and I started writing in my journal, and for some reason, I wrote, "I'm crazy. Julia's crazy. All my friends are crazy."

I hadn't realized it, but she was watching me write and she said, "You think I'm crazy?"

"I think you're crazy in a good way. See, I wrote that I'm crazy, that all my friends are crazy."

She was silent and then she said, "You know I brought you up there to spend time with me, not my father."

"I'm sorry," I said. "He kept asking me to do things."

"You could have said no."

"I'm sorry . . . I didn't want to be rude."

"So you were rude to me. You were *my* guest."

I didn't say anything. I was in over my head. I regretted having gone with her. I was a weak person. I had gone so I could meet a famous writer. We were both silent. Then she said, "I'm not angry at you, I'm angry at him. I can't stand the man, but I visit him once a year because he's my father."

I left her at the station in New York, and vowed that I wouldn't have anything more to do with her. I had enough problems. Alone on the train to New Jersey, I wrote in my journal, "Julia would kill me if she knew this but I like her father more than her. She gives me the creeps. Scary to write this, but she reminds me of a brooding spider."

In October, Julia left for California for eight days and

sent me a package with eight presents. I was to open one present each day she was gone. I opened them all at once. They were strange presents: a Jackie Mason tape, fancy pencils, expensive fudge, potpourri, a little travel alarm clock, beautiful rubber erasers to go with the pencils, a thermometer to put out my window, and a small desk ornament—a tiny globe. The letter with the presents thanked me for going with her to her father, but then ended angrily: "You didn't have to be so cold on the train. You didn't have to tell me that we were only friends. Don't be so pompous. Who do you think you are?"

I considered throwing the gifts away, but I thought this would bring me bad luck. So I stored her presents in my closet and pressed on with trying to write my book.

My son's mother sent me more photos to look at—we had talked on the phone a few times—and I wrote back telling her that I would come see them both very soon. I kept hoping to go on some Kerouac-like writing jag and finish the book, but no such jag occurred.

At the end of October, I received a phone call from a woman who said that she was helping to organize a literary symposium of young American writers to be held in Sweden, at Gothenburg University. The symposium was jointly sponsored by the university and by a Swedish literary magazine called Nista. The woman had a slight accent. Her name was Sara Sundstrom.

She told me that I was one of twelve candidates whom they were considering. She was calling from New York and wanted to interview me. Selection for the symposium was based on this interview and a sample of my work. If chosen I would receive an all-expenses-paid trip to Sweden in March. I readily agreed to be interviewed and we made an appointment to meet in New York in two days.

That night Julia called. She was just back from California, and her voice was ebullient. She said, "Did you receive my package?"

"Yes," I said and thought of mentioning the angry tone at the end of her letter, but decided not to—she was sounding friendly, and I didn't want any conflict.

"Did you only open one present each day? I wanted you to think of me each day that I was gone," she said.

"I opened one each day. The Jackie Mason tape was the first," I said. I didn't like to lie, but it was a sort of half-truth. The Jackie Mason *had* been the first thing I unwrapped. "It was an interesting assortment, thank you . . . How was your trip?"

"Terrible. I was practically blind the whole time. I had a problem with my contact lenses, they were scratching my eyes—I had to go to an eye doctor. I don't like to go to doctors I don't know."

We talked for a little while longer, I told her about the symposium in Sweden, and then we rang off. I thought to myself that my friendship worked fine with her over the phone, but that in person it was a disaster.

Sara Sundstrom called back the next day, but I wasn't in, and she left a message on my machine asking me to bring a photograph of myself to our meeting. She didn't leave a number where I could reach her.

The following night, around nine o'clock, I met with her at Birdland on Broadway, up near Columbia, as we had planned. She was sitting at a table next to the large window that looked onto the street. She was a blonde woman in her mid-thirties. She was small and had handsome features. Her skin was a little worn from the sun. She seemed very European: mature and cool. She stood up to shake my hand and then we both sat down. She said, "I don't have much time, so we have to do this quickly."

"All right," I said. Her attitude was as if I had requested the interview. She already had a drink, and I didn't bother to order one.

"Do you have your writing sample and the photograph?"

"Yes," I said, and smiled, drawing them out of my backpack. I wanted to appear friendly and outgoing so that I could get a free trip to Sweden. I handed her two chapters of my novel and the photograph. She put them in her bag, and then she put on the table a small tape recorder. She pressed record and began to ask me questions: What would you offer to the symposium? What new things could you say about writing and literature in America today? Who are your influences? Are you calm in front of a large audience asking you questions?

She was stern and almost mean. I tried to give concise and intelligent answers, but I struggled. I said things like, "I'd love to come and talk about American literature. There are so many American writers I've loved, I can hardly name them."

Then the phone at the bar rang. The bartender answered and said to us, "Is one of you a Dr. Sundstrom?"

"That's me," she said. She went up to the bar and took the phone for just a minute.

When she came back to the table, I said, "You're a doctor?"

"I have a Ph.D.," she said.

"In what?" I asked.

"The Russian language," she said. It was the very end of the cold war, and there was something spooky about her being a doctor of Russian. I was about to ask her who had called, but she said, "So you'd like to come to

Sweden?" It was the first time she smiled at me, and she seemed to soften.

"Yes, very much," I said

Then she told me that she needed cigarettes. She glanced out the window and said she was going to run across the street and get a pack. I looked out the window. Across Broadway there was a little tobacco and newspaper shop.

She picked up the tape recorder and her bag and said, "I'll be right back." She smiled at me. I sat at the window in Birdland and watched her cross the street. It was night, but Broadway was well lit by the streetlights and the headlights of the cars.

Something was wrong. She had told me we didn't have much time, but suddenly she's going across the street for cigarettes. I wanted to follow her, but I wondered if I was just being paranoid. If I joined her across the street and she was simply getting a pack of cigarettes, then I would blow my chance at a free trip to Sweden by acting as if I didn't trust her.

She went into the store. The lights on Broadway changed, and the road filled with traffic. I tried to watch for her through the cars and buses, but it was difficult to see the other side of the street.

When the lights turned red again there was a clear view, but I didn't see her coming out of the store. I was getting anxious. The light changed once more, and I couldn't see across the street, and she didn't return to the bar. I asked the bartender if she had paid for her drink, and he said she had.

I ran across Broadway to the newspaper store, but she wasn't there. I asked the proprietor if a blonde woman had come into the store, and he said yes, but that she had left several minutes ago.

"She's not in the bathroom? Do you have a bathroom?" He looked at me like I was crazy. I ran back across Broadway to Birdland.

"The woman I was with, has she come back?" I asked the bartender.

She hadn't. She had taken off with my photograph and my two chapters. I had other copies, but the idea that she had walked off with them sickened me. Something grotesque was happening. I had no way to find her. She had never given me a phone number or an address where I could reach her.

I called my agent—I didn't know who else to call—from a pay phone on Broadway. I said to her, "That person who was interviewing me for that symposium in Sweden . . . I know this sounds crazy, but she just stole two chapters of my novel."

"Are you sure?" my agent asked. She probably thought I was drunk. I told her what happened, and she said, "Go to the police. This way we'll have a record in case those pages get published somewhere."

I went back to Birdland and asked the bartender where the closest precinct was. It was over on Amsterdam, the 24th. The station was in the middle of some tough-looking projects.

Except for a sergeant at the front desk, the station seemed deserted. The sergeant was a portly, soft-looking man with glasses and a bald head. His desk was elevated. I looked up at him and said, "Excuse me officer . . . This is very odd, but I'd like to report something stolen."

"What?"

"I'm a writer . . . and somebody just took off with two chapters of my manuscript."

"Fiction?"

"Yes," I said.

"Really?"

"Yes."

"This is right up my alley, then—I'm a fiction buff!" He smiled happily at me. "I love to read. I'd like to write a book someday. As a cop you hear a lot of stories . . . But I have to say you're the first writer to come in because somebody stole his writing."

He made a phone call, and another officer came into the room, a heavyset woman. She led me to a desk and typed up my report and gave me a receipt. I took the train back to New Jersey.

The next day, first thing in the morning, I went to Firestone Library on the Princeton campus and did some research. There was no magazine called *Nista* in any listings. I did, however, find the phone number of Gothenburg University.

I rushed home, made the international call, and was connected to the English department. It was late in the afternoon in Sweden, and a secretary put me through to the head of the department, a man who spoke perfect British-accented English. I said I was an American novelist connected with Princeton University and asked if his department was having a symposium in March of young American writers.

"No, no such symposium."

"I heard that there was going to be some kind of panel . . . might it be held by another department?"

"No other department except this one would be interested in American writers."

"Have you heard of a literary magazine called Nista?"

"No."

"Is there such a word as "nista" in Swedish?"

"No."

"Thank you for your help," I said. "There's been a misunderstanding."

"Perfectly all right," he said, and he laughed and we hung up.

I don't know what the professor made of such a strange overseas call, but my mind was reeling. The whole thing was a mad hoax. I felt sick. Who would hate me enough to arrange such an elaborate trick?

The following day, a message was left on my machine by a man with a phony-sounding foreign accent. He spoke with great urgency: "This is Dr. Bohanson. I am the editor of *Nista* magazine. I received your writing! It is very important that I speak to you! I am in Boston airport. Call me!"

That was all he said. He didn't leave a number. Boston airport. Not even Logan airport. Who was doing this to me?

The next morning I stepped out to get the paper and, when I came back, there was a message from Sara Sundstrom: "Dr. Bohanson wants to speak to you about your writing. Why don't you call?" She didn't leave a number. She had never given me a number.

Their torture of me was strange and absurd. The woman's voice was hateful. There was no way I could get any writing done. I was no closer to finishing my novel and seeing my son. I needed to clear my mind, so that afternoon I drove to the ocean.

I went to Asbury Park, a place I had often gone to for its downtrodden beauty: the rusted Ferris wheel with each car bearing the name of a Jersey town; the deserted boardwalk; the closed-up fudge and taffy shops; the warped and gigantic wooden casino, which looks as if it's going to topple into the ocean; and, of course, the Atlantic, gray and enormous and indifferent.

It took me an hour to drive from Princeton. When I got there, I sat on the beach. It was a cool November day, but the sun was bright. I was all alone except for a few stragglers on the boardwalk, and I stared at the ocean. Then I got on my knees, bent my head to the ground, resting it on my hands, and started praying. I was agnostic, but I prayed to God to help me. I was overwhelmed by everything. I needed help. I dug my hands into the sand. They got entangled in something wet and I lifted them up. Attached to my fingers were damp strips of disintegrating toilet paper, and on the paper were little black bugs. I screamed and thrashed my hands in the sand to get the bugs and paper off me.

I went running off the beach and into the bar of the Empress Hotel, across the street from the boardwalk. This wasn't a good thing for me to do. I was young, but I had quit drinking the year before and knew being sober had enabled me to write my novella and to graduate. But I didn't care. I ordered a beer and a shot of whisky.

The Empress was a transient hotel. Like the rest of Asbury Park, the Empress had probably been glorious in the fifties—it looked like something from Miami. The bar still operated, and the drinks were cheap. It was afternoon when I got in there, and I drank for hours. At some point I sat at a table with a borrowed pen and a piece of paper and wrote a long drunken letter to my son. I gave him lots of advice and apologized that I hadn't been able to come see him yet.

I remember looking up from the letter to see that I had been joined at the table by an old woman. She must have been seventy; her hair was gray and her eyes were crazy.

She told me that Abraham Lincoln was Jewish—you could tell because of his name, and that she had taken an

accounting course with Frank Sinatra in Jersey City in the
1930s. At some point, she said she wanted to have sex with
me if I wore a condom. She said she hadn't had sex in years.

I was crazy drunk and agreed to have sex with her. When
we stood up from the table, I saw that she was incredibly
tiny. She was about four foot eight and used an old broom-
stick for a cane. She was wearing a housedress. I realized
then that I was completely mad, and there was no way I
could sleep with this woman. I told her that I was starving,
that I had been drinking for hours. I suggested we go to a
restaurant and have dinner rather than go to her room. She
said, "They won't let me in any restaurant the way I look.
You go and come back. I'll be waiting."

I went to another bar, spent the rest of my money, and
then got into my car and blacked out.

I came to on some restricted roads of the Fort Dix military base. I have no idea how I got in there. I found my
way out and, half-conscious, half-drunk, drove back to
Princeton. I am beyond fortunate that I did not kill
anyone. Somewhere I lost the letter I wrote to my son.

I drank for a week. I went to a psychologist and told
him about getting a letter with a picture of my son, *Nista*,
the miniature old woman I had almost slept with, and
everything else. I asked him to put me somewhere to
sober up. He said he wasn't sure if I had a drinking
problem or if I was chemically imbalanced.

He put me in a psychiatric hospital that had an alcohol
unit, covering all my potential problems. After a humiliating week on the locked-up psychiatric ward, I was trans-
ferred to the alcoholic wing.

I told my life story to the group, and afterward the head
doctor said to me, "You're an alcoholic and a maniac.
Someday you're going to have a florid psychotic moment

and end up in Bellevue. But because you're smart, when you come out of it you'll be able to talk your way out. But then it will happen again. If you don't go on lithium you'll lose your mind and never write that book."

The doctor was chewing Nicaret gum while he gave me my life sentence. I refused to go on the lithium.

The doctor came by my room the next day and gave me articles about manic-depressive, alcoholic artists who commit suicide without lithium. He tried to convince me by saying, "I want to help you be a writer who can write."

But I kept refusing the drugs. He performed numerous tests on my blood, nervous system, and brain. He did this to a number of patients, milking their insurance companies for all he could get.

It was the closest I've come to jail: I couldn't leave the place against doctor's orders unless I wanted to absorb the expense of my hospitalization, which was something like a thousand dollars a day. I was stuck there until my insurance ran out.

The day after Thanksgiving, my father, whom I told all about Sara Sundstrom and *Nista*, called me at the hospital. He said, "There's been a break in the case. I know who was involved with stealing your writing."

"Who?"

"Julia."

"How do you know?"

"A woman called here yesterday looking for you. She said she was with *Nista* magazine. And I asked her for a number where you could reach her. I didn't let on that I suspected anything, and I heard her whisper, 'Julia, the father wants a number.' She gave me a California number. I had a feeling it was phony, and I called it for you. It was an optometrist's office. I asked where they were located—

Berkeley. Why would she give an eye doctor's number? Then a few hours later Julia called to wish you a late, happy Thanksgiving. I didn't let on anything."

I felt incredibly grateful to my father. "Thank you for solving this," I said. "Julia went to an eye doctor in Berkeley."

"Don't do anything about it, especially from there. You don't want to provoke her. She's crazy."

"I won't do anything."

"How was the Thanksgiving meal they gave you?" he asked.

"Horrible," I said.

"You'll be out soon," he said.

"I hope so," I said.

I hung up with my father. The pay phone was in the lounge. It was the rest hour before dinner, which was the only time we were allowed to receive and make phone calls. I went to my room and lay on my bed.

I went over in my mind all that had transpired between me and Julia. When something like this happens to you, you don't see the odd trail of evidence accumulating, but now, like a constellation, it was all laid out for me. The Swedish sailor remark when we first met. The music teacher story. The kiss at her door. The prank phone calls. The botched weekend at her father's. But who was Sara Sundstrom? What kind of friends did Julia have that would go along with her? Who was the man who had called me, claiming to be Dr. Bohanson?

I felt a weak, impotent rage. What could I do to Julia? I got off my bed and went back to the phone and dialed her number. She answered, and we exchanged the usual greetings. I wanted to act as if nothing had happened to me, to show her that she hadn't affected me in the least.

"I'm just returning your call," I said. "How was your Thanksgiving?"

"Uneventful. And yours?" she asked.

"Very nice," I said. They had served us artificially flavored pumpkin pie. "Whatever happened to the party with Woody Allen?" I asked.

"He canceled this year," she said. "How's your book coming?"

"Great," I said. "Almost finished. How's your writing?"

She talked about her book for a while, and then, as if it had just occurred to her, she asked, "What ever happened to your trip to Norway?"

"Oh, you mean Sweden," I said. Norway. She was purposely feigning ignorance. She had masterminded the whole thing. Here was my small chance at revenge, to act as if it had meant nothing to me. She was probably dying to hear me describe my confusion and bewilderment and fear. "Well, the trip didn't happen," I said, laughing. "It was just some silly hoax."

Silly. I intended that word to be a dagger into her heart. But then I realized she had probably watched me run frantically out of Birdland to that news store. Most likely she had been right on Broadway, and from a pay phone had called the bar to ask for Dr. Sundstrom. And she had chosen Birdland for its big windows, so that she could see me sitting there, answering questions like a fool. I imagined she had listened to the tape recording.

"Oh, that's a shame," she said. "You deserved a trip like that."

"Well, it was just a stupid hoax," I said, and despite all my acting, it was terribly scary to speak to her. I was locked up, but she was the insane one. My dad was right. I didn't want to provoke her. I was afraid it would make her do something more drastic, and she had already proved very capable of hurting me. I then said, "I better get going, my mom is calling me to dinner." A few patients, men and women, all clothed in sweatpants, were starting to gather by the ward's locked door. In ten minutes we would be led down the hall to the cafeteria.

"All right, Jonathan," she said. "Call me. Come into the city so we can get together."

"Okay," I said, and we rang off. I placed the phone on the cradle and wanted to strangle Julia. I saw my hands around her neck. Her eyes would have to meet mine, acknowledging her punishment and acknowledging that she hadn't gotten away with anything. But it didn't feel good to think about hurting her. I wasn't used to feeling violent, to wanting to really hurt someone.

After forty days, I was let out of the hospital. I didn't hear from Julia and didn't call her. I was told that the best way to deal with obsessed people was not to initiate any contact, to starve them of yourself until they became obsessed with someone else.

I started trying to write again, but still couldn't get anywhere. I kept thinking of the famous writer's words: "Maybe it isn't supposed to become a larger story." The fact that he was Julia's father made his offhand remark even more ominous. The deadline for handing in the book passed. I was still 30,000 words short.

The new year came. On January 23, I wrote a desperate letter to Joyce Carol Oates, my teacher. Essentially, I was asking her to help me write my book—a ridiculous request. I didn't know how I could possibly mail the letter, but didn't know what else to do. I needed help. I had to finish the book so that I could go see my son.

Then before I mailed the letter, I opened a Hazelden

book of daily meditations, which a friend had given me in the hospital. At the top of each day's meditation was a quote from a famous person. For January 23 it read, "No person can save another."

The author of those words was Joyce Carol Oates.

I didn't have to mail my letter. She had answered me.

From that point forward, I started to write and didn't stop until it was finished. Julia took one more shot at me, though. A letter arrived on February 22, posted from Berkeley:

The signature, while nearly unintelligible, looks like "Sara Sundstrom." It was a letter from a fictional literary magazine, signed by someone with an assumed name,

```
                    Nista
               Nonnensgatan 32
               Stockholm, Sweden
                                    Berkeley
                                    15 January
     Dear Mr. Ames,

     Dr. Bohanson has asked me to write you to inform
     you that we have made our choices for the panel
     for our symposium in March.

     I am afraid your qualifications for our agenda are
     sadly lacking. While we both agree that your
     writing contains a certain juvenile charm, our
     responsibility is to deliver something a bit more
     substantial.

     Off the record, may I also offer a bit of personal
     advice for future interviews. When someone asks
     you, what, if anything, you can contribute to a
     serious literary symposium, you might think of
     something other than that you would "love to go".
     I am afraid I was not impressed by your enthusiasm
     for a free trip to Europe, when you could hold the
     promise of so little in return.

     Still, thank you for your interest in Nista, and
     as we say in Gothemburg, "Många Hälsningar"!
     Regards,
```

written or dictated by a madwoman, and yet I was hurt by the criticism of my writing.

I had thought the whole problem with Julia had come to an end, but holding that letter in my hands, I was devastated.

I had to end this somehow. I wanted revenge, but thought it best to forgive. My plan was to forgive and ask for forgiveness.

The side of me that wanted revenge imagined that by being morally superior I would come out ahead. But I tried to repress that thought. I wanted to act purely so as to stop her strange attacks against me.

I phoned Julia at her work number. After our initial greetings, I said, "I know this comes out of the blue, but I just wanted to call and tell you I'm sorry if I hurt you or led you on in any way."

Her voice took on a low, hushed, deeply appreciative tone, she said, "Thank you . . . This means a great deal to me . . . I want to talk to you more, but things here are busy right now. Can I call you back in half an hour?"

"I just really wanted to say that I was sorry—"

"Are you telling me that you don't want anything to do with me?" Her voice was now harsh, angry. The change in tone was rapid.

"I just want to say I'm sorry—"

"I want to speak to you in half an hour," she demanded.

"All right," I said, weakly, and we hung up. Half an hour later she called me. She asked me how my work was coming; she said she was nearly done with her book. I was sick of this banter, of being afraid of her, and I finally said, "What's been going on with you?"

"What do you mean?" she asked. Her voice was immediately odd and defensive.

"I know that you are involved with Nista magazine," I

said. It was exhilarating to finally get it out. To show her that I knew the truth.

"What are you talking about? You're very strange." She was shouting.

"I know that you're involved," I said.

"You're sick . . . I don't know what you're talking about . . . What are you accusing me of?"

"I know that you're involved with Nista magazine." My voice was calm. She was hanging herself.

"You're sick . . . I don't like this . . . I don't like you . . . Why are you saying these things—"

She hung up the phone.

I was wiped out, destroyed. I lay on my bed. Five minutes later, the phone rang. I didn't pick it up. It was Julia. I listened to her leave a message on the machine, her voice was contrite, practically a whisper: "Jonathan, I understand if you don't want to be my friend, but I'd like us to be friends. I want to talk to you. Please call me . . . I think you're a really good writer . . . If you don't call, I understand. But please call me."

I have never spoken to or seen Julia again.

Epilogue

I finished my novel and met my son. I became very involved in his life. I became his dad. He's now fifteen years old. He has my last name. He's a wonderful boy.

For several years I waited for my florid psychotic moment. In my mind I called it the FPM. One night, I was alone in a diner in New Jersey, and a very overweight man approached my table. He said, "I read your book." I looked at him. "I liked it," he said.

I knew him from somewhere. Then I placed him—the head doctor from the psychiatric hospital. He was still talking down to me like I was his patient. But there was something wrong with him. He was heavy when I knew him, but now he was obese.

"Thank you for reading it," I said. "Are you still at the hospital?"

"I don't practice anymore," he said, and gave me a strange smile. I sensed that he had lost his license. That's when I stopped waiting for the FPM.

In 1989, a few months before my book came out, Julia sold her novel to the same publisher. This was incredible to me, but fitting. I had told my editor this whole story and one time, when I went to see him, he informed me that Julia was visiting her editor—there were troubles with her manuscript. My editor showed me the office where Julia was meeting with her editor. The door was slightly ajar. I walked past to try and catch a peek of her, but wasn't able to. My editor didn't want me to make trouble, so I left the building before her meeting was over.

Her book came out a year after mine. The reviews weren't very good. They all mentioned that she was the daughter of the famous writer. She hadn't escaped his shadow. In a bookstore, I looked at her novel. The epigraph was from Balzac: "How fondly swindlers coddle their dupes." I glanced through the book. I didn't expect to find my two chapters. Who knows what she did with my photograph. Drew a mustache on it? Horns? Cut it up?

Her book ends with a man, a famous writer, sitting by himself on a plane to Stockholm. He is going there to collect the Nobel Prize. The empty seat next to him is supposed to be for his ex-wife, but she didn't show up at the airport. He isn't terribly upset because they fight a great deal, and he's actually relieved to go to Stockholm without her. Under the seat in front of him is his briefcase, and he believes that his acceptance speech, which he has slaved over, is inside. But it isn't. The speech has been stolen by his ex-wife. She has stolen his writing.

And the last word of the last line is: Sweden.

Notes

1. Regarding the letter sent to me by *Nista*: there is no street called Nonnensgatan in Stockholm. I think the hidden meaning could almost be: Nonsense Street. Många Hälsningar, directly translated, means, "many salutations," but is not a phrase used in Swedish letter-writing. Furthermore, Gothenburg is misspelled.

2. The names in this essay have been changed, unless they were false to begin with.

Commercial Intermission
Book Jacket Flap Copy I Wrote for My Other Books

(You should, I hope, find this amusing—if you read all three passages a joke emerges.)

For the hardcover of
The Extra Man
(Scribner 1998)

Jonathan Ames, whose debut novel *I Pass Like Night* was enthusiastically praised by Philip Roth and Joyce Carol Oates, has followed up with a brilliant and comic second novel.

Louis Ives, the narrator of *The Extra Man*, fancies himself a young gentleman fashioned after his heroes in the books of F. Scott Fitzgerald. He dresses the part— favoring neckties, blue blazers, and sport coats. But he also has a penchant for women's clothing, a weakness that causes him to lose his job at a Princeton day school after a bizarre incident involving a colleague's brassiere. Thrust out of Princeton, he heads to New York, where he rents a cheap room in the madly discombobulated apartment of Henry Harrison, a failed but brilliant playwright who dances alone to Ethel Merman records, sneaks into Broadway shows, and performs with great style the duties of a walker—an escort for the rich widows of the Upper East Side.

The two men, separated in age by more than forty years, develop a relationship that is irascible mentor and eager apprentice, and they form a bond the depths of which neither expected. But Louis, when he's not with Henry, has fascinations that lead him to an unusual community on the fringes of the sex world of Times Square. He develops a secret life there, which he fears will be his undoing and which he must keep hidden from Henry at all costs.

A hilarious yet moving story about friendship and longing, *The Extra Man* is an original and unforgettable novel by one of America's most talented young writers.

For the hardcover of *What's Not to Love?: The Adventures of a Mildly Perverted Young Writer*
(Crown 2000)

"Jonathan Ames is one of the funniest writers in America," so says Jonathan Ames, who is actually writing this flap copy, which is the publishing industry term for the boastful fluff you read on the inner portions of most hardcover book jackets. So let the truth be known: Most writers write or at least rewrite their flap copy. And why not? They are writers after all. For the flap copy on my last novel, I had the audacity to pronounce that I was one of America's most talented young writers. My mother read that and was very proud, pointing it out to me. I then said to her, "I wrote that." But she was still proud; she probably didn't believe that I wrote it. In fact, she doesn't believe most of what I tell her, but that's probably because she couldn't take it if she did believe me. Which is a good way to describe this book, this comic autobiography: It's the kind of book one's mother shouldn't read, though there are several passages where I profess my great Oedipal love and desire for my mother, which she might find flattering. What else recommends this book, or, rather, what recommends me, since this book is about me. Well, I'm bald and ribald, I'm like Rabelais and

Danny Kaye, sometimes I'm straight and sometimes I'm gay. Well, not really. I'm almost never gay, but it rhymed nicely with Kaye, and also I tend to be depressed rather than gay. But I do like to make others laugh, so if you're standing in a bookstore, I hope you'll find this book funny and I hope that you'll move on to my introduction, where I'll further implore you to keep reading, with the idea that you'll eventually purchase the book, which is the point, by the way, of flap copy.

For the paperback of *What's Not to Love?*
(Vintage 2001)

Jonathan Ames, who describes himself as "the George Plimpton of the colon," takes you in this endearing memoir, on a vivid exploration of his life and his body. From the recounting of his late puberty (age 16), to his early fatherhood (22), to his early thirties (early 30s) worries about balding, impotence, and depression, Jonathan Ames bares his soul and drops his pants. He is a hero for the twenty-first century, swearing to get by on his own without Viagra, Rogaine, or Prozac! And his heroic adventures, you'll find, are varied and heartwarming—high-end colonics, barroom brawls, European travels, and unstoppable nosebleeds are just a few of the things he gets himself into. *What's Not to Love?* is clearly a memoir from one of our funniest and most daring writers.

Part IV:
Criticism
(Well, actually, compliments)

John Lurie and the
Lounge Lizards
New York Press, 1997

*I almost killed a man at the Mercury Lounge the other night. I
was there to hear John Lurie and the Lounge Lizards. But
really I had no business being at that club—unlike most people,
I have almost no interest in music. This is because I have a great
fear of technology. As a teenager, I didn't consider myself dex-
terous enough to put a needle on an album. In my twenties, I'd
buy cassettes, but I was always a klutz and I'd break the plastic
covers and the tapes would fall apart or the tapes would come
undone in my boom boxes and I'd be driven mad. And now in
my thirties, I'm absolutely frightened of the CD and want
nothing to do with it.*

Also I never go to hear live performances because I
don't like crowds and cigarette smoke, and I'm too cheap
to pay a cover charge. So I'm very ignorant of music, but a
friend of mine invited me to accompany her to hear John
Lurie, and she was treating—so I went.

I stood in an uncomfortable crowd for thirty minute,
until finally the Lizards came on stage. There were eight
of them—a cellist, two guitar players, a drummer, a bongo
player, a tenor sax, a pianist, a trumpeter, and Lurie himself on alto sax.

They began to play and I was immediately drawn in. Their music was astounding. Sometimes it was jazz and all kinds of jazz—blues, bebop, big band. Sometimes it was funk, sometimes it was rock, sometimes it was classical, and sometimes it was like two birds chirping—when Lurie and the other sax player playfully tweeted a duet at one another.

All the pieces seemed rehearsed and yet spontaneous. They played their music like a loose garment that fits beautifully. And their songs weren't indulgent and overly long like some jazz I've heard (I've snuck into the Blue Note a few times), and each number was like a story: there was a tangible beginning, middle, and end. It was really quite amazing. I loved it. Also, Lurie is going bald in a good way and I like it when famous people are bald. And almost all of them were wearing ties, which I prudishly approved of. The cellist, a quiet-looking woman, was also wearing a tie and her face betrayed absolutely no emotion, no affect, but this made me think that she must be a tiger in bed. So I was having a great time—the music, Lurie's balding, the sexy cellist, but there was one terrible problem: the man I wanted to kill.

He was a Frenchman who was standing right in front of me. He was wearing an expensive gray suit, he was about six foot three (unusual for a Frenchman), he had a full head of black hair, and he had very broad shoulders. I could hardly see the stage. This was bad enough, but he was also talking the whole time to a countryman of his, who had a Julius Caesar haircut, and they were doing a lot of French laughing. Lurie would be playing a beautiful solo and these two Frenchmen were carrying on as if they were sitting at a cafe on Boulevard de Montparnasse.

I wanted to say something to these two, particularly to

the one in front of me, who seemed to be the leader. I once knew French—thirteen years ago I was a male au pair in Paris—but I could hardly conjure up a single phrase with which to chastise these two. All I could manage was one word: I kept hissing at the back of the tall Frenchmen, "Alors!" I think it means *so*. I was saying so with an exclamation mark and they didn't turn around. They couldn't hear me. I said it about twenty times. Then one time, I said, "This is not Boulevard de Montparnasse!" But again they didn't hear me or pretended not to. My friend glanced at me a few times, she didn't know what I was doing, but mostly she was into the music.

I started thinking that I might give the tall one a karate chop right between his shoulder and neck—it was the part of his body I was obsessing on since it was in my direct line of vision. Then I started thinking I might give him a Vulcan death-pinch, which I had once given to a boy in the third grade on the playground with disastrous results—the next day the kid developed an actual pinched nerve and I was in big trouble. I was called to the principal's office and my parents had to meet with the other boy's parents. I'm lucky it was the seventies and not the nineties, otherwise I might have been sued or charged with sodomy, since sodomy seems to cover all acts, including most likely Vulcan death-pinches. As it was, in the third grade, in the 1970s, I wasn't charged with anything, but I was ordered to write an apology note in my best handwriting.

But the tall Frenchman's shoulder was so thick that I thought my death-pinch would have little effect, and also it was rusty since I hadn't used it in twenty-four years.

Then the Julius Caesar Frenchman left. I surmised that he was going to get a drink at the bar. I was able to see the stage from where he previously stood and the tall one, thankfully, had no one to speak to. I relaxed and enjoyed the music.

Then Julius Caesar came back. He handed the large Gaul a beer. The large one then fished out his wallet and gave his friend some money. He went to put his wallet back inside his interior jacket pocket, but he missed and the wallet fell to the ground, but he didn't know it! Then he shuffled his feet for some reason and the wallet was behind him and right at my feet. I had been watching him so closely because I hated him. I discreetly put my foot over the wallet. Then I bent down as if to tie my shoe. What to do? Revenge was mine! They were already talking again! They were rude! I was sure that the wallet was loaded—he had a fancy suit and rich looking hair. But I was only evil for a second. I tapped on the man's shoulder—the very shoulder I had imagined death-pinching. He turned and I presented the wallet. He looked at me as if I had lifted it and he grabbed it quickly out of my hand.

"I found it on the floor," I protested, and then added, to show my sophistication with the languages of the world, "Alors!"

"Oh, thank you," he said graciously with a French accent, then he turned back to the stage. But this whole wallet episode gave he and his friend more ammunition for conversation.

He owed me now, so I tapped him forcefully on the shoulder, "Alors," I began. "Would you please be quiet. And as a reward for my having found your wallet, I would like it if my lady friend and I could stand in front of you. She can't see very well"—this was a lie, but a good one— "and also please stop talking. This is fantastic music and I want to listen to it."

The two Frenchmen were mortified by moral and cultural superiority, or they thought I was nuts, but either way they obeyed my orders. We switched places, and I had a good view of the stage, but then I closed my eyes, the better to listen to the music. My friend, who was somewhat oblivious to all that I was going through, liked our new position; it was a little closer, and she swayed happily to the sounds of the glorious Lizards.

Several minutes went by and I heard no annoying French chatter and I was a little surprised by how obedient the two men were, so I turned around and they were gone. I had scared them off—gave them something to talk about when they were back at the cafes on the Boulevard de Montparnasse.

Shtupping

NEUROTICA: Jewish Writers on Sex, edited by
Melvin Jules Bukiet, W. W. Norton & Company
Bookforum, 1999

I wonder if my Gentile readers know what shtupping *means. I know it's fairly common, but it may have slipped past some people's cultural radar. So, first of all, shtupping is Yiddish and Yiddish words often sound like what they are trying to convey. And shtup (the root of shtupping), to me, sounds a little bit like a grunt or a swift human motion that meets some mild resistance, perhaps causing a grunt. So, you sweet, innocent Goyim, that's a hint. But I'll be more direct. I'll give it to you in context, like something from the SATs, and without a doubt you should be able to decipher its lusty meaning: "The man went to rinse off in the bathroom. He was feeling good about himself. 'I gave her a good shtupping,' he thought proudly."*

So, my title explained, let me proceed. Why are we all so mad about sex? Why can't we get over it? I'm sick of sex. I'm sick of thinking about it. I'm sick of my friends thinking about it. We all get momentarily distracted by things like the Tour de France or stamp collections or a painful cuticle, but we always come back to sex. Nothing else demands our attention this way. Somebody should write a letter to the editor about this. There should be a rally, a strike, a sit-down, a town meeting, an orgy . . . See back to sex. I start to get somewhere, make some progress, and then my mind turns a corner and I want to kiss a woman's buttocks, fondle her breasts, smell her armpit, and have her praise my penis. By the way, a note to women readers, Gentile and Jewish: Try to say something nice about your lover's penis. Not every time you make love, but once in a while. Gaze at it fondly, praise its shape, say it's just the right size. Anything will do. Chances are if you're sticking with the guy there's something about his penis that you like, so find that one thing and proclaim it. You know how much you appreciate it when a man at the beginning of an evening comments on how pretty you look, well it's the same for men with the penis. They need reassurance about their genitalia, the way a plant needs water. Many of you know this, but some of you women forget or you think that the man is cocky, literally and figuratively, and doesn't need the old pat on the back, a little stroking, literally and figuratively, but every man is weak in this area and a kind word from you will do wonders. Enough said.

Now, about the book that has provoked me to go on above the way I have—*Neurotica: Jewish Writers on Sex*— let me just say that I liked it quite a lot. I recommend it. But who am I to recommend something? I don't know, but let's put that philosophical conundrum aside, and we'll all assume that my judgment has some validity. So what recommends this book? Well, not the premise. Here comes the negative stuff. First the negative and then the positive. My negative comments are where I, as a critic, show that I have some intelligence, a cultivated aesthetic sensibility, and a distinguished worldview. Or something like that. Except in my case, my criticism is not coming from the small part of my brain where my intellect is housed, but rather the cranial lobe where I have stored my inherited shtetl mentality, which tells me that Jews should keep a low profile and not attract attention. I learned this from my mother. She hated it when a Jew made the headlines for doing something bad. She felt that one bad Jew would get all of us in trouble, and trouble for Jews meant devastation, slaughter, pogroms. And I have to say that one area where Jews seem to make a lot of headlines for being bad is in the area of sex. Elizabeth Taylor. Monica Lewinsky. Marv Albert. All Jews. All sex-crazed. And this all adds to the anti-Semitic portrait of Jews: we have wild libidos that make us crave Gentile flesh (in medieval times anti-Semites thought we wanted to eat their children, in modern times they just think we want to eat them out.) So when I saw this book, with its subtitle *Jewish Writers on Sex*, my shtetl reflex was: Don't add to our *tsures*, our problems. They already think we're sex-crazed, don't feed their prejudices. After all, I haven't come across any books with subtitles like: *WASP Writers on Cocktail Parties and Not Communicating Well with Your Loved Ones* or *Catholic Writers on Coming from Overly Large Families and Turning One's Back on the Church*.

So perhaps the premise of this anthology is faulty according to my shtetl thinking, but the result is actually quite wonderful. The table of contents of this book reads like a baseball lineup of all-time great Jewish-American writers, as well as promising newcomers. You've got well-known Hall of Famers Henry Roth, Woody Allen, Bernard Malamud, Erica Jong, Philip Roth, Cynthia Ozick, Isaac Bashevis Singer, Saul Bellow, and Jerzy Kosinski—and all of their selections are very strong. My favorites were Henry Roth's piece, an excerpt from *A Diving Rock on the Hudson*, which deals with brother-sister incest; Woody

Allen's "The Whore of Mensa," a comic masterpiece, and the best spoof of the private detective story that I've ever read; and Malamud's "Still Life," one his Fidelman stories, which are tales about a young libidinous Jewish painter in Rome.

Of the pieces by writers who are not as universally well-known just yet as the ones mentioned above, I loved Helen Schulman's "P.S.," a melancholic yet comic mixture of a story about an older woman and a younger man; Benjamin Taylor's excerpt from his novel *Tales Out of School*, which depicts an incredibly charged scene of homoeroticism between a bully and his Jewish victim; and Sandi Wisenberg's "Big Ruthie Imagines Sex without Pain," a beautiful song of a story about the trapped soul and sexual longing of a woman who wears a size 18.

So while many of the pieces in this book are quite moving and jarring, there's also a great deal of humor. There's a lot of shtupping and a lot laughing, and who doesn't like to shtup or laugh? For me, the two things happen to be related. If a shtup is good I find that I laugh afterward, that something comic and mirthful in me is released, and this is sort of what happens while reading the best of these stories. They made me enjoy thinking about sex, even if I don't want to think about it.

Of Breasts and Transhistories

The Woman I Was Not Born to Be: A Transsexual Journey, by Aleshia Brevard, Temple University Press

New York Press, 2001

In the late eighties and early nineties I was obsessed with women's breasts to an appalling degree. Every woman I saw I wanted to nurse on. This obsessive state of mind, which I've since outgrown (now I want to go down on all women—much healthier, I think), was very painful. The world was filled with boobs I couldn't have! I was like that desolate baby chick from the children's book, who, accidentally ejected from his nest, staggers about in a Beckettian landscape looking for his mommy.

I was living in Princeton, New Jersey, during this difficult period and had a lovely girlfriend, but her breasts—for the idiot I was at that time—were too small. The poor girl, a wonderful artist, sensed intuitively my condition—I had the decency to never say anything about it, but women are emotional tuning forks, they pick up everything—and she painted this large canvas of a stupendously endowed woman rising out of the sea. She hung it over my bed, perhaps for me to look at while I mounted her, which now that I think of it is like the remedy that Dr. Richard Von Krafft-Ebing, the famous nineteenth-century German psychiatrist, recommended for a shoe fetishist: His wife's high heel was to be nailed to the wall over their conjugal bed so that he could peer at it and be aroused sufficiently to perform his marital duties.

I didn't like my condition and I thought of contacting the Kinsey Institute and asking to be allowed to nurse on one hundred women lined up in a gymnasium. I thought that might heal me once and for all; the idea being to demystify the breast, to get my fill. Later, I did attempt such a cure on my own when I moved to New York in 1992 and frequented the suckling booths of a peep show on Forty-third Street, though I was often concerned about getting TB from the nipples of those women. They didn't seem to wash their boobs between clients, but I never developed a bad cough, and I think the cure worked on my breast problem—by 1993, after just a few months of steady nursing, I was interested in all parts of the female anatomy, including the penis. Turns out that right next to the peep show on Forty-third Street was a legendary tranny bar, Sally's. So I cured myself of my bosom condition and then right next door, I developed another problem, which took me years to get over. But this is one of the strengths of my character: When it comes to sexual fetishes, I can't be pigeonholed! I'm always changing, always growing!

Anyway, I've digressed, let me go back in time to late October of 1990, when I was still that wandering chick looking for the perfect nipple. I was flying back from Los Angeles and a friend picked me up at the airport in Philadelphia. It was around ten p.m. and I was tired, but on our way back to Princeton my friend, an older man, wanted to stop at a gay bar in New Hope, PA—the Provincetown of the Keystone state.

So into this gay bar, called the Cartwheel, we ventured. Being straightish, I didn't feel entirely at ease as we penetrated the establishment, which is often my reaction to gay bars. It's like how I, as a Conservative Jew, feel in Orthodox synagogues—I almost belong, but not quite. So I was very pleased when immediately on approaching the large circular, cartwheelish bar, a gorgeous, older blonde woman said to me, "Where have you been my whole life, baby? Look at those blonde eyelashes!"

She was sitting on a barstool and right away gathered me into her arms—she was a big woman, about six feet tall in a low-cut blouse and stylish skirt—and she began to make love to me, in the old-fashioned sense that is.

She looked to be in her late forties, had a beautiful smile, bedroom eyes that ate you up, glamorous long legs, and very important to the young, twenty-six year-old Jonathan—an ample, delicious bosom. Her breasts were as big as the ones my girlfriend had put in that painting! It was just about the quickest pickup of my life. She held me against her lovely, comforting chest, and we chatted happily and spontaneously. We were kindred spirits: she wanted to mother and I wanted to be mothered.

Well, our bar-side lovemaking went on for about an hour and then my friend, who brought me there, wanted to get back to Princeton. I kissed my new lady friend goodbye and she gave me her number, written on a Cartwheel napkin, and we promised one another that we would get together—a promise tinged with erotic possibility.

During the car ride home, my friend expressed his wonderment at my ability to pick up—or rather to be picked up—by the only woman in the bar. I was also impressed with myself, but guilty, too—my girlfriend the artist was waiting for me at home! I was a cad. But how could I have resisted?

Over the next two weeks, this older woman and I had

two or three quasi-erotic phone conversations. She lived a few towns away from Princeton and was acting in a local theater company—she had gone to the bar with some gay members of her troupe. We talked about getting together, but I kept postponing this: I was scared about cheating on my girlfriend.

I felt unfaithful, though, just by possessing that Cartwheel napkin—it seemed to burn inside my desk drawer where I had it hidden beneath unpaid bills. I would often look at that napkin, with its hastily scribbled name and phone number, and become guiltily excited—should I call or not call? Should I arrange an encounter? But then, in what felt like a heroic moment after a therapy session, I threw the number away! For all my faults, I loved my artist girl, and I never again saw or spoke to the woman from the bar.

Now let's fast-forward. The girl and I broke up two years later and I moved to New York, as I said, in 1992. I took my cure at the peep show and picked up my new fetish-condition at Sally's. Over the next several years, I wrote a novel, which was very much inspired by my tenure as a Sally's barfly. The book, *The Extra Man*, came out in 1998, and since that time I've often been solicited to provide blurbs for books with sexual content. For example, a few months ago, I was contacted, via email, by a publicist for Temple University Press who was hoping that I might read and blurb one of Temple's forthcoming books—the memoir of a transsexual. I happily assented and the book, in galley form was sent to me—*The Woman I was Not Born to Be: A Transsexual Journey*, by Aleshia Brevard.

I loved the book and found it absolutely fascinating and it inspired me to read several other transsexual memoirs.

These personal histories, like Ms. Brevard's, are very similar in structure to that classic literary model the bildungsroman, the coming-of-age novel. In fact, there is such a wealth now of transsexual memoirs that they are deserving of their own category, maybe "transhistory" or "transromance" or "genitomemoir." Well, I'll leave it to the Ph.D.'s, but I think I will go with my first suggestion.

The basic outline of the Transhistory is as follows: a boy or girl very early on in their life feels terribly uncomfortable in their gender role and there is a sense that some terrible mistake has occurred, that they were meant to be the other sex. Attempts are made—by parents or society—to reform them and they learn to repress as much as possible their instincts. Eventually— like the protagonist of the bildungsroman—they leave the home, their small world, and venture out, usually to a big city. There they begin to privately or publicly masquerade as the other sex, until eventually the masquerade goes beyond costume and posture and becomes permanent—especially in the latter part of the twentieth century with the advent of synthetic hormones and plastic and sex-change surgeries.

The third act to transhistories—first act: gender-dysphoric childhood; second act: the move to the big city and the transformation—is the aftermath of the sex change. In most of the books I've read, whether it be female-to-male or male-to-female transsexuals, the writer will not proclaim that great happiness has been found or that all their problems are solved, but they all do seem to express this feeling that they've done all they can (penises removed, breasts implanted; penises constructed, breasts removed; myriad other surgeries; great physical and psychological suffering) and they have come, finally, to a place of self-acceptance and peace. These are the success stories, though, and it takes a lot of courage to write them, but what of the transsexuals for whom gender reassignment doesn't work? To tell their story would take even more courage, if they even had the will to pen such a tale.

Aleshia Brevard's memoir follows this basic transhistory model and I'm happy to say that her tale is one of the success stories, and is one of the most amazing memoirs—transsexual or otherwise—I've ever read. Here's the Hollywood plot summary: Born in the late thirties on a farm in the south, as Alfred Brevard Crenshaw, but called Buddy; quits the farm and runs away to the West Coast, landing eventually in San Francisco, where he becomes a drag queen at the famous Finocchio's; performing as Lee Shaw in the late fifties, Buddy is perhaps the first Marilyn Monroe impersonator and achieves such a level of fame that MM herself comes to his show; during this time he meets the love of his life, a man named Hank, and so that they may be married, Buddy undergoes in 1962, at age twenty-three, a sex-change operation; as Aleshia the relationship with Hank sadly falls apart, but she goes to college, studies drama, and is twice voted "Actress of the Year"; after college there's a brief marriage, then a move to Los Angeles and a career as a B-movie and soap-opera actress and Playboy bunny—becoming the first transsexual Hollywood starlet, but all the while never revealing to Tinseltown her previous life as Buddy Crenshaw; there's also a second marriage and the role of mother to three stepsons.

This life story, which I've summarized with the barest-bone details, is told with incredible wit and grace and feeling. Especially moving is her portrait of her mother, Mozelle, this Southern woman who never stopped loving and supporting her child. Here's an incredible example of her mother's devotion (the day after the surgery):

... I was curious about the appearance of my vagina. I'd never seen one—and now I had my own. In fact, I had a brand-new one! I'd bought the darn thing sight unseen. I wanted to see exactly what it looked like.

The day after surgery, I asked for a hand mirror and tenderly positioned myself for my first peek at a vagina.

"GOOD GOD!" I shrieked. "What have they done to me? This looks like something you'd hang in your smokehouse ... after a hog killing."

I'd never seen anything so gross. It was swollen, red and WRINKLED . . . This thing needed to be ironed . . . I started to cry, which only made matters worse.

Mother rang for the nurse.

"You're perfectly normal," they both reassured me. "That's how you're supposed to look."

Who did they think they were fooling? I was having none of it.

"Like THIS?" I keened . . . This thing had folds! I was suddenly reminded of that unattractive rear view as I herded home the cows.

I was truly upset.

"We'll show you," my mother volunteered.

My mother and the Westlake Clinic's charge nurse both lifted their skirts, presenting me a view of not one but two naturally born vaginas. By golly, they did have folds. There were four outer labial folds on each vagina. Satisfied that I was normal, I drifted off to sleep.

• • •

Well, I absolutely adored this book and all the while as I read it I kept wondering why the name Aleshia Brevard was so familiar to me. I had this vague feeling that maybe I had spoken to Aleshia on a phone-sex line or something; it was kind of haunting. And I kept looking at her sexy pictures in the middle of the book and I found her, as Hollywood casting agents had, very beautiful—that's the other aspect of transhistories: incredible before-and-after photos. Then I got to the end of the memoir and there was a brief mention of having been in a small theater company in Princeton. She was the woman—though I couldn't quite recall the name, was it Aleshia Brevard?— whom I had met at the Cartwheel! I promptly emailed the publicist at Temple University Press: "I love the book and will happily give it a blurb. But there's something curious going on—I think I've met Aleshia. Can you ask her if she remembers meeting me at a bar in New Hope, PA, ten years ago?"

A few hours later the publicist forwarded an email to me from Aleshia Brevard. It was one line long: "Where have you been, baby?"

No Quiffs, Ends, or Buttocks about Tit!

Now Dig This: The Unspeakable Writings of Terry Southern, 1950–1995, by Terry Southern, edited by Niles Southern and Josh Alan Friedman, Grove Press

Bookforum, 2001

Where have all the ballsy writers gone? What's happened to the hard-drinking, ass-pinching American scribbler?

And, by the way, I'm not just talking about the ass-pinching of females, because Ginsberg, Burroughs, and Capote all qualify as ballsy. Furthermore, since I'm being politically inclusive (see previous sentence), we haven't just lost ballsy male writers, either. There used to be interesting (ballsy) women writers, too, like Lillian Hellman, Dorothy Parker, and Gertrude Stein. All of which leads me to ask: What the hell is going on out there? A whole breed has died off and nobody seems to have noticed. The Discovery Channel should be on top of this: "Writers with Charisma and Balls Have Disappeared!"

I don't know if it's global-warming, less nutrients in the soil, or estrogen in tap water, which would make women less ballsy, as well. But just in case you're not up on the latest science, let me explain: women pee out their birth-control pills into toilets; and toilet water, being water, eventually gets absorbed into the atmosphere, and then comes back down as a hormonal rain of sorts, which could explain the androgyny of Vermont, Canada, and the singer

Prince—he's also quite north, in Minnesota. Prince, being an artist, may have intuitively sensed what was going on and hence his song "Purple Rain," which was originally titled "Pink Rain," but the marketing people at his record company convinced him otherwise.

Aside from the possible scientific explanations for the death of ballsiness, there is an economic one, which I think may be the real cause: high rents. It's very hard to be a ballsy writer when you can't afford to live anywhere. It makes you absolutely nervous and insane and takes all your guts away. I have to say this is the case for yours truly. If I could pay a 1954 rent of fifty-eight dollars a month, I might actually be a ballsy writer. But I'm so crippled by my enormous twenty-first-century rent that I can barely get out of bed, let alone raise hell, which is what you need to do to qualify as a ballsy writer. You have to be a hell-raiser. You have to care about political things and you have to be able to afford booze, not to mention days lost to hangovers. But if you're worried all the time about having to go to live with your parents as a thirty-seven-year-old (something which is looming for yours truly, please send checks in my name to Thunder's Mouth Press), then to hell with hell. You only have one goal: to come up with the rent. You don't have time for political causes or all-night orgies.

Anyway, I've been led to all this serious conjecture about the Death-of-the-Ballsy-American-Scribbler after reading *Now Dig This: The Unspeakable Writings of Terry Southern*, which is a posthumous collection of writings by, well, Terry Southern. Now this guy was the ballsy writer of all ballsy writers. He had a good time, pinched a lot of asses, and raised a lot of hell! He's considered a founder, if not the founder of New Journalism (Thompson and

Wolfe followed his lead), and some of his credits include: four novels, the most famous being the comic-erotic novel *Candy* (a spoof of Candide); the screenplays for *Dr. Strangelove, Easy Rider*, and *Barbarella*; scads of articles for, to name a few publications, *Esquire, Rolling Stone, The National Lampoon*, and *The Nation* (back when those magazines were ballsy magazines; wait a second—could there be a connection between the death of the ballsy writer and the ballsy magazine? Would somebody at the Discovery Channel please get on this! I don't like the burden of having to educate people, I'm not ballsy enough!); and friendships with just about every interesting person who was running around in the latter half of the twentieth century.

But in getting ready to write this review, I mentioned the name Terry Southern to people in the Quality Lit game (a phrase of Southern's; he had a particularly wonderful animus for *The New Yorker*), and he seems to have the reputation of a writer who fell short—"Oh, yeah, Terry Southern," they'll say, as if they feel snootily sorry for him. Then they mention booze or Hollywood, and there's no doubt that both those things can kill a writer's work and kill the writer, and this may have been the case with T.S., but he certainly did not fall short! That is absolute bullshit. There's no quiffs, ends, or buttocks about tit! This guy was amazing and I wish he was still around swinging his balls and if you haven't read him, then pick up *Now Dig This* and you'll get a great introduction to one of our country's most unique and compelling writers.

The thing I admire most about Southern is that he was spectacularly hyper-versatile, which is in full display in this collection: New Journalism pieces, serious book reviews, comic-erotic riffs, skits, letters, and fiction. In short, Terry Southern could do it all; he was like a radio station that played rock, jazz, and classical music. Some of my favorites in this book are his account of the Democratic Convention of '68, which he attended with Burroughs, Ginsberg, and Jean Genet; a piece about private detectives, which includes information about the drug case against Lenny Bruce; and a tribute to Kurt Vonnegut, which ends up being, primarily, a description of a Parisian brothel, Le Maison de Lange, and its house specialty, a supremely exotic blowjob ritual called Le Cercle des Enfants du Paradise.

So rush out and pick up *Now Dig This*, and if you have a little something extra in your pocket after you buy the book, well then do write that check for yours truly.* For what it's worth, I'd think you were really ballsy for doing so.

*Editor's Note: Checks made out to Jonathan Ames can now be sent to Jonathan Ames c/o Thunder's Mouth Press, 161 William Street, NY, NY 10038

Part V:
Essays with Sexual Content
(A warning or a recommendation, depending on your personality)

The Eulenspiegel Society
New York Press, 1996

In October of 1992, around the time of the presidential election, I was trying to write a novel about someone with lots of sexual perversions. It was to be a veiled autobiography. But I also needed to do some supplemental research. A friend, a woman who liked to bind and slightly strangle men with their own neck-ties, recommended that I attend a meeting of the Eulenspiegel Society.

"It's a support group for people into S&M," she said. "There'll be good material for you."

"Perfect. I'll go so I can write about it," I said, my usual excuse for anything perverted I like to do.

I called the Eulenspiegel Society and the answering-machine tape told me that the group was meeting that Tuesday night at eight o'clock and the topic of discussion was submissive men and their toys. The group met at 24 Bond Street, an interesting coincidence, I noted, for an S&M society.

I arrived a little before eight and the meeting was being held in an actor's studio and theater. In the narrow lobby of this theater, S&Mers were lined up to pay admission. I joined in and on the wall to my right there was a row of head shots of midwestern waiters and waitresses—the current acting troupe—and there were also some old photos of Frank Langella in a play during his youth.

At the entrance to the theater, I paid my five dollars to a diminutive mistress-type wearing a leather bra and high black boots. She gave me a little pamphlet about the society.

"Thank you," I said. "It's my first time here." I was being friendly. But she didn't acknowledge me. She was in her role. I admired this.

I entered the theater. It was a typical boxlike performing space. Black walls, black curtains in the back, and a high ceiling. For the meeting, chairs were arranged in a circle on the stage floor and people were seating themselves.

I took a seat, and feeling shy, I studied my pamphlet, which told me the origin of the society's name. It had come from a passage in a book by Theodore Reik, called *Masochism in Modern Man*. The passage was reproduced and I read that in German folklore there are many tales about a young lad, a rogue, named Til Eulenspiegel. He liked the pain of walking up hills because he knew there would be pleasure in going down. But then when going down a hill, he thought of the pain of going up the next hill, so he realized it was much more pleasurable to go up a hill. His discomfort became joy. This, according to Reik, was the essence of masochism, and the tap root of the Eulenspiegel Society, which was originally founded by masochists. Along with the passage from Reik, there was a nice little ink drawing of a smiling German boy, someone's idea of Til, and his lederhosen were dropped and he was proffering his rear for a spanking.

The meeting was called to order by a large black mistress.

She had light chocolate skin, a kind mouth, and wonderful gigantic breasts held in by a leather halter. She welcomed us to the society, newcomers and members alike, and she said with enthusiasm, "We're here because sex and role-playing are fun!"

Then we had to go around the circle and introduce ourselves and tell everyone the role we liked to play and the things we liked to do.

"Howard, submissive, I like paddling and nipple torture."

"Cheryl, dominant, I like to be worshipped."

"Steven, switchable, I like to be lit on fire, and I like flogging."

And so it went. When it was my turn, I said that I was undecided, and no one gave me a hard time. They were understanding, tolerant. It was kind of like a twelve-step group, except that at the Eulenspiegel Society one's madness was being embraced, rather than rooted out. I felt guilty for being a sneaky writer looking for material, but in my own way, I belonged. I can take on a perversion if I am surrounded by like people. It's the same thing with sports. I can switch the teams I root for with great ease. I'm like a tree frog—I adapt to my surroundings, whether they be sports or fetish oriented.

Around the circle there were about twenty people, mostly middle-aged men who spoke intelligently and with feeling about their roles and their particular fetishes. There was also a couple from New Jersey, as plain as you could get, but the man was dressed just like his wife in a green dress and red wig, which added an interesting twin-spin to their relationship. There was one young man whose head and body were completely shaved and he was wearing a leather diaper. He was banging his knees together in happy nervousness. I was intrigued by an attractive young Hispanic couple who looked shy and said they were first-timers. And besides the Mistress and her assistant who had given me the pamphlet, there were only two single women. They were friends and looked like office types. They wore simple blouses and skirts that went to the knee.

After our introductions, the Mistress told us that toys could enhance submissiveness, and then she said, "I mentioned it at the last submissive men's meeting—did anyone bring toys?"

"Show and tell!" said one of the middle-aged men, and everyone laughed. It was a benign gathering, I felt. People sharing a hobby. It wasn't dark or devious. The high school equivalent would have been the chess club.

"I have something," said a tall man in his fifties, who was casually dressed in corduroy pants and a sweater. He had an earnest face and he wore wire-rimmed glasses. He took a paper bag from underneath his chair and from it he removed a rubber hair brush with plastic bristles with red tips. "I bought this in a regular drug store, Duane Reade," he said. "It was *only* four dollars." The economy of this was very important to him. It *was* a good price. "The bristles are extremely firm and the handle is . . . serrated." He held up the brush for the group to look at. "Only four dollars," he repeated.

"See," said the Mistress, "you don't have to order from the catalogs. We all know how expensive they are. You can be *creative* with everyday items and turn anything into a toy." She looked at the man and his brush, "Have you tried it out yet?"

"No," he said demurely.

"Demonstration!" shouted a Eulenspiegeler. We all laughed good-naturedly.

The hairbrush man was brought into the center of the circle. He was smiling. All eyes were on him. He was popular. The Mistress ordered another man to bring a chair into the circle.

"Take off your glasses," she said to the hairbrush man. He put them on the chair. "Drop your pants." He dropped his nice corduroys. "Underwear too." Down came his briefs, they were clean. I had a direct view of his cheeks, which were sinking inward from years of gravity and were covered with wispy gray hairs. He was told to bend over the chair and I was prepared to be horrified, but he discreetly tightened his weak buttocks to keep things closed.

The mistress strode behind him and she was wearing a black mini-skirt, and I was treated to a whole other kind of ass. Each cheek was like a large, filled laundry bag. I found it quite appealing.

She began to smack him with the brush, and with each stroke he and the chair galloped an inch forward.

"Hold still!" she finally shouted, and I thought that this was all pretty good for the five dollars I had paid. Like the brush man, I appreciated a bargain.

I watched his cheeks blush, even through the strands of hair. I realized it looked like my father's ass, which I hadn't seen in years. I wondered if my rear would turn out so flaccid. After five minutes of being smacked, the man was allowed to pull up his pants. He turned and faced my side of the room. He was smiling after his beating, happy to have broken in his new brush, but he had no erection. A small purple penis hid in thick, dark, unkempt old-man pubic hair. That's too bad, I thought. Potency problems. But he seems happy.

He pulled up his pants and sat down gingerly. The brush was passed around for us to look at. I had seen similar models and I passed it quickly, though I didn't think I could get germs from the handle, but, nonetheless, I did feel a little squeamish.

After this paddling, the Mistress walked about the circle and then addressed an obvious favorite of hers. "I know someone who's wearing toys right now," she said to a small man in his forties with just a fringe of brown hair around his nicely shaped narrow head. He was wearing a shirt and tie and his pants were worn several inches above his hips. He had the look of an engineer. Obeying the Mistress's command, he stripped down in front of us and his body was chalk-white and hairless, and he was wearing a metal chastity belt! It was silver and as thick as a paperback novel, covering mostly his groin area, and was clamped about him with some kind of circular belt.

Under his chair was a little duffel bag and from this he took out two metal clamps, which he attached to his nipples, but the clamps mostly sucked up white flesh since his nipples were meager and as small as a cat's.

The Mistress sat down and he stood in the middle of the circle and fielded questions from the group.

"How do you urinate?"

"Special grill."

"Can you get erect?"

"Semi."

"Do you bathe?"

"Yes."

"Does it rust?"

"No. Stainless steel."

"How long have you been wearing your chastity belt?"

"Four weeks with a two-day break."

"Who has the key?"

He pointed to the Mistress. He had answered all the

questions with a passionless, scientific detachment. When he was done, he sat down and I saw how the belt cut into his thighs.

After that the group began to have general sharing and the boy in the leather diaper was profoundly narcissistic and wouldn't stop talking about himself in the most boring way, and I found this tiresome and I left. I didn't think anything would top what I had already witnessed.

The next day I met an older friend of mine for coffee. He was a seventy-two-year-old former actor and was mildly loony. He looked like Richard Burton, had Burton lived another difficult fifteen years or so. We were in our favorite Greek diner and looking at our newspapers, which we liked to do between bouts of conversation. My friend wasn't a Republican—he said he was a monarchist, that his ideal country would have a King and also a Bishop to instill moral order—but it was the fall of '92 and he hated the upstart Democratic candidate, the forty-six-year-old Clinton. I, on the other hand, loved Clinton.

My friend was reading about the imminent election, and he said, "I can't stand this Clinton. He wants to let gays in the military. He'll destroy it. They should especially leave the Navy alone. They're happy homos the way they are. If you bring these things to the surface it causes too many problems. Clinton doesn't understand that we need hypocrisy."

"We need hypocrisy?"

"Yes, it keeps people from getting at each other's throats."

"I like Clinton," I said.

"You're young. You're sick. The whole country is sick. There's too much sex going on. It's clear that this Clinton is a sex fiend and that's why you like him. He needs to be locked up. All young people need to be locked up, but not with one another. That may be the only solution."

"Chastity belts could be a way to lock people up, but let them be free at the same time," I said, thinking of my visit the night before to the Eulenspiegel Society.

"Yes, that's not bad," said my slightly mad friend. "We should look into this. Get a machine shop to mass-produce them and sell them at church bazaars. First I could give a sermon on the virtues of chastity and then we could peddle the things. I wonder how much it costs to make a chastity belt? I'll write a letter to Cardinal O'Connor. We can get the Church to finance it and we'll sneak a profit."

Well, like most great plans, that one never came to fruition, and now four years later Clinton has just been elected to a *second* term, and I was thinking that I should look in on the Eulenspiegel Society again. I'm still writing my veiled autobiography about someone with perversions and I thought a Eulenspiegel meeting would be good for me. I went back on a Tuesday night to Bond Street and the topic was long-term S&M relationships. At the start of the meeting two upcoming events were announced—an evening about interrogation, how to do it, and a whipping workshop, with emphasis on flogging with some discussion on the use of the single-tail whip. As four years before, I was again struck by the hobbyist nature of the group.

For the discussion on long-term relationships there was a panel of four couples fielding questions. There was a much bigger crowd than the meeting I went to in '92—S&M seems to be booming along with the economy—and there was lots of laughing and clapping going on. The panelists were in front of us on the stage and the rest of us sat in a small bleacher section.

The first question from the audience was: "Do you stay in your roles twenty-four seven?"

One of the panelists, a young, chubby, voluptuous woman in a skimpy black dress, said, "I always know that I am his, even when we're apart. So I am submissive all the time."

But another panelist, a sensible bald man in leather, said, "You have to be realistic, you can't beat someone all day long." Everyone laughed.

A young couple, affectionately looked at as the novices on the panel because they had only been together one year (everyone else had experienced at least six years of commitment), were a dominant woman/submissive man pair. The woman, who was very overweight, but had a pretty face and a bright person-ality, told the story of their relationship: "We met at one of the clubs and I was tying up a friend of mine. She was on a table and I looked over and there was this blonde guy. He was cute—he wore a collar. He helped me with the ropes. *We met over my friend*," she said and she had to stop a moment because everyone laughed and applauded at her joke, and then she continued, "and we've been together ever since, for one year. But we're not in our roles twenty-four seven. I only dress him up a few times a week—and he looks better in my things than I do, and we're the same shoe size, so that saves money—but when we do do it I think it's important for us to really get into our roles, to make an effort, to rein-force why we're together, and cross-dressing, I find, is really helpful. Makes our roles very clear." She then slapped her blonde boyfriend and he smiled.

I stayed for about an hour and then I left. There were no demonstrations like last time with the hairbrush and the chastity belt, and so I got bored. When something's not your hobby, you can only take so much. Also, the couples were a bit self-congratulatory. They were sort of gloating that they were in long-term relationships and I found this grating. I guess they are to be applauded, but I just wasn't in the mood.

The next day, to keep things mirroring the events of four years past, I called my old nutty friend. I hadn't spoken to him for several months and it was time to check up on him, and also I wanted to hear his views of the election. After we had exchanged our initial greetings, I asked, rubbing it in, "So what do you think about Clinton winning?"

"I think Clinton is Hillary, and Hillary is Clinton. Cross-dressers! This way he can commit all his crimes and not be impeached. You can't impeach the wife, though I wish you could."

"Cross-dressing can be a sign of a healthy relationship," I said, thinking of the young Eulenspiegel couple.

"Cross-dressing is for criminals like Clinton to hide their identity."

"Clinton doesn't commit any crimes," I said. "That whole Whitewater thing is just hot air."

"You voted for him again, didn't you?"

"Of course," I said.

"There's really something wrong with you. You're not getting any better. Why don't you go hang out at a VFW. They'll knock some sense into you."

My friend was wacky but that was a pretty good idea. I was tired of the Eulenspiegel Society. I need new material and so I wondered what kind of meetings they have at the

VFW. If there's a sex angle there, especially if the vets are old gay sailors, I could be the first to discover it, like an anthropologist meeting an untouched tribe on the Amazon. Could be very interesting.

Some Thoughts on the Crapper

Gawk, a now extinct Internet
magazine, 1997

This morning I woke up with a good-sized erection. I was next to my girlfriend and the slight contact of her leg caused this to happen. My girlfriend likes it when I have a morning erection. She likes my penis. She says it's fat. Not long, but fat.

For my taste it's too pink and rather ugly. My girlfriend once saw a thickly muscled, whitish-pink dog, the kind that has small eyes and was once used in beer commercials, and she said, "That dog looks like your penis." I objected, though secretly I concurred. I also think that I see things growing on my penis and a doctor friend of mine told me that all men have skin-plaque on their penises. I'd like to dip my penis in some flossing-mouthwash solution and remove that plaque. Actually that's not a bad idea. Johnson and Johnson, which has a fitting name, should come up with some sort of penis-wash that removes penis-plaque. Johnson-Wash. It's a winning name.

Unfortunately and one of the points of this essay is that I almost dipped my penis in the toilet bowl this morning. I had my morning erection, as I mentioned above, but I also had to take my morning crap. Lately my bowels have been regular and good because I was taking these herb tablets and psyllium tablets, but generally my digestion is poor. Though I try to take my own advice, which I once gave to a semi-constipated girlfriend: "Be grateful for whatever comes out." I dispense this advice, because if you know anything about health, you know how essential and vital it is to get the waste out of us. Detoxify at all costs.

So this morning I walked into the bathroom and was worried about my erection. I tried to do a yoga breath to make my penis wilt. Men will understand why I needed my cock to go down, but women might not know that you can't have a bowel movement if you have a hard-on. Hard-ons take precedence over everything. They override all other functions. It's Darwinism at play.

So if you don't let your erection wilt completely what happens is that when you sit on the toilet and push your cock down into the bowl to piss, you get erect again. At least I do. The pushing down must excite me, even though I don't want to be excited. So I really need to let my cock go down, but I'm almost always too impatient to let the thing deflate completely and I end up with a big erection just when I need to shit and then things get quite complicated. I really am an idiot. I never learn. I make the same mistakes over and over again in life. Don't fall in love with people who psychologically resemble your parents—yet I do it every time. Don't drink alcohol, you're alcoholic—yet every couple of years or months or days, I think I can handle a drink. Don't try to take a shit when you're semi-erect, you'll wreak havoc—and yet I do it every time. It happened this morning. I was semi-erect and hoped that this time it would be different. I pushed my penis down toward the water to piss before shitting (a necessary order of events) and the thing became rebelliously erect again. I was presented with my usual problems.

My cock expanded and the head of my penis was speeding for the underlip of the bowl, where all sorts of horrible micro-organisms and stray pubic hairs collect. And this was my girlfriend's toilet, which she shares with her roommate—*a man*! I knew that all sorts of his weird stuff was caught in that underlip. So just before my growing cock kissed that lip, I hurriedly pointed it down but then it skimmed the cold germ-infested water, which was at hightide. Why is life so insane? I then yanked my wet-with-toilet-water cock straight up, but now I was in danger if I pissed of having urine hit me in the face. So I took my cock, like a gear shift, and sought a compromise position: I skirted the very top of the cold water and aimed the nozzle to shoot at a target just below the toilet lip. I let the urine flow. I hoped my aim would be true, that I would fire just below the lip and not shoot over the edge and splatter against the wall. This was a real worry because when I piss out of an erection my accuracy goes down markedly. I'm like a shotgun when erect—I scatter fire.

But disaster was averted. The urine stayed in the bowl. I was able to relax now and my penis went down. It was blessedly soft. So then my sphincter relaxed—a kind of chain reaction—and I was able to release my bowels. But how tawdry life is. Why must I shit? I have to remember, though, that we all defecate. I think it would be very helpful to people if we saw movie stars going to the bathroom. Self-esteem across the nation would skyrocket.

But since there are no public service announcements of this sort, I was shitting and worrying like crazy about the noises I was making, the wheezing of gas that was going on. I was terribly frightened that my girlfriend had awakened and was listening to me—her room is right next to the toilet and the walls are paper thin—so I hurried my bowel movement. I then flushed, got off the can, and while washing my hands I realized that I wasn't finished. I had double-clutched my shit. I hate when this happens. I'm so anxious to get it over with that I rush and then flush and think I'm done, but I'm not. Then the person outside the toilet hears me crap again and flush again and they can't believe what's going on in there. You see, whatever toilet I'm on someone is always listening to me and feeling loathing for me—when it comes to shitting I'm afraid that I have some paranoid schizophrenic tendencies, but only in this one arena. Anyway, a double-clutch on the toilet means double the time in the bathroom and double the embarrassment. But things can actually get worse: there's always the fear, which is sometimes realized, that the second flush won't work so soon after the first flush. Then you have to wait for the tank to refill—like waiting for your cock to go down; patience, you idiot!—and flush a *third time*!

Well, I sat back down on the toilet this morning, finished my movement, felt like a fool, flushed again (it worked), washed the hands again, and returned to my girlfriend's room. She was still asleep. It was only eight o'clock in the morning and I had already been to war.

I crawled back into bed and masturbated a little to soothe myself after my nightmarish start to my day. My girlfriend woke up a few minutes later and reached for my cock. She held on to it like a pacifier and said in a sleepy voice, "I love how you're so erect in the morning."

I didn't let her know that this was an artificial morning erection, nor did I tell her what I had been through. This is an example of human isolation. We can never fully be known. But it's better that way. Why puncture her happiness by revealing to her the hell of my inner life? It might be her only dose of joy all day long. She squeezed my cock tight. "I love it," she said, sweetly.

"I know," I said, "I know you love it."

The Gay Nineties
New York Press, 1998

"That's Annie Sprinkle," said my friend. We were at a publication party for the book Miss Vera's Finishing School for Boys Who Want to Be Girls.

"Are her breasts real?" I asked; Annie Sprinkle's bosom was enormous in a very attractive way. Her cleavage was the length of a yellow legal pad.

"Oh, yeah, they're real," said my friend with authority; he's a connoisseur of performance artists and porn stars. He's a forty-year-old casting director and has been running around New York for twenty years trying to get laid. And he does pretty well. "Have you seen Annie Sprinkle's work?" he asked.

"No, I'm a Philistine," I said. "But I've heard of her."

"In one of her videos she ejaculates a white liquid when she has an orgasm."

"From her breasts? Breast milk?"

"No from her pussy. She's a female ejaculator. I'd love to have a woman come like that in my mouth."

"But what's the white stuff? Yeast?"

"Don't be disgusting," said my friend.

"I wasn't trying to be disgusting," I said, "but all the liquids I've encountered down there are usually clear."

"Well, she shoots white stuff. I can't explain it."

"I guess that's why she's called Annie Sprinkle."

In addition to Ms. Sprinkle, there were lots of other celebrities at this party—all the Matriarchs and Frontiers–women of Sex. Leading the bill was Veronica Vera, the author for whom the party was being thrown, and the self-proclaimed dean and founder of the world's first cross-dressing academy, which has the same title as her book. And since this is the gay nineties, I should make it clear that Miss Vera, as she is known, is a biological female.

Throughout the party, held at 304 Hudson Street, she was on a small, elevated stage overlooking all of us revelers. She's a lovely mature brunette, who epitomizes the adjective "Rubenesque." She was wearing a beautiful pink gown and a sparkling tiara. And like Annie Sprinkle, Miss Vera has an inviting bosom. It's not as big, but it looked very comforting to my needy eyes. When she addressed all of us from her royal perch, she said, "I feel like a princess."

To celebrate this publication of her first book, she had several of her students and friends come onstage and model jewelry. This was when all the Matriarchs of Sexuality came out. There was Candida Royale, a curvy, movie-starrish blonde, who looked to be in her early forties.

"She was a porn star in the seventies and now she produces porn," said my friend, the expert.

There was Dr. Susan M. Block, another forty-something blonde. She had wild eyes and was wearing red panties and a red bra and a feathery scarf. Her name was familiar to me and I realized she was a Doctor of Sex; I had called her 900 number years ago and spent a lot of money.

Then a stocky, gray-haired woman in black pants came

onstage. "She teaches women how to masturbate with dildoes," said my friend. "They sit in a circle."

"You know everything," I said.

Then there was Kate Bornstein, a tall, glamorous post-operative transsexual. Also blonde. According to my friend, she's a monologist who talks about getting a sex-change so that she could be a lesbian. "She published an article in the *New York Times* about it," he said. "And she went to Brown University back in the sixties."

"Well, Brown has always been very liberal," I sniffed.

After the jewelry show, it was back to simple drinking and gawking. There was a nice crowd to look at—several cross-dressers, publishing types, sexy young waitresses. My friend and I went to the free cheese plate, which I found disappointing. I had been hoping for fancier hors d'oeuvres and purposely didn't eat dinner before the party.

While munching on a cracker with a cube of cheddar, I said to my friend, "All these famous sex women are kind of old." Now it's not polite to remark on a women's ages, but I thought it was interesting that Vera, Sprinkle, Block, Royale, the dildo professor, and Bornstein could all be classified as middle-aged.

"What's wrong with that?" asked my friend.

"Nothing," I said. "It's social commentary. They're feminist pioneers who have survived. And pioneer life is very rigorous, so they're to be commended."

"I like older women," said my friend, not really listening to me.

"Me, too," I said. "They're much more understanding of impotence."

Then somebody walked past me and squeezed my ass. I turned and a cute face smiled at me. The lighting was dim, which was very thoughtful for all the cross-dressers present, and my ass-squeezer appeared to be a girl dressed as a boy. She had a page-boy haircut and was wearing a tweed coat that was extremely narrow at the waist. She walked away from me and smiled over her shoulder. My friend witnessed the whole transaction. "Was that a girl dressed as a boy?" I asked hopefully.

"No, I think it was a boy dressed as a boy, but in a feminine manner," he said, and then he left me to go to the bathroom.

I resumed my gawking at the crowd and then my ass was pinched again. It was her. I looked at the face closely—it was him. He took my arm and squeezed it.

"You're very beautiful," he whispered and he spoke with an English accent.

"You're very forward," I said.

He tried to kiss me. And he had to aim up, since I had a good six inches on him. I moved my mouth and he caught my manly chin. "I don't kiss on the first minute," I said.

"Come get a glass of champagne," he said, and wove his arm through mine and led me to the bar.

"I won't have any, I only drink temperance beverages, but you can have one," I said. And since he was holding on to me like a woman, I thought I should do the gentlemanly thing and order his drink for him. When the champagne came it was twelve dollars—there my chivalry ended.

"I forgot, I spent all my money on a taxi," I lied. "I'm sorry, but you'll have to pay for it." And he didn't protest at all, which was only right since he had invited me to the bar. He sipped his champagne and said again, "You're very beautiful."

I wanted to correct him and point out that I am balding. But I realized that the lighting, good for transvestites, was also good for my hair. My comb-back of my front-fringe over my enormous bald spot was working in such dim light. So I let him remain deluded.

"What do you do for a living?" I asked.

"I design costumes and make corsets," he said.

"Are you wearing a corset now?" I asked—this explained his feminine and narrow waist.

"Yes," he said.

"I had to wear a corset as a boy," I said.

"Of course you did," he said, and he went to kiss me again, and he got my ear. I didn't have a chance to tell him that my childhood corset was for back spasms because then a friend of his, a very tall Scandinavian boy with yellow curls, joined us. He was wearing a coat with a sumptuous fur collar. Introductions were made and then Yellow Curls said, "You're very blonde."

"So are you," I said, and I wondered if from his angle above me if he could see the bald spot.

"Are you going to be our new friend?" he asked with a jaded smirk.

"One never knows," I said.

His cigarette, because he was so tall, was held at the level of my eyes. I was blinded by the smoke, but stoically didn't say anything. Then the corset-maker reached out and stroked my chest, and Yellow Curls winked at me. These two were the kind of dandies I had only read about. If I wasn't careful some kind of drawing-room prison rape was going to take place.

I saw my friend in the crowd looking for me. This was my chance for an exit. "I have to go," I said. "My friend knows no one here. He'll panic."

My small suitor quickly pressed upon me his card. "Thank you," I said and dashed over to my friend.

"Let's go," I said. "Those two would have taken me to an opium bar. My virtue was in danger."

At the coat check, we were given gift bags filled with cosmetics and shampoos, courtesy of Miss Vera. It was a very nice touch and a pleasant ending to a fascinating party.

When I got home I looked at the card the boy had given me. There was a family crest under the his name and when I examined it closely I saw that the two angels holding the patriarchal shield were wearing corsets.

Friending
Edifice Rex, an Internet
magazine, 2000

*I have a dear friend, R, who for the last year has been in
something of a slump with women. His happiness is important to me—I care for the fellow—so I gladly and frequently
serve as a sounding board. Chiefly what I do is listen to him
while he attempts to decode the behaviors of the women he's
trying to court. The most recent case was interesting, I think,
because R several times in our conversations used the word*
friend *as a verb.*

"Jonathan," said R, calling me on the phone, "I need
your help with the latest girl I'm interested in."

"I will strain every nerve," I said, enthusiastically.

"We had a first date. Good dinner, good conversation.
We're in the same field. Then I walked her home. There
was that awkward moment, but I leaned in and got a little
kiss on the lips. I left feeling fine."

"So far, so good."

"I called a few days later and suggested another
dinner and she counter-proposed a coffee. But no firm
date was set because her schedule is hectic. I sensed that
by suggesting a coffee instead of dinner that she was
friending me."

"Friending. That's very interesting. I see what you mean."

"But then there was an interesting development. I ran into her at Barnes & Noble and she kissed me on the cheek and told me to call. So would a woman who kisses me on the cheek at a bookstore be friending me?"

"I don't think so. I think that clearly indicates physical affection."

"That was my thinking. So I called and last night we had another date. Everything was fine. She laughed at my jokes; she seemed to like me. Then I made a move to walk her home, but she said I didn't have to. But you have to walk the woman home. I insisted, but inside I was dying. At her door she barely gave me a kiss on the cheek. I came home and took two sleeping pills. But then two days later, I got a phone message. Let me play it for you."

What I heard was a sweet young lady's voice telling R that she'd had a lovely, fun time and looked forward to seeing him again.

"That's very positive," I said.

"She wouldn't leave a message like that if she was friending me, right?"

"I think it's unlikely that she's friending," I said, though it wasn't easy for me to use this grammatically incorrect term. "I think you should feel encouraged."

Well, R called her again. He asked her out for a drink. She said she was having dinner with a friend that night and could the friend come also for a drink. R balked, said he'd prefer to see her one on one. He tried to set up a date for another night. She said her week was very busy, but that she'd call him when it cleared up. The young lady has never called.

"In the end, I wasn't even friended," he said.

"It's for the best," I said. "You wanted to be girl-friended not friended. Probably better to have it this way, otherwise you'd feel conflicted. Now it's clear where you stand."

"I know where we stand, but I feel like I'm sitting."

His voice was rich with melancholy. Shortly thereafter we rang off. I had to leave him to lick his wounds, but I'll be there, ready to be his friend, to friend him, the next time he calls.

Penis Enlargement
Gear Magazine, 2000

The first time a girl puts her hand in my pants, I'm always hoping that my penis will feel big to her, substantial. But sometimes the new girl in my life will put her hand down in my pants at the precise moment that my erection—because it has a life of its own, the damn thing—has temporarily gone down. "Why couldn't she have grabbed it ten seconds ago?" I often wail in my mind. In these tragic moments, I hope that the girl, while she's holding my small offering, is forgiving and understanding of the male anatomy.

My particular male anatomy—my penis that is—is an adequate size, I think. I'm no Kentucky Derby winner, if you know what I mean, but I seem to cross the finish line admirably.

Still, I wouldn't mind being a little bigger and that's because sometimes I have been bigger. Once or twice a year, I notice that my penis is significantly larger. With about the frequency of a lunar eclipse, I will observe, as I am about to mount a woman, that I am more endowed than normal. "Why can't I be like this all the time?" I have wondered during these unusual priapic episodes.

So having said all this you can understand why I was

very intrigued when an editor at *Gear* sent me on an assignment to meet a female hypnotist, Laurie Straub, whose specialty is penis enlargement, or rather, I should say, Penis Enlargement, which is how it is referred to in Ms. Straub's brochures.

Before meeting Ms. Straub, I spoke to her on the phone, and she told me, "I don't want to mislead you—I can't enlarge your penis in one session. My program is a twelve-week program. What you'll be getting is an introduction."

"So I won't significantly change after one meeting?"

"No, but you will feel *something*. Probably a tingling sensation in the scrotum. And since you'll be in an open, suggestive state we can throw something else in to work on while we're at it, if you like. But not cigarette smoking. That would take two sessions. What most men like to do is get their penis enlarged and stop procrastinating," she said.

"That sounds ideal," I said. "It would be great to have a larger penis *and* pay my bills on time."

Ms. Straub is a tall, statuesque, good-looking woman in her mid-thirties, who bears a resemblance to the actress Renee Russo. My hypnosis session was held at her fashionable New York City apartment, but before she put me under, we discussed, as we sat in her living room, how exactly she goes about enlarging penises.

"I know more about your penis than you do!" she said good-naturedly. "A lot of people say that the penis is a muscle. It's not! It's soft tissue filled with blood. Three cylinders of soft tissue. One forms the head, two others form the shaft. Soft tissue expands more easily than muscle; that's why it can be enlarged. It's like fat."

"Three cylinders," I said, flinching. "I didn't know that."

"And I bet you didn't know that your penis is actually up in your body a couple of inches. If you try to make it bigger through surgery, they cut ligaments to drop it and you have to wear weights attached to your penis to keep it down. That's no good. And to make it wider it's even worse—they insert fat. Then the penis is lumpy. Not like you want it at all. My method is completely natural."

Ms. Straub was led to natural Penis Enlargement through her work in natural Breast Enlargement, which has been a staple of the hypnosis market for several years now, whereas expanding the penis is brand-new—Ms. Straub is just about the only practitioner in the country.

The principle behind expanding breasts and penises, according to Ms. Straub, is that hypnosis "taps" the part of the brain known as the hypothalamus. By controlling the hypothalamus, hypnotists put you into a state of relaxation, which Ms. Straub describes as being a place between wakefulness and sleep. The hypothalamus, according to Ms. Straub, along with being able to relax a person, also controls the pituitary gland. Ms. Straub believes that her program enables people to stimulate their pituitary gland, which will then release hormones—creating a sort of second pubescence—and this release of hormones can increase the size of your penis or breasts depending on what you have, breasts or penis that is.

Furthermore, her program works on stimulating nerves and increasing blood flow. She operates on the principle that we can get our bodies to do anything—from overcoming disease to increasing the size of our penises.

But her approach isn't simply physiological. There is also a psychological angle to the whole thing. Through hypnosis, she hopes to guide men back to earlier emotional traumas that may have inhibited the growth of their penises. Her twelve-week program, which consists of listening to tapes twenty minutes a day, is, she said, "a lot about undoing issues that keep you smaller."

"Almost all men," she explained further, "when they were little boys saw their father's big penis, and then they would look at their little one. This is very intimidating. Or a girl in the sixth grade says, 'You have a small dick.' And you hold on to that. I had one client tell me about his son coming into the bathroom and saying, 'Daddy, you have a big penis.' And I told him, 'I hope you told your son he has a big one, too; otherwise, he's going to come see me in twenty years!' So one of the main goals of my program is to get men feeling good about themselves. If they feel good, they can make their penis bigger."

We then decided it was time for me to be hypnotized. She pulled a chair alongside my own and asked me to close my eyes. With soothing New Age music tinkling in the background, she talked me through a relaxation of my whole body and then had me slowly clap my hands together as if they were drawn by magnets to one another, which was her way to test her control of me. She hadn't hypnotized me with a swinging watch, like in the movies, but just with the sound of her voice, which is why she is able to market her program through the sale of cassette tapes.

So once my body was relaxed and my mind hypnotized, she had me visualize that I was in a bathtub and that warm, beautiful, magical water was swirling around my penis, and that my penis felt healthy and good. Then she told me my penis was getting longer and longer as the water whirled and swirled. In my mind's eye, I then saw my penis emerging out of this turbulent bubble bath (I added the bubbles) and it was wonderfully large. And in real life, sitting in that chair, I was getting a hard-on in my pants and I wondered if Ms. Straub noticed this. You can have thoughts like this while hypnotized—your mind is very much your own, just suggestible.

For several minutes—though it was hard to judge time—she kept talking in her soothing voice about my elongating penis and the swirling magical waters, but she would also emphasize that I was growing in a healthy way, that everything else was staying the size it should. I knew that she was referring, without saying it directly, to my prostate. In this day and age of ubiquitous prostate cancer, this must be a delicate subject for Ms. Straub. I'm sure that concerned clients have asked her if their prostate gland would enlarge through her program, and so she kept telling me that only the parts of my penis which could healthfully expand were expanding.

She then brought me out of the hypnosis and it was like coming to after a very good massage. I was supremely relaxed.

"How do you feel," she asked.

"Very good."

"Did you feel anything in your scrotum or penis?"

"I became aroused. Is that normal?"

"Most men just feel a tingling. But it's not too abnormal. Some men ask me if they can masturbate during the tapes. I tell them no."

This seemed prudent, and I pressed on with our discussion. "Since this is your business, I have to ask you: Do you really think bigger is better?"

"Men ask that all the time. And all women will say size doesn't matter, but they're liars. They try to be gentle. They'll say to their boyfriends, 'It's not the size of the bait, it's how you wiggle a worm.' But when we women get together we say a whole other thing."

"So women *do* talk about size!"

"Well, mostly we do talk about what they do with it," said Ms. Straub backtracking somewhat, retreating into the female version of the Mafia code of silence, "but we do say it could be a little longer, a little wider."

"Have you increased the size of your husband's penis?" I knew Ms. Straub was married. She had told me on the phone when I first called her that her husband was her business partner.

"I've got to benefit from this, too!" she said, laughing. And then she said, becoming more serious, "My husband was very helpful in developing the program, because he has the parts. I could read the medical texts, but I don't have the parts. At first, he was skeptical, but then his penis started to grow and he was surprised."

"Have you increased the size of your breasts?" Asking this question, I was allowed, within the context of serious journalism, to look fully at Ms. Straub's rather lovely chest. She was wearing an open sport coat over a tight black shirt, and she further opened her sport coat, revealing to me the appealing bounty of her bosom.

"I made them a cup size bigger and I made them rounder. They used to sag. I went from a *B* to a *C*. Most women increase by one cup size." She looked down at her breasts; I looked at her breasts. Life was pretty good; she closed her jacket.

"How much do men increase?"

"One to two inches in length, and one to one and a half inches in girth. I have over a 90 percent success rate. But if it doesn't work, my tapes come with a money-back guarantee."

Ms. Straub then showed me before-and-after pictures of the first men she experimented on. They were all close-ups from the waist down, and some of the photos showed men with small flaccid penises in their before pictures and then larger flaccid penises in their after pictures, and some of the photos showed men with erections before and after, and there was no denying from all of these pictures that everyone had grown.

"Is your goal to increase the size of the flaccid penis or the erect penis?"

"Both," she said.

"What is the correct way to measure one's penis?"

"I always tell my clients to measure from the pubic bone. Some guys say to me over the phone, "I have a nine inch penis." But they're probably measuring from the anus."

"What would you say is the average length of the male penis?"

"Five and a half to six inches."

I kept a poker face, not revealing whether I was average or not, but I recalled having measured myself in high school (when rulers were much more available), in the manner Ms. Straub had described, and falling very much in the average category. "Half a foot sounds better than six inches, don't you think?" I said, and Ms. Straub smiled. "How do you advertise your business?" I then asked.

"It's not big word of mouth with Penis Enlargement. People don't want to admit that they've gone in for it. But Viagra has helped me tremendously because now people will talk about penises . . . So all my business comes to me through publicity—like magazines or radio, and my website, which is the best way for people to find me . . . And I know people do my program to make their penises grow, but it's a lot more than that. It helps them be happier, reach their other goals, their body goals, feel more confident. Once you get your penis to grow, the rest of life is cake."

"I can see that," I said, and I felt this was a good place to end my enjoyable interview with Ms. Straub and I thanked her for her time.

Then that night, before going to sleep, I mysteriously felt compelled to take a bubble bath. But having no bubble bath, I used shampoo and that worked quite well. And when I was in my lovely bubbly tub, I closed my eyes and imagined the water swirling and my penis growing and growing. In the physical realm, my hand helped advance my mind's inner vision, and several moments later, when I opened my eyes, I looked down and thought to myself, proudly, "Not bad. A good half-foot!"

(Ms. Straub's program, called Mind Quest, can be contacted via post at 204 East 11th Street, Suite 165, NY, NY 10003; via phone, toll-free, at 1-877-439-8363; or via email at www.hypbody.com)

The Pop (definition: cum-shot) and My Pop (definition: dad)
Gear magazine, 2002

The Premise: My editor at Gear had the idea to send me to L.A. to be guest-director of two porn videos being produced by Vivid Films—the most successful maker of adult movies in the country. I was to then write about my experience, and Vivid, by giving me this opportunity, would get free publicity. I didn't understand, though, why a professional porn company would allow an amateur to screw up the screwing, and it turned out, once I got to L.A., that my role wasn't really guest-director, but more of a guest-gadfly, like a UN peace observer, which was fine with me. I didn't feel qualified to direct a porno: I can hardly take pictures with a throwaway camera. So the following is my report from the front lines of porn, where I was joined for a few hours by my father, a porn fan and a senior citizen, who happened to be visiting L.A. at the same time.

Day 1, December 4, 2001
The Setting: A soundstage in Chatsworth, CA—The Valley. The soundstage is in a little industrial complex; its neighbors—computer companies, small factories— unaware, most likely, that porn is produced inside. The stage is the size of a warehouse and divided into small,

fake rooms, primarily bedroom sets. There are also dressing rooms and a lounge for the actors and crew to hang out in.

8:20 A.M.
First conversation with Robby D, the director, who is a short, powerfully built fellow with a glistening shaved head, tattooed arms, and a prankster's smile.

"So, as you know, I'm supposed to be guest-director," I say, shyly.

"I understand that's to be a loose term."

"I'll probably mostly observe," I say, immediately capitulating.

"That's a good idea," he says.

"But, if it's all right, I'll ask you questions, and sort of follow you around."

"Fine, ask whatever you want."

"So what does a director do?" I ask, stupidly, but you have to start somewhere.

"Fuck the chicks."

"Really?"

"Nah, you think I want to fuck these girls after they've been getting fucked all day? What do I do? A director has to know who to put on the bottom and who not. You have to know that this one guy, if he gets on his back, he loses wood. You have to know what people can do."

We are in the lounge, which has a table filled with snacks. Robby D. eats a pop tart. He offers me one. I decline.

"There are some things in the scripts I was wondering about that don't make sense," I say. I had read the screenplays on the plane ride out. Robby D. cowrote them with a porn-writer named Beth Ann Rafael.

"That's because it's porn," he says. "I purposely leave holes in the script. Better to let the guy at home wonder what's going on, fill in the spots himself. If you make it too clear, they don't get it."

Synopsis of the Two Films, *C-Men 1: Pussies in Heat and* *C-Men 2: Bush Piggies:*
In the first film, three superheroes are under attack from four female villains who look like cats. If a regular man makes love to one of these "bad pussies" he's turned into a stuffed animal. The superheroes don't get turned into stuffed animals, though, because of their super-powers, but they *are* in danger, and so they make all the bad pussies disappear when they ejaculate on them and then in the film's climax they make the bad pussy's leader, Kitty Kat, blow up when one of the superheroes farts on her. In the second film, there are again villainous women, and in this one they look like pigs. After a man makes love to one of these pig-women, she then aims her ass at him and his head blows up. The superheroes don't blow up immediately—because they're superheroes—but they get Tourette's-like symptoms and eventually their heads *will* blow up unless they use their super-semen and super-powers to make the evil women, led by Panting Patty, turn into smoke.

8:50 A.M.
Conversation in the lounge with Eric Masterson, porn actor, who bears a striking resemblance to the actor Matthew Perry. Many people in porn seem to be the double of someone in the other Hollywood, like porn is an alternative universe—the old upside-down, Bizarro world in DC comics. I name this alternative world *Hollygetwood.*

"How'd you get into porn?" I ask.

"My wife, Wendy Divine, got into it. So I was like if you're doing it, I'll do it. But for a guy it's not easy. You have to be able to get wood when they tell you to get wood. But I get paid to get off, so I can't complain."

"Is this industry hard on you and your wife?"

"We just care about each other so much that we make it work. She leaves in the morning or I leave and we know what the other person is going to be doing—having sex with somebody else—and we say, 'Have a good day.' We're just really in love."

"Do you ever work together?"

"Yeah."

"How's that?"

"Good and sometimes not good. Good because we get into it, but then sometimes, like if I know she's sore I'll feel bad about us having to do it, whereas with another girl, though I wouldn't want to hurt her, I'm more like, 'Well, this is what we have to do.' But I feel bad if it's my wife."

"Do you worry about STDs?"

"We all get tested for HIV every thirty days. And for the bigger companies, like Vivid, it's condom only. So I try to work mostly with places like Vivid . . . But sometimes someone will come up HIV positive. So then they do a family tree to figure out who the person was with. And if you were with the infected person, you get quarantined and can't work until the tests are all clear."

Mark the Saint, the skinny, rough-looking, but kindly Production Assistant, walks up to us. "What are you guys talking about?"

"STDs," says Eric.

"We've all got 'em," says Mark. "I got one right here." He doesn't indicate where, but it's a good joke.

9:15 A.M.

In dressing room, with April, who will act in the first sex scene of the day. The makeup woman is putting on April's pig-face. April is twenty-three, has been in the business three years, and has done hundreds of porn films. "I stopped counting after two hundred," she says. She has a beautiful lean body, an incredible ass, small, well-shaped breasts, and a pretty face, though she has bad skin, but the makeup covers her acne pretty well.

"What do you think of today's script?" I ask.

"Haven't read it," she says, "but it should be easy. I only have a love scene."

My heart breaks a little when she says "love scene."

Robby D comes in the room and tells the makeup woman that April can't have pigtails—they're too suggestive of a young girl. The pigtails are undone and Robby has April try on her pig-snout. Pigtails: not okay. Pig-snout: okay.

"I look silly," she protests. "I can't wear this."

"You have to wear it," Robby says. "It's your character. You're a bush piggy."

Eric comes in the room. Eric will be in April's love scene. Robby D says to them, "First scene is easy. You come in and start fucking." Robby D leaves the room; I follow him. He says to me, "The things you can get these girls to do."

"You mean put a pig nose on?"

"And take a dick in the ass."

Robby likes to be gruff, to shock, but mostly he's joking around, playing a part—a coarse porn director.

10 A.M.

Sex scene, Eric and April, a shabby, cheap-looking apartment set.

Eric is in a superhero outfit—blue and white cape,

white tights, and a blue tunic. April is wearing six-inch heels and a fishnet body stocking—her fat pink nipples protrude through the fishnet and there's a large hole cut out for her pussy (she has a piercing down there and a small strip of hair). She's wearing her snout and her pink pig makeup. She looks very sexy.

April says to Robby, "You using my favorite filter?" This must be a filter that doesn't show the bumps on her face.

"Yeah, but you're looking better. Just don't pick your skin," he says sweetly. Then he feels her pussy to see if she's wet.

April gets on the bed and has "pretty girl" pictures taken. These are still photos that are done before the girl's makeup or hair is messed up or she has come on her. The photos are used for the video boxes, magazines, posters, etc.

Eric opens a small toilet case and pops a Tic-tac. In the case are condoms, lube, tic-tacs, desensitizing cream, and other items, probably some Viagra. It's his kit that he takes on all shoots. He's very professional.

The sex begins. Eric and April kiss. Then Eric goes down on April's pussy; he's still in costume.

"Give me some oinks," Robby D says to April. He's manning the camera, which is propped on his shoulder. Several lighting crew guys stand around. Mark the Saint hovers with paper towels. Jim, a big building of a man, watches the action on a monitor, letting Robby know if things are in focus. Shylar, the Production Manager, pops in and out, keeping an eye on things.

"I don't know how to oink," she says.

Eric keeps eating her pussy.

"You have to oink," Robby says. "And put your fingers in your pussy and then in your mouth." She makes some good oinks and fingers herself while Eric licks her.

For a few minutes, they shoot Eric eating her pussy at *soft* angles—for the soft-core release of the film, which goes to the *Playboy* channel and other outlets, and so you only see the back of Eric's head or April moaning, no genitals in soft. Then they shoot it for hardcore, with a big lamp, held by Jim Fillmore, the head of lighting, shined right on April's pussy and the camera zooming in so you see everything—pink lips, clit, juice, saliva, Eric's tongue.

"Open her up," Robby D tells Eric. "Let's see the meat."

They finish the pussy-eating and Eric has to get out of his costume. April sits on the bed waiting. Robby D farts a couple of times. Everybody laughs. The farting aspect to *C-Men 2*, it occurs to me, is perhaps partly autobiographical, and I sympathize—I, too, often have gas problems.

Eric is struggling with his costume.

"He's Captain Hebrew," says Shylar.

"Why Captain Hebrew?" asks Robby.

"His cape looks like what Rabbis wear."

April is bored.

"Jonathan," Robby D, says to me. "Go keep April's pussy wet." Everybody laughs. April smiles at me. If only. Then Robby D asks me, "What position do you want them in?"

He's playing along at my being a guest-director, but I'm at a loss. Then I say, "Well, I think it would be hot if they're doing missionary and her arms are above her head and he could gently hold her wrists down."

"Can't do it," Robby D says. "Can't show a woman being restrained. And at that angle we wouldn't get penetration. This isn't like the sex you have at home. You have to know the laws and you have to think of camera angles."

Eric gets out of his costume. April gives him a blowjob. He doesn't wear a condom for the blowjob. Robby shoots at hard and soft angles. Eric's cock is pretty big, but not too big, which I find reassuring. April makes a lot of wet slurping noises while sucking him. I wonder if blowjobs are always this loud. I haven't ever really noticed before. Robby D asks April for a stringer—a line of spit that runs from her mouth to his cock.

After the blowjob, Robby D tells April to do a "reverse cow-girl." This means she sits on his cock with her back to him. Eric puts on a condom and lubes it up. April sits on him and I watch his cock slide right in her, no resistance.

After a few minutes of this, they go to doggy-style, but April has to stop.

"It hurts," she says.

"You sound like my wife," says Shylar. He's a skinny, long-haired, unshaven fellow.

"How *is* Catherine?" Jim, the monitor guy, asks Shylar.

"Her back is fucked up," says Shylar, speaking of his wife.

Mark the Saint brings April some lube. Eric remounts her. They keep shooting. Then Robby D tells Eric to do a FIP—a fake internal pop—for the soft-core sequence, which means he pretends to come inside April. Then Robby tells him for the hard to pull out and "jack and pop on her back and ass." Eric pulls out, struggles with the condom, but then successfully jacks and pops on April's ass. The photographer takes a few quick pictures of the come, then Mark the Saint gives Eric a paper towel. Eric cleans himself and April, which seems very nice to me.

Then they have to do some dialogue from the script. This is when April is supposed to aim her ass at Eric and give him Tourette's.

Robby D instructs April: "You're a villain. Be animated."

"I can't," says April.

"Yes, you can," says Robby D.

"I'm a porn star, not an actress," says April.

"Just be animated."

"I don't know what animated means."

I'm not sure if April is joking or not. They shoot the scene.

Afterward, I ask April if she enjoyed the sex.

"It was all right," she says. "I like sex with my boyfriend better. I like to grind. But for the camera you can't grind. You have to show penetration and sometimes the angles hurt."

"What's your boyfriend think of you being in porn?"

"He's a mainstream actor. He doesn't like it. We don't talk about it."

I ask her how much longer she wants to stay in the business. She says five years and then she wants to start a family.

She goes to take a shower and Mark the Saint says to me, "This is your first time on a porn set, right?"

"Yes."

"Did you have to leave when they were fucking?"

I figure that he thinks I might have needed to vomit, like someone going to a morgue for the first time—it *was* strange to see another man's cock sliding in and out of a pussy. And the pussy looked so vulnerable—stretched open, punctured. "No, I didn't have to leave," I say.

"I can't believe you didn't get wood," he says and walks away. Oh, that's what he meant, I think. I wonder if something is wrong with me that I didn't get wood. The sex didn't affect me at all. I just felt bad for April. There was nothing erotic about it for me. Then again, I don't find porn erotic, so it makes sense that I wouldn't find the making of porn to be a turn-on. Watching Eric and April fuck was more like the Science Channel to me: "This is what a human penis looks like going inside a human vagina." But if it was my human penis going in April, then that would have been erotic. Then I would have gotten wood. At least I hope so.

12:10 P.M.
Parking lot. Conversation with Marty Romano, who will be in the next sex scene with the *C-Men 2*'s star, Cheyenne, who is on the cover of December's *Penthouse*. Marty is a big, tough-looking guy in his thirties—he's a biker with dark brown hair, a goatee, and many tattoos.

"Do you like working in porn," I ask.

"Hell, yeah," he says, smoking a cigarette. "I get to have sex and I get paid for it. And women hardly sleep with me in the real world, but here I get to fuck somebody like Cheyenne."

"Do you ever worry about not being able to perform?"

"Nah, I love sex. And if I need to I can always take a Viagra. But with Cheyenne I won't need shit. Some guys shoot cayberjack in their dicks. If I did that I could fuck the whole crew."

"What's cayberjack?"

"This shit that makes your dick hard."

"How do you spell it?"

"I don't know."

"Are your friends like, 'I can't believe you're a porn star'?"

"I'm not a porn star."

"You're a porn actor?"

"Yeah."

"How come you're not a star?"

"I'm not good-looking, I'm out of shape, I don't have a big dick, and I'm covered in tattoos."

12:30 P.M.

Sexual Harassment

Shylar, who's a sweet guy, has a sex toy. He's walking around the lounge with the thing. It's a white plastic dildo with a viewer and a light, a kind of periscope that you can put up a girl. He spots April.

"Hey, April, I want to look inside you," Shylar says.

"No way," says April. "That's gross."

"Come on, I give you work all the time," says Shylar—he hires the actors and the crew.

April goes with Shylar to the bathroom and Robby D joins them. They don't fully close the door. I see Robby D kneeling in front of April and looking in the viewer. He sees me spying on him from between her legs and closes the door.

On a porn set, it's hard, I imagine, for girls to complain about sexual harassment. It would be a kind of oxymoron.

Later, I spot Shylar. "What it look like inside April? Pink?"

"Yeah, but I couldn't see much. But I can put that thing on eBay now and make some money, if I wanted, especially with her pussy juice on it."

1:00 P.M.

Sex Scene with Marty and Cheyenne. Cheyenne is a wholesome, pretty brunette with breast implants, which lessens her appeal for me. They're on a set meant to look like an auto shop. The auto shop is where Cheyenne and her evil bush-piggies hang out. Marty's motorcycle is in the center of the set. Marty is just a guy who comes to the shop; he's not a superhero; after he has sex with Cheyenne he will blow up.

Marty's on a couch. Cheyenne gives him a blowjob, but she has to take a break because her jaw hurts. When the blowjob is done—filmed for six minutes—they go to reverse cowgirl. Shylar comes alongside me. "Watch Robby D," he says, "he's got a bad habit. He always grabs his dick." I see that Shylar is right. Robby while hoisting the camera with one hand is massaging his dick with the other. Over the next three days, Robby D is always grabbing his dick. But that's all right—everything goes on a porn set.

Shylar and I watch Marty's dick go in and out of Cheyenne's pussy. All the crew, about ten guys, watch, and also some of the girls, the other actresses. Cheyenne has very large purple lips. A beautiful pussy. I notice that Marty doesn't seem to have any balls.

"Is Marty castrated?" I whisper to Shylar.

"I don't know," says Shylar. "There are a couple of guys in the industry with no balls."

Marty and Cheyenne switch to doggy-style and one of the crew whispers that Marty has acne scars on his ass. Another guy says, "I got something worse than scars, I got this huge hemorrhoid I'm working on. I wish somebody would take a sledgehammer to the thing." Marty and Cheyenne keep fucking. Mark the Saint is sitting on the floor, his back against the wall, and he's sleeping.

Cheyenne is really screaming and moaning. Then Robby stops filming. Blood is pouring down Cheyenne's leg. She's having her period. Somebody wakes up Mark the Saint and he rushes over to her with a paper towel. Somebody says that towel could go for a lot on eBay.

I hear Cheyenne say to Marty, "You made me come and that opened things up, that's why the blood came out." She goes to the bathroom to put in a new sponge. I learn that a lot of the girls, like Cheyenne, have numerous orgasms. It's not just the guys who enjoy the sex.

Cheyenne comes back from the bathroom. They

resume doggy-style. It's time for *the pop*, but Marty can't do it. The whole crew is waiting for him to come. The pop is kind of sacred, the set always gets silent for the pop.

Marty's really struggling. Cheyenne tries to help him. She blows him, jacks him. At one point he just hugs her. He needs some tenderness. The still photographer takes some pictures, he's kneeling by Marty and Cheyenne. Robby D farts explosively on the squatting photographer's head and the guy leaps up like he's been electrocuted. Everybody laughs and moans, "Robbbbyyyyy . . ."

"I parted your hair with that one," Robby says.

"Fucking burned off my hair," says the photog.

Finally, after about forty minutes, Marty's ready. Robby D tells him to shoot on Cheyenne's left ass-cheek and tells Cheyenne to arch her ass and give him a good target. Marty explodes. There's a hell of a lot of sperm, which seems to make up for the delay, and I figure that Marty must have balls somewhere to come that much.

2:30 P.M.

Conversation with Cheyenne in parking lot. She has the same accent as the actress Geena Davis.

"Do you enjoy working in porn?" I ask.

"I do. I wouldn't continue if I didn't. I get off in most of my scenes. I love it, but it's not something I want to do forever. I'm contracted for six more films."

"Are you dating anyone?"

"No. I want to have something steady, but it's hard not to make someone jealous if you're in this business. And my own values are monogamous, so I can't expect a guy to put up with me being in porn. That's why I'm moving on to dancing. This way I can make good money *and* not have sex *and* have a relationship."

A lot of porn stars make very good money on the stripping/dance circuit. They also have websites where they sell their pictures, panties, and anything else a guy could fetishize.

Summary of the Rest of Day 1

Cheyenne, despite having her period and being sore, has sex scenes with two more guys and has several orgasms. One of the guys, T. J. Cumming, is a young blonde fellow. "I always play the delivery boy," he says. Everyone bad-mouths T.J. behind his back because supposedly he's appeared in gay porno films. "It's just not socially acceptable to do gay films and straight films," says a cast member who asks to not be identified.

Cheyenne's other sex scene is with a big, burly fellow named Steven St. Croix, who does a great Christopher Walken impersonation and laments that his porn career has ruined his chance to do mainstream work. He drives a BMW and brings his small, nervous dog on the set. Hours before their sex scene, Steven keeps going down on Cheyenne while they are shooting some dialogue. At one point, he is kneeling in front of Cheyenne with her pussy in his face and Robby D, who has been trying to set up the action, says, "What are you doing? Do you know how many dicks have been up there today?" (Cheyenne has been with Marty and T.J.)

The whole crew laughs at Steve and he just keeps his face in her pussy and he's smiling. I happen to be standing right behind Cheyenne and can't see her face, but from her posture she doesn't seem offended by Robby D's remark. Then Dale DaBone, one of the superhero porn stars, who looks just like Rob Lowe, says, "That's why he keeps eating her pussy, he really wants to suck cock."

The whole day's shooting lasts fourteen hours. Around nine P.M., Mark the Saint asks me again if I got wood. I lie and say that I did.

December 5, 2001
Day 2
Vivid Girls

On the second day of shooting, they work on *C-Men 1*. The superheroes are again Eric, Dale, and Steve, but all the girls—the bad pussies—are new, and they are all Asian, led by Kira, the star, which means she has the most sex scenes. Kira, like Cheyenne the day before, works exclusively for Vivid, which utilizes the old Hollywood studio system of signing stars to long-term contracts. Vivid was the first porn company to do this and by doing so they created a brand name, Vivid Girls, which has established their dominance in the industry.

9:10 A.M.
Conversation with Fujiko, Mikotan, and Mina, the three bad pussies, in the dressing room.

Fujiko, bad pussy #1, is a Japanese porn actress. I've been told that she's only recently arrived in the U.S. She's quite lovely, with a gorgeous oval face and very large, natural breasts. She's wearing high heels, a fishnet body stocking, and her cat makeup is already on.

"How long have you been in the U.S.?" I ask her.

"Two months. I have visa."

"I have a Citibank Visa," quips Mikotan, bad pussy #2, who is Asian-American, and is having her cat makeup applied. Mina, #3, sits quietly in another chair, waiting her turn.

I laugh at Mikotan's remark, but keep talking to

Fujiko. "How do you like doing porn here in the States?" I ask.

"Having so much fun here," she says, in her accented, more or less fluent English. "Japanese dick is purple. I like pink. Caucasian is pink. I can smell the difference between black, Caucasian, Asian."

I don't really know why she's telling me this, but she's very chipper and friendly.

"What do they smell like?" I ask.

"White like butter. Japanese—soy sauce. Korean—kim chi. Chinese—miso. Black like baby powder. I smell under the balls."

I wonder if I can arrange to have Fujiko blindfolded and have her do a smell test. Then she says to me, pointing at my white eyebrows, "You're so blonde."

"It's good for jogging at night," I say. "Reflector strips on my forehead."

"But what color are you down there," she says and points at my groin.

"Orange," I say. All the girls shriek. Mikotan tells me I should say auburn. Fujiko leaves the room. I ask Mikotan if I can ask her some questions.

"Okay. But I don't have to suck your cock."

"No. Unless you fall in love with me," I say, and I wouldn't mind if she did fall for me. She's gorgeous—perfect skin, full mouth, great figure, smart, witty.

"Yeah, I'll give you a blowjob if I fall in love with you or if I want to see your orange pubes."

I feel some wood developing, but I press on with my questions. "So are you Japanese?"

"Half Japanese, quarter Chinese, quarter Samoan."

"How old are you?"

"Twenty-four."

"How long have you been in porn."

"Three years part-time. I'm really a computer programmer. Java, e-commerce, normal Asian girl stuff. Yada yada yada."

"Do your parents know you do porn?"

"Yeah."

"Do they mind?"

"My mom doesn't mind. My dad likes porn but not anything I do. When I told him, he slammed the phone down."

"Do you enjoy it?"

"Yeah, I'm divorced and I don't feel like dating. But I like to get laid once in a while, so if I'm going to have mindless sex, I might as well get paid."

Mikotan then leaves the room and I'm left with Mina, who is very petite, less than five feet. She is quite beautiful. She has full round breasts from implants, but they look good on her.

"How long have you been in the business?"

"This is my first film since 1995," she says.

"Why did you drop out?" I ask.

"It was very hard on my system, because I'm so small down there. I had lots of yeast infections, all that thrusting gets all the bacteria up there. So I only do girl-girl now. For pictures I do boy-girl but for movies only girl-girl."

"What have you been doing the last few years?"

"Just being married."

"Does your husband mind you doing porno?"

"No, he likes to watch me."

11:30 A.M.

My Dad Comes to the Set

My dad shows up and I introduce him to the three bad pussies. He gets his picture taken with Mikotan and she puts his hand on her breast. He's smiling broadly. He's seventy-three years old, has a white beard like Hemingway and he's wearing his dirty, yellowed baseball cap with pins from all the places he's visited. No pin, I imagine, though, for coming to a porn set. With his hand on Mikotan's breast, he says, "You're warm."

"I've been working," she says.

We go and watch Kira having sex with T.J. on a medical gurney. My dad is very quiet and respectful. It doesn't seem too weird, for some reason, to be with my father and watch T.J.'s cock slide in and out of Kira's pussy. It's just so clinical. Robby D is up on a ladder above T.J. and Kira.

"Open up . . . say ahhh," Robby tells Kira, indicating she should spread her legs more and expose more of her vagina.

"Stop fucking like a pussy," he tells T.J. Everybody picks on TJ. His face is beet red. Probably from Viagra.

"I like girl on girl," my dad whispers to me.

Damn, I think, *my dad likes what everybody likes. How typical.*

"He should touch her breasts," my dad whispers.

"Yeah," I say. Kira's breasts are unnaturally large from implants. She looks like the actress Tia Carrera.

Later, when they're done, my dad says, "I'm exhausted just from watching. Your mother told me not to come home with any strange ideas." He sits down on the bed where Eric screwed April the day before.

I introduce my dad to Jim Fillmore, the head of lighting who looks like Kris Kristofferson. "If anybody asks," Jim says to me, "tell them your dad is senior correspondent."

I like that and this gives me an idea: my dad should write a little something about visiting a porn set. I suggest this to my dad and he agrees to give it a try. "It's like role reversal," I say to my dad and Jim Fillmore. "Father comes with son to work."

"Yeah, father *comes* with son," my dad says and Jim laughs. My dad then tells Jim about the advances he's seen in porn, from 8mm to video. "Next step will be *smellervision*," says my dad. Jim laughs.

Later, my dad gets his picture taken with all three bad pussies. Mikotan says to the other girls, "He's a married man. We can't get him in trouble."

"Get me in trouble," says my dad. "Get me in trouble."

My dad comes away with a Polaroid of him and the girls. I walk him out to the parking lot. He's going to make color Xeroxes of the picture and send it to all his old buddies in New Jersey. He calls my mom on his cell phone. "I'm all worn out," he tells her, "but I'm still alive. There were a lot of cables I could have tripped on."

A few nights later, I celebrate Hanukkah with my parents. I tell my dad that I already gave him his present.

4:20 P.M.
Fujiko's Sex Scene with Steven St. Croix

Fujiko is giving the most incredible blowjob to Steven. She spits on it, rubs it up and down, twists it, just really goes at his cock with incredible gusto, and Steven is writhing in a chair, trying not to come.

All the crew watches in disbelief at this blowjob, except for Mikotan, who is reading *PC Magazine.*

Robby D is playing with his cock the whole time he films. When it's over, he says to Fujiko, "What are you doing the rest of your life?"

"I'm available," she says, and wipes spit off her chin. "I'm a saliva machine."

"Where'd you learn to suck cock like that?" Robby asks.

"In school. We train in Japan. I paid four hundred American dollars to learn how to do this."

"I would have taught you for free," says Robby.

"Maybe she can teach Cheyenne," says Steven.

For the rest of the day everybody talks about Fujiko's blowjob, and I think it's interesting how in Japan they train their porn stars like the way they train sushi chefs or sumo wrestlers. It's all very Zen.

Day 3
3:30 P.M.
Conversation with Shylar while Kira has sex with Cheyne Collins, a big beefy guy.

After the oral sex, Kira refuses to do anal with Cheyne, says he's too big. Robby films them having regular intercourse.

"It's in her contract to do anal every movie," Shylar tells me, "but she backs out almost every time. She's only done two out of eight. So next year she'll owe six anals, but you can't force a girl. She's got her own mind."

"How would you characterize the girls in the business?"

"All different kinds. All fucked up in the head, they have to be. Half are on drugs, a quarter have fucked up childhoods, and a quarter are normal and just like sex. But what's normal? The money's not that good. They get eight hundred dollars for a boy/girl scene and a thousand for anal . . . These Asian girls are great, though, real slutty."

"Your percentages are low," says Jim the monitor guy, listening to us. "Seventy percent are fucked up from childhood, twenty percent are on drugs, ten percent are normal."

Shylar nods his head in agreement with Jim's adjusted tally.

"What about the guys? Are they fucked up?" I ask him.

"Yeah, they're sex addicts. But we're all fucked up in this business. We have to be. We're all undedicated film-makers. If we weren't crazy we'd be in the mainstream. We're right in Hollywood. We could be making good money . . . But I do like porn. You don't have to be anal, you can be yourself, let it all hang out . . . Last night it got crazy, though. Steven was getting another blowjob from Fujiko and Dale was fucking Mikotan and Mina. And we weren't even shooting. That usually doesn't happen. I saw Mina's husband looking for her. I tried to run interference. But he said he was going to watch Dale fuck his wife. He wanted to watch."

5:00 P.M.
Sex Scene with Dale and Anne Marie

This scene really gets to me. Anne Marie is twenty years old and only been in the business a few months. She looks like she's sixteen. She's utterly angelic—a beautiful, sweet face, large brown eyes, soft lush hair, olive skin, and one of the prettiest, most perfect bodies I've ever seen. She's a Latina from the Valley, just over the mountains from where we are shooting. She told me she wants to stay in the business a year, pick up some good money, and then quit.

"Do your parents know?"

"My mother knows. But what can she do? I'm on my own. My dad doesn't know. He would freak."

"Do you date?"

"Not really. It's kind of lonely. I date guys in the business; they don't freak out. But I like porn; it's pretty fun. You go to different locations, meet different people. I like the acting. And for a couple of hours I make really good money."

"Do you enjoy the sex?"

"It's hard with people watching but it feels good. And I always wondered about going with a girl and never would have if it wasn't for porn."

Anne Marie then tells me that all her friends from high school already have one or two kids, so by comparison she's not too wild, or at least she wasn't in high school when they all started getting pregnant.

Anne Marie and Dale start their sex scene. They begin with a blowjob. Just as he turns on the camera, Robby turns to those of us watching and says in a sad, sincere whisper, "She's too young. Somebody save this girl from herself."

I find it terrible watching Dale's enormous, ten-inch dildo-like cock go in her mouth. Anne Marie keeps gagging on it, but she works hard.

Later, when her ass is in the air for doggy-style, she looks so beautiful. While she's in that position, they have to pause for Robby to put a new battery in his camera and Dale keeps going in and out of her to stay hard and she props her face on her forearms, waiting. Sex and her beautiful body seem sacred and I feel like she's letting both be destroyed. A fresh battery in place, Robby does a close-up on her pussy. I look at it on the monitor; she really does look like an oyster or a flower, her lips these petals.

When they're ready for the pop, Robby wants Dale to come on her face. Anne Marie says no quietly.

"You don't do facials?" asks Robby. "Come on, you can do it."

"All right but I don't want it in my eyes."

Robby turns to us and says, "Didn't even have to debate that one."

I'm dying.

"I can't beat off on her face if the kid doesn't want it," says Dale.

"Come on tell him how much you want it," says Robby.

"It's all right," Anne Marie says in a very small voice.

"Don't worry," says Dale. "It won't go in your eyes. I came once today." Dales looks at us watching and winks. He has no idea if it will go in her eyes.

For some reason, though, they end up doing the pop on Anne Marie's ass and I'm relieved. Robby tells Dale, just before he comes, "Let's see the DNA . . . Let's see what your kids look like."

6:00 P.M.

Conversation with Jim Fillmore after Anne Marie's Scene

Jim has been working on porn sets for twenty years. He has long gray-brown hair tied in a ponytail. He often walks around with an unlit cigarette in his mouth.

"How do you deal with watching these pretty girls having sex?"

"If you wave a steak in front of a dog and never give the dog the steak, he learns that he can't have it. It always looks good but he can't have it. It's like that. Crew and talent never mix. But if you're a director you can get a blowjob, they all do."

"What do you think of the girls in the business?"

"Girls come and go, but guys, if they can do it, last forever. A girl has maybe ten years. Twenty to thirty. Then they leave, get a millionaire. A sugar daddy. Or they go into dancing, some good money there. But thank god for porno. At least they're treated nice here. Somewhere else where they'd be taken advantage of they don't get lunch. At least here they get lunch."

"What do you think of the guys in the business?"

"We're all, guys and girls, just a bunch of harmless criminals. We like to think we're bad but we're not. When they had the riots a couple of years ago, I thought this was my chance—the cops are all occupied. But all I came up with was riding my bike 120 miles per hour and I couldn't even do that. So we're all harmless . . . And people here can talk about anything. It's a refreshing crowd that way."

"What do you think of Anne Marie? She's so pretty. Sweet."

"Too sweet. Some girls come in here so wholesome it's unnerving. But it won't last long. The face changes. They get this whore face. A face that's seen too much."

6:45 P.M.
The End
Robby very kindly wants to have me be an extra in *C-Men 1*. They set up a bar and I'm in there with several other extras, all of whom look like they were found on skid row. Robby has me sit at the bar next to Mikotan, whom I'm to try to seduce, but then Dale DaBone, in his yellow superhero outfit, will tell me to get lost and he'll pick her up.

These are my last minutes on the porn set. I've been on the inside of an industry designed, primarily, to give men something to masturbate to, and I've had a very good time. I really like the people. It has been like hanging around a circus troupe. They're vulgar and crude, but also very nice; they have been generous to me—talking to me, welcoming me. Mark the Saint had told me that working on a porn movie is like going on a camping trip: you get close to one another. I agree with him. I will miss these porn people.

We begin shooting the bar scene and I talk to Mikotan.

She encourages me to feel her breasts, to stroke her thighs. I happily obey her orders and then I lightly pinch her large brown nipples through the holes of her fishnet top. I feel them get erect between my fingers. Her nipples get wood! And there's a chain reaction—I get wood! I get wood! She smiles at me. I cup her breasts. I like this business. I tell her she's beautiful. Then Dale DaBone strides over in his superhero outfit, his super-weapon in his shorts, and he tells me to get lost. I don't want to leave Mikotan, but I have a role to play. So, grimacing like a loser for the camera, hamming it up, I make my exit and my career in porn comes to an end and yet I have finally arrived. I got wood.

Going to Work with My Son

by Max Ames

Gear magazine, 2002

All my life I have been attracted to porn flics, starting when I was about seventeen years old. My first exposure was to a black & white flic shown at a party held in honor of a fellow who returned from a tour of service in France after WWII. The returning G.I. regaled us with stories of communal toilets and amorous adventures in French brothels. As years went by various films came into my possession—but the hard part was borrowing a 8mm movie projector upon which to show them. I remember once when I was babysitting at my sister's home and my grandfather came in, took one look at the screen, turned around, and said, "Fooey!" In retrospect, I am probably fifteen years older now than my grandfather was then. However, I continued to acquire films and when I chanced on one in color I was truly hooked. When I was single, I would enjoy hosting a party of mixed couples to view what I termed "training" films. And although my memory is clouded I recall having dallied with a young lady or two who was "turned on" by one of my "training" films.

Recently, I had an opportunity to actually watch the filming of a modern porn film when my son offered to have me accompany him to a set. I was impressed by the voluptuous nature of the female leads and by the staying power of the males. I always thought that they made these films in segments because I could not believe how the male leads could tarry as long as they could. I will say that part of me hoped that I might find a plot which at least attempted to portray romance or rose-colored reality, instead I found anything but. It was more like a TV documentary on horses being serviced. Where was the least bit of gentleness of lips brushing lips or a hand tenderly cupping a breast? But, regardless, I found it interesting and entertaining to watch.

When I was a little boy my father would take me to work with him and I can truly say that going to work with my son was equally enjoyable. If one lives long enough some of our dreams are fulfilled and being a guest on a porn set was one of them for me.

Part VI:
Essays without Sexual Content
(A warning or a recommen-
dation, depending on your
personality)

A Dog's Life
New York Press, 1997

I was in the Jacuzzi and the jets were working on my Thanksgiving hemorrhoids. It was the day after the big meal and I was pretending I was a movie star or a star writer; after all, I was in the city of stars—Los Angeles. My sister had given me a plane ticket to be with the family for the holiday and now I was living it up, staying in her beautiful house, which rests at the top of a canyon. I sat alone in the Jacuzzi and looked down and east from my mountainous perch to the famous sprawl of the San Fernando Valley. The air was perfectly clear because of a rainstorm the night before—no smog—and I could see for miles all the way to the red-pink San Gabriel mountains, and the farthest range even had snowcaps. Every now and then you get a glimpse in L.A. of the beauty that brought all the people there to destroy it.

A number of my relatives had come west for Thanksgiving at my sister's and I was rooming with my step-niece, Andrea, a precocious eight-year-old blonde. She had the top bunk and I was down below. She needed some rough stuff at night, but after that she was all right— I'd let her bomb me for half an hour with all her stuffed animals, about a hundred of them, and then she'd be exhausted and nod off.

So I was happy in that Jacuzzi, happy to be in L.A., but the trip had gotten off to a difficult start. Our first night all together, Wednesday, my cousin Francis's dog attempted suicide. Francis is in the fine arts business and wherever he goes he brings along his little pet beagle, Puccina, a female who has the nervous personality of a Chihuahua. Francis was staying in a hotel and had to leave Puccina at my sister's that first night. The dog cried and barked and went mad as soon as Francis left. Andrea loved the little dog and wanted to take care of it. She insisted on having the beagle sleep in her bed. So I tucked them both in and went to the commode. Then when I was brushing my teeth, I heard scuffling in the bedroom.

"No, Puccina, no!" screamed Andrea, playing the scolding mommy. The neurotic dog yipped and whined.

I completed my toilet and as I came into the dark bedroom, Andrea wailed, "PUCCINA!" And this time, her voice was frightened, not scolding. Then there was a sick gurgling sound. I couldn't see a thing. I fumbled for the light switch, then found it. I saw the dog hanging from the top bunk. Andrea had fastened Puccina's leash to the bed post. The dog must have thought I was Francis and had leaped off the bed—hanging itself. She dangled in the air, choking, her eyes bulging. Her little white belly was exposed and pathetic; her four paws waved helplessly. I was stunned by the gruesome sight of her neck swelling. Then Andrea screamed and I moved across the room like an Olympian and gathered the body up and rested Puccina on Andrea's bunk. Puccina was alive! I had saved her!

My mother and sister came running into the room in their nightgowns. Their eyes were wild, frightened. They were wondering if they had made a mistake letting me bunk with Andrea. "What's going on?" my mother asked.

"Puccina, longing for Francis, attempted suicide," I explained quickly before they rushed to judgment like the LAPD. I then pantomimed how I had found Puccina dangling from her gallows. I held out my hands like paws and bulged my eyes. And there was something morbidly comic about my performance that caused my mother and sister to double over in laughter.

"Oh, god, I have to pee," said my mother, and she raced out of the room. Whenever I send my mother into hysterics, she pees in her pants.

My sister decided that Puccina should stay in my mother and father's bed. So the lights went out again; Andrea attacked me for a bit and then quickly fell asleep. I lay on the bottom bunk unable to sleep because I could hear Puccina moaning down the hall. I was pissed off and I determined that Francis should be called to come fetch his dog and sneak her into the hotel. I walked down the hall barefoot to tell my mother this and stepped in a little puddle of urine. Fucking Puccina!

I went into my parents' room and my father was fast asleep. My mother was petting Puccina, attempting to soothe her. "This is too much," I said. "We have to call Francis to come get her. This dog is impossible. She's keeping me up. I can't sleep. *And* she went in the hall. I stepped in her urine!"

"That was me," said my mother. "I thought I cleaned it all up."

"Oh, god," I said, wiping my foot on the throw rug. "If I'm going to be funny, you really need to wear a diaper or something... this Thanksgiving is getting off to a terrible start."

My mother didn't like me chastising her for her incontinence and she said, "Just be grateful you're not where you were ten years ago."

I harrumphed and went back to bed. I lay in my little bunk and thought about Thanksgiving 1987. In mid-November of that year I had gone on a cocaine and alcohol binge brought on by sadness, depression, and personal problems, not to mention despair. I ended up on a locked psychiatric ward in a private South Jersey hospital. It was a nightmarish place—they let all the nuts chain-smoke in the common room, but all the windows were sealed tight so you couldn't jump out and escape, and the fucking smoke was killing me. I was supposed to be detoxing, not retoxing.

After a week on the locked ward, I was sent to the substance-abuse wing of the hospital. My roommate, Frankie, was a dwarfish manager for a Burger King and moonlighted as a drug dealer. He had done so much cocaine that his brain was shot and there was nothing left inside his nose. There were so many holes in his septum that his snoring at night was like a wind chime.

After being roommates for a few days, he told me that he had been "cheeking" his medication for weeks, and planned to take all the pills on Thanksgiving when we had no counseling sessions. He showed me his huge stash of antidepressants, anticonvulsants, and antibiotics. I looked at all the little white pills and he said, "When it comes to drugs I save 'em like a Jew."

He didn't know I was Jewish and I didn't think now was the time to inform him. More importantly, I was worried that he would OD and if I didn't do anything I'd be partially responsible for his death. But the worst thing to be in any kind of penal colony is a snitch, so I confided with an old alcoholic woman on the ward who nobody bothered with and she snitched for me. Our room was raided Thanksgiving morning and they found his stash.

After hours of counseling, he was let free, but I didn't know it. I was back from the dreary Thanksgiving lunch and was standing in our room looking out the window at some yellow weeds by a highway, daydreaming about escape. Then suddenly there was a horrible stabbing pain in my neck. I turned and the little coke weasel had his toothbrush jutting out of his fist. The pointy end with a hard rubber pick was aimed right at me. He had found the best weapon he could. They kept our razors—we only shaved under observation.

"I'm going to kill you, you narc!"

"I saved your life, you would have OD'd."

He took another swing at me and almost put a hole in my shoulder with the toothbrush. The little anti-Semitic fuck knew how to fight. I had about seven inches on him and I threw a measly punch that glanced off his pointy head. I was in danger. He was full of venom and I was full of depression. He charged me and slammed me against the window, but the glass was strong and didn't break. He buried his face in my belly and he was pummeling me with his fists and the toothbrush and then he bit my stomach like a wild mongrel.

This got to me. Human bites are very dangerous! More dangerous than dog bites. I pushed him off me, swung out my fist and caught him on the jaw. This is what happens when you let yourself get put into rehabs—you meet the wrong kind of people. He staggered back onto my bed. Some blood came out of his mouth. I don't like the sight of blood.

"My tongue!" he sputtered.

Then the orderlies were in there and seeing the blood excited them, gave them a chance to be violent, and they threw me against the wall. Frankie was sent to the "quiet room" and then back to the psych ward. What happened to me over the next few hellish weeks is a whole other story. Mostly I pretended I was Papillon and would run laps in the tiny courtyard where they let us get fresh air, trying to build up my strength for my escape. And then my insurance ran out after forty days and they released me.

Well, I thought about all this while I lay in my cozy bunk in L.A., and I did feel grateful, as my mom had said, but it occurred to me that my two Thanksgivings ten years apart weren't so different: each time I had saved a dog's life.

Forty Dollars
New York Press, 1997

*The other day there was a banging at my door. A desperate voice
was breathlessly exclaiming, "You don't know me . . . I'm your
downstairs neighbor . . . Please, I need your help. I'm very sick!"
I looked through the peephole and saw a man with long hair. His
head was down, his hands were against my door.*

"What's the matter?" I asked, a little frightened. I'm
new to my building. I didn't know if he was my neighbor
or not.

"I have a terrible fever, I have AIDS," he said. "I need
help, I'm going to faint." His face looked up at my peephole. He was gaunt, skeletal. His eyes were desperate.
How could I pretend that he wasn't there? How could I
play at being a New Yorker? I opened my door. "Thank
you so much," he said, and he almost collapsed into my
arms. I led him into my kitchen. "Please, sit down," I said.
He slumped into a chair. I wasn't afraid of him; he must
have weighed ninety pounds.

"This is so embarrassing. I'm so sorry to do this. But I
need help." He held his face in his hands and he sobbed.
He almost fell off the chair.

"It's all right," I said. "You don't have to be embarrassed."

His face had small scrape-like lesions. His teeth protruded from his gums. He was wearing blue pants, a turtleneck, and a light wool sport coat. His shoes had tassels. I asked what I could do for him. He told me his story. His roommate was at work; he was overcome with fever; his doctor was at Montefiore Hospital in the Bronx and wanted him to come in immediately. But the EMS wouldn't take him to the Bronx—they would take him to a local hospital, where he would receive terrible shots. His doctor in the Bronx had a new, less painful treatment for his fungus. He had called the Ninth Precinct but they told him that they weren't a car service. He needed twenty-eight dollars to get to the Bronx.

"I'm so sorry," he said when he finished his story. "This is so humiliating."

I took out my wallet. All I had was twenty dollars. I offered this to him.

"Oh, God," he wailed, "I need twenty-eight. It always costs twenty-eight."

"I only have twenty."

"They won't take me for twenty," he sobbed. His skull-like face was racked with panic and misery.

"You go back to your apartment," I said. "I'll go to my ATM and get the rest of the money."

"I'll come with you. The fresh air will be good for me. I haven't been out for days. I may have to lean on you. You can help me get a taxi."

We walked to Avenue A. He put his arm through mine. He wasn't steady on his feet. He asked me questions about myself. I told him I was a writer. He asked me if he could borrow my book sometime, if he could come up and talk to me sometime. I said yes to both questions. I thought of my friends who have died of AIDS.

He told me that he had been diagnosed in 1987, but had only taken sick in the last two years. He was a former airline steward with American; he was suing them for firing him when he became ill with pneumcystitis. They had at least reinstated his free-flying privileges. "But I can't go anywhere," he said.

We waited on line at the ATM. People stared at him. He put on sunglasses and he kept pulling up his pants around his narrow torso. He was trying to arrange himself properly. He looked like he had been handsome once.

In my bank account I had seventy-three dollars. Some checks were arriving soon, but I had planned to live on the seventy-three and the twenty in my wallet for about a week. I took out forty dollars and gave it to him. I didn't think to get change at a store and give him twenty-eight.

"I feel like I've made a new friend," he said. He gave me his phone number and his name and his roommate's name. He told me that his roommate would give me the forty dollars that night. He told me that sometimes his roommate left the fax machine on so if I called I might hear a beeping sound, but that I should try again later.

I offered to hail him a cab. He said he'd like to walk to Houston Street and get one there; the cool air was making him feel good.

"I'll walk you to Houston," I said.

He put him arm through mine and he held on to me. At Houston, he said he could cross the street by himself and he would get a cab going in the direction of the FDR. I was suspicious, but I didn't insist upon coming across the street with him. He threw his arms around me and hugged me and thanked me. "I'll come visit you," he said, and then he started to cross and I headed back on Avenue A. I told myself that I wouldn't turn around and see if he was really getting a cab. I wanted to trust him *and* I didn't want him to see me being suspicious. And if he was stealing from me, did it really matter? The noble thing would be to not look back.

I made it halfway down the block and turned around. He was nowhere in sight. It seemed unlikely but it was possible that could have already gotten a cab.

I walked home and wasn't sure if I'd ever see that forty dollars. I was left with only fifty-three for the week, but I knew I had a lot of practice at that kind of thing and my refrigerator had some food in it. I thought, too, how I could borrow money from a number of friends if I had to, but I'm sick of doing that and I have too many debts. I got home and put the whole thing out of my mind.

That night I was having dinner at a friend's house. There were four of us: myself, another man (the host), and two women. I told them what happened. One of the women, a painter, a good friend who lives two blocks from me said, "I know that guy. He's come to my door twice. He always says he's your neighbor and he asks for a real specific amount of money. The second time he came I said I was going to call the police and he disappeared fast."

The host said, "Jonathan, you're a New Yorker. What were you thinking?"

My other woman friend said, "You did the right thing. It's only forty dollars. He needed it for *something* . . . The only problem is you might be less giving the next time someone approaches you."

I used my host's phone to call the number the man had given me. I got a fax machine.

When I went home, I was still hoping against all evidence to the contrary that the forty dollars might have been slipped under my door but it wasn't there. And I found out the next day, just to be sure, that no one bearing the man's description lived on the floor below mine.

I was a little angry, but not too bad. The guy was a great actor. It was a great performance: he deserved the money. I had really believed that he would be coming up to my kitchen to visit with me, and I had imagined how I would make him tea and talk with him and it would be a way to be with my friends who have died, who, like the man, were so pitifully devastated toward the end of their lives. I wish I had given more to them.

The man conned me, but still it had been a chance for me to help someone, and I wouldn't have been able to live with myself if I hadn't opened the door to him. So I wasn't broken up about the money, but I did worry, as my friend said, that maybe I was going to be less generous to the next person that came along. But I thought about it and I realized I wouldn't be because of something I did once. Thirteen years ago, I was walking on Fifth Avenue, it was winter, and I was wearing an old army jacket and a black cap and I suddenly decided to sit on the sidewalk and put my palm out. I wanted to see what it was like to beg. I was twenty years old and did things like that. I put my back against a building, pulled my knees to my chest, and lowered my head. My open hand was extended. It was late in the afternoon, around four-thirty. It was cold, but there were a lot of people on the street. I looked at everyone's shoes. I dared to glance up a few times and people would see me for a second or just ignore me all together.

I kept my hand out but I was burning with the most incredible humiliation. I could hardly take it. I didn't know I had so much pride. I wanted to tell people that I was pretending, that I wasn't someone who had to beg. I only sat there for five minutes, no one gave me any money, and then I leaped up and for the first few steps that I took I felt weak and pathetic until I literally shook off the humiliation like some kind of cloak. Ever since, I've given change to almost every person who asks me.

But forty dollars is a lot more than the twenty-five cents I usually give, and the timing wasn't great for me, since I was in between checks, but I think of the man's teeth, how they were like teeth in a skull. He needed the money for *something.*

I Love You More Than That
New York Press, 2000

I went out to Queens to take my great-aunt Pearl to the doctor. I took the G train all the way from where I live in downtown Brooklyn to her neighborhood, Rego Park, which is right next to Forest Hills, which must be right next to Long Island. I always forget the exact geography, but it's way the hell out there. I was on the subway a good fifty minutes, about twenty-three stops. I drank a coffee and read the paper.

I got off at Sixty-third Drive and started walking the several blocks to my great-aunt's building. I was a little hungry and remembered that in my backpack was a bagel with cream cheese I had bought with my coffee but had forgotten about. It was almost one P.M. and I hadn't eaten anything all day. So I started in on the bagel, especially because I knew I'd need strength to get my great-aunt to the doctor's. My blood sugar is all nutty and if it dipped while I was with her I'd be in trouble. She's three-quarters deaf, and when she walks she teeters and careens, even with her cane, and she makes everything worse by being stubborn. She's eighty-eight years old.

So I chewed that life-saving bagel and was thinking about my great-aunt, how she's prideful and brave, but her body is falling apart, getting weaker, and as I often do, I wondered how much longer can she live alone. She won't wear one of those alarm bracelets, and every time I call and she doesn't answer I fear the worse.

The city sends her a woman now who comes Monday through Friday, from nine to one, which leaves my great-aunt alone on the weekends, and so she hardly goes out of her tiny one-room apartment until the woman, Mary, shows up again Monday morning. Then maybe together they'll walk to the library or to a bench or to the market. Mary, who is a sweet Haitian woman in her early forties, has been coming for about a month. My great-aunt needs her very much, but pretends that the city has sent Mary only to help with her housekeeping, that she's a cleaning lady of some sort.

Then, as I kept walking, I wondered who will take care of me if I manage to get old. My son, whom I've been a part-time dad for? He loves me now, but what if that ends? And why should he help me? It's like that Harry Chapin song—and it's terrible when songs are true—but I haven't always had time for my son, and so maybe later he won't have time for me.

So will there be anybody who loves me enough to look after me? And if not, will I be able to pay for someone to take care of me? I have no money at thirty-six; how much will I have at seventy-six?

And so my morbid, self-pitying thinking went, and I was licking the cream cheese, with its fat and its fake white color, out of the corner of my mouth, and just a few bites before this bagel was saving my life, my sugar, but now I thought of it clogging my heart and how I'd pay later for this bagel-with-cream-cheese when I was old and deteriorating and in pain. I saw myself lying on the floor in an apartment in Queens—inherited from my great-aunt? all that I'll be able to afford, her subsidized rent?—paralyzed by a stroke, an aneurysm, a something, just lying there, a thousand bagels-with-cream-cheese my undoing, and I'd pass the time on the floor by thinking how once I could chase girls—I could!—and all the while, too, I'd be hoping that someone would come save me, knock on the door, remember the old man in 6V.

Well, I still ate the whole bagel—the folly of youth. And I passed a lot of old people on the sidewalk. Queens is like one big nursing home. But I was defiant. I ate that bagel! I won't get old! I'll be healthy up until the moment I die!

I rang her buzzer, 6V. The door clicked open. I took the elevator—which often is broken, further trapping my great-aunt in her crowded, antique-filled apartment—to the sixth floor. Mary opened the door. She's a handsome, kind woman. We had met once before.

"I'm glad you could come," she said. "I don't like the way she looks. She's not herself today."

My great-aunt came out of the bathroom. She's tiny, a little less than five feet now, having lost a few inches over the years. I hugged her to my chest as I always do and stroked her reddish-white hair. We parted and she said, repeating the symptoms she had told me over the phone, "I have knitting needles every couple of minutes running from neck, up my head and into my face. Knitting needles. I haven't slept for three days."

"Sounds terrible. We'll see what the doctor thinks," I said.

"What?"

I shouted this time and she caught it. I had called the doctor that morning and got her an appointment by convincing the nurse to let us come in, even though there wasn't an opening until the next day.

Mary had to leave and she and my great-aunt hugged goodbye. "She's sugar," said my great-aunt. I called a taxi. I helped my great-aunt on with her sweater-jacket, and her fingers were too shaky to manage the buttons, so I leaned over her from behind to button it, the way I used to help my son with his jackets when he was very little. We got in the elevator and she almost tripped on the way out—the elevator hadn't stopped even with the floor, it was dangerous, and my vigilance had been lacking, I didn't have her arm.

"I almost fell," she said, nervously. A few years ago, she broke her ankle and she worries about falling again.

We got in the waiting taxi without incident. The doctor was over in Forest Hills, about eight blocks away. It was a quick ride. While I paid the driver—a man with an odd orangish wig; I only saw the back of his head—my great-aunt opened her door and started getting out. "Wait for me," I said.

"I can manage," she said, obstinate.

"Famous last words," said the bewigged cabby.

I got the change, raced out my door and around the cab, and sure enough she was out; she had managed. Disaster averted. I helped her up the curb. "How much did you tip him?" she asked.

"A dollar," I shouted. It had been a four-dollar fare.

"Too much," she said. "A quarter would have been enough. Are you rich?"

I piloted her into the small, shabby office of her doctor.

"I have knitting needles in my head," said my great-aunt to the receptionist.

"Just have a seat, Mrs. Klein," said the woman, using

my great-aunt's married name from the early sixties. She was divorced twice, the first one when her husband came back loony from World War II. Besides her two marriages, she also had many "gentleman-friends" leave their shoes under her bed, as she likes to say. For a long time, she was a manicurist in a barbershop in one of the old men's clubs off of Park Avenue.

We sat down in the waiting room for a few minutes. Two other patients came in—first an ancient Jewish man wearing a yarmulke, a stained yellow shirt, and a wide black tie, and then an old Russian woman, doubled over with osteoporosis.

The receptionist, who was also the nurse, led us into the one consulting room, which had a little closet-like changing area attached to it. I helped my great-aunt with her sweater and shirt and with her back to me she removed her lopsided bra: one cup is filled with foam padding to compensate for the breast lost to cancer fifteen years ago. She put on a blue paper smock and then the nurse and I helped her onto the examining table. It seemed like she would slide off and break something before the doctor got there, but she held on.

The nurse left and I sat on a stool and looked around; the little room was crowded with boxes of insurance forms and there was dust everywhere, the look of neglect. Then the doctor came in: a man in his sixties with a weak chin and bald head, but clear smart eyes, though tired. He examined my great-aunt and he told her things, most of which she didn't hear, so I'd repeat crucial phrases for her; she seems to hear me when she can't hear others. "It's most likely a pinched nerve, probably caused by arthritis," he said.

"What? Did you say a pinched nerve?"

"Yes, a pinched nerve!" I shouted. The doctor looked at me appreciatively.

He checked her lungs, holding the stethoscope to her back, and all over her were little things, brown and dry—how uncomfortable her skin looked. And I admired this doctor, tending to the old, tending to my great-aunt. He wrote her a prescription for anti-inflammatory pills and gave us a sample box, as well, enough for two days. He had her take one of the pills with water. "I know she lives alone," he said to me, and she didn't catch a word. "So don't worry, these won't make her drowsy or groggy. She won't fall down because of them." Then he patted her on the back and left the room.

"A nice man," she said.

She went to get dressed, and called me into the little closet space to hook her bra. Then I buttoned her shirt and helped her with her sweater. "What would I do without you," she said and kissed me.

We left the office and she insisted on walking to a restaurant, where she'd treat me for lunch. She refused to let me get a cab. As we walked, about ten minutes per block, she practiced her Christian Science, as she likes to call it, even though she's Jewish. "I don't have a problem. I don't have a problem," she said, and she walked a couple of steps, feeling proud of herself. "It works!" she said. But then she had an attack of the shooting pains and was flinching on the street, we had to stop our slow walk, and she muttered, "Damn, knitting needles," and then she conceded, "Well, I have a pinched nerve. But at least I don't have arthritis. That's one good thing." I thought it was best not to tell her what she had missed of the doctor's diagnosis.

It took us about forty minutes, but we made it to a diner

on 108th Street—Rego Park's main thoroughfare, which my great-aunt calls "Little Moscow." In addition to being a giant nursing home, Queens is also amazing for its United Nations diversity: on 108th Street, you see the greatest panoply of ethnicities anywhere in New York, it's like an Olympic village, though Russian Jews do predominate.

We got a booth in the diner and she ordered a Coke and a hamburger with raw onion. She ate the whole thing. Thinking of my heart and the cream cheese bagel, I had tuna fish salad and lentil soup.

We were there awhile; she's a slow eater, but finally the meal was over. We hadn't talked much, since I'd have to shout, which isn't so good in a restaurant, but I did ask her at one point, "WHO ARE YOU GOING TO VOTE FOR PRESIDENT?"

"Democrat," she said. "What's his name?"

"GORE."

"Yes, I'll vote for Gore."

She gave me money to pay and told me to leave a one-dollar tip. It was a thirteen-dollar bill. I let her amble out on her own for a few steps and threw another dollar-fifty on the table, then caught up to her. We have this problem with tipping whenever we go out. She still tips taxis a quarter and for all meals she leaves a dollar. Her tipping hasn't kept up with inflation.

We went to a pharmacy and filled her prescription. The beautiful Russian woman behind the counter asked my great-aunt her birthday for the insurance form, and my great-aunt said, "February twenty-second, nineteen-nineteen." I know she was born in 1912; for most of her adult life she's been subtracting a number of years. Even now I guess she prefers people to think her eighty-one instead of eighty-eight, which is not unreasonable.

It took us another thirty minutes to get to her building, about four blocks away, and again she refused to let me get a cab. "Don't make me an old lady!" she said. We stopped on a bench halfway there, so she could rest. She kept getting the knitting needles. I rubbed her neck and watched some twelve-year-old kids play handball in a schoolyard. They were all calling each other "nigger" and "bitch." My great-aunt heard nothing.

We got to her apartment and she was exhausted, trembling. Too much walking. I helped her undress and she got into her narrow bed, which is also her couch. I put the phone on her little night table, but even with the extra-loud ringer, she doesn't always hear it. And then next to the phone, I put a glass of water and the pills the doctor prescribed. Then I kissed her on the cheek and said, "I love you."

"I love you more than that," she said. And then I left the apartment—I had an appointment in the city—and I pulled the door locked behind me. It always feels cruel to leave her. To her and to me. What if I never get to see her again? I always think that maybe this time is the last time. But I steeled myself—you have to walk away from the people you love—and I pushed the button for the elevator so that I could go.

Bice
Cabinet, 2000

When I was a little boy, I liked to pick my nose. In fact, I've enjoyed picking my nose for most of my life. This is not something to be proud of, but telling you about my nose-picking brings me to the word "bice." Perhaps it's not clear how this brings me to bice, but I will try to explain.

The good and clever editors at *Cabinet* asked me to write about a color. I said I would do this. I am a writer and writers usually say yes when editors offer you work. So the idea was that they would choose the color for me and I was to respond. But they didn't give me the color right away, they told me they would call me back in a few days. Fine, I said, and I looked forward to this. I saw it as a version of that classic word association game—the psychiatrist says to you, "Just tell me the first thing that comes to your mind after I give you a word," and then he says, for example, "Cereal" and you say, "Morning," and then he says, "Picnic," and you say, "Apples, no—French kissing," and nobody figures anything out, but the game is fun to play.

So I waited for my color, to which I was going to respond to with immediate first-thought, first-feeling sensitivity and clarity and enthusiasm. I did find myself, though, cheating and mentally preparing my essay in advance, hoping for blue, about which I could write about my grandfather's eyes, or red, the color of my hair, my son's hair, my great-aunt's hair, my grandmother's hair, numerous uncles' and cousins' hair, and I envisioned an essay with the winning title *A Family of Redheads*, or just *Redheads*.

Then the phone call came. The *Cabinet* editor said, "Your color is bice." I was silent, mildly ashamed at a deficient vocabulary, as well as a deficient knowledge of colors. Blue and red were striking me as quite pedestrian now. "Do you need to look it up?" asked the editor. "Don't worry if you do. I didn't know it either. It was my colleague's idea . . . Do you want something easier? Like yellow?"

I felt tempted to say yes. My eyes are often yellow because of a dysfunctional liver, and I immediately thought about how I could write about my liver and about the body's humours. But steeling myself, showing a flinty courage, I said, "No, bice is fine. I have a good dictionary. I'm on it. You can count on a thousand words on bice from me."

We rang off.

I opened my dictionary—it's an *OED* for the field, so to speak; it's about the size of the Bible, as opposed to the colossal, numerous-volumed regular *OED*. I found bice, though, out of curiosity, I checked my *American Heritage Dictionary,* and there was no bice. Good thing I have my *Junior OED*.

What I encountered in the dictionary was this: "pigments made from blue, green, hydrocarbonate of copper; similar pigment made from smalt, etc.; dull shades of blue & green given by these."

Well, my immediate response to bice was straight out of the ethers of my long-ago childhood; it was Proustian; it was tactile; it was visual; it was beautiful, sad, and lonely. It was better than blue or red or yellow. What I saw in my mind's eye, my soul's heart, was the standing, tube-like copper lamp that used to be beside the couch in the living room of the house I grew up in. And every night, I would sit on this couch, in the darkness, alongside this unlighted lamp, and I would watch television all by my very young (six, seven, eight, this went on for years) lonesome yet happy self. I felt a solitary contentment in the darkness watching my programs before dinner, my mother cooking in the kitchen beside the living room, and all the while as I absorbed the stories from the TV and soaked up the radiation from that ancient, large contraption (TVs, like cars, were made uniformly big back then), I would pick and pick my nose and then wipe my small treasures in the tubing and grooves of that long lamp. And no one saw me doing this because I was in the darkness. And the effect of my salty mucus—like sea air on a statue—was that the copper lamp slowly, in streaky spots, turned greenish blue. To everyone but me this was a mystery. "Why is this lamp eroding?" my father would sometimes ponder.

On occasion, showing largesse, I would put my snotty treasures on the underside of the wooden coffee table in front of the couch and our dog Toto, named by my older sister after Toto in the *Wizard of Oz*, would come and bend his red and brown Welsh terrier neck and happily and aggressively lick up the snots. I can still see him in my mind, craning to get under the table. And my parents and relatives would notice this and everyone thought that he must like the taste of wood.

I was clandestine in my actions, but I didn't feel too

much shame about any of this—nose-picking was too much something I had to do. But as I got older, the lamp was looking more and more terrible, and there was talk of throwing it out. I secretly tried to clean it, but the blue-green streaks would not go away. But I didn't want this lamp to be forsaken by my family; things back then, objects, were nearly animate to me, dear even, and to lose a thing from the living room, my special room of TV and darkness, would be terrible, I wanted everything to stay the same forever; and, too, I felt horribly guilty that I was killing this lamp. So I pleaded with my parents on its behalf, told them I loved the lamp, and it wasn't thrown away. With this reprieve, I tried not to wipe my snots on it anymore, to only coat the bottom of the coffee table and feed my beautiful dog, but sometimes I would weaken, and I'd find a new unstreaked spot—I could feel them with my fingers—and so I'd make my mark, my hydrocarbonated snot—there must be hydrogen and carbon in my mucus, all the elements of the world must be in me, in everyone—would mingle with the copper and make a union, a new thing, alchemically, chemically, pigmentally, and that thing was the color bice, a good color, I think, because it has brought back to me that TV and darkened living room and childhood and lamp and coffee table and beloved dog—all things gone a long time ago. All things that didn't last forever.

GERMS!

Open Letters, 2000. Stories for Open Letters, a now-dormant Internet magazine, were to be written in the form of personal correspondence.

December 24, 2000

Dear Lauren,

Yesterday was a germ disaster. Truly incredible. Every time I left the house I was directly splattered with influenza microbes as if my fellow humans were mist-machines and I was an orchid.

The day began happily enough. I slept quite late, moving in and out of dreams, until I finally got out of bed around noon. Then I ejected myself into the world, where I proceeded to have a lovely lunch at Cafe Melange on Atlantic Avenue, dining on a smoked salmon sandwich. My phone-therapist had told me that a daily intake of salmon is good for depression. I found this to be excellent news. As you know, I have put up over the years a legendary resistance to his recommendations about antidepressants, but I embraced this salmon-cure. "The perfect remedy for a Jew like myself," I had said to him. "It makes me wonder if pork is good for depressed Christians. Muslims probably need lamb."

So of late I've been absorbing lox more than usual, since I'm having my annual winter suicidal-ideation fest, brought on by light deprivation and family gatherings.

Anyway, I had enjoyed the first half of my Cafe Melange sandwich, lapping it up like some people gargle Paxil, but I was full and I asked the waiter to please wrap up the remaining half, thinking it would be wise to spread out my dosage across the day. So the waiter carried off my plate and I continued reading my newspaper when suddenly there was a volcanic sneeze. I feared for the worst, and it was the worst that had occurred. I looked up to see my waiter in the after-throes of a nasal explosion, his head turned politely away from my plate—but had he turned in time? Most definitely not! I once saw a science show on PBS which captured, somehow, in slow motion, the distance that the average sneeze travels. I clearly remember seeing on the television—a chilling image that has haunted me for years—thousands of particles flying out of a person's nose and spreading a good fifteen feet in all directions. It turns out that the structure of the average human nostrils, while baring a resemblance to a double-barreled shotgun or twin cannons, has the shooting ability of a Gatling gun: its fire—microbes, not bullets—blankets and decimates everything within 180 degrees.

So, it was clear that my salmon sandwich had been terrifically violated, and there was no way I could eat it now, and this was upsetting on a number of levels:

(1) I had wasted money—I should have cleared my plate. Also, I enjoy eating at Cafe Melange because the prices are reasonable. For $5.95 you get a smoked salmon sandwich, a nice heap of coleslaw, some mixed dark green salad, and a pleasing complement of olives. But now my pleasure at a bargain was destroyed—for $5.95 I had only gotten to eat half a sandwich!

(2) The waiter would think I was nuts if I tried

confront him—very few people saw that PBS sneezing special—and so I felt a pathetic impotence when he brought me back my sandwich neatly wrapped in a little bag. It's like I'm a closet neurotic or something—I should have stood up for myself, for my sandwich. I even carried the thing all the way home and put it in my refrigerator, for some odd reason going through the motions as if I would eat the thing later in the day. Maybe I was trying to lessen the blow. "Act as if," they call it, in New Age circles. But, still, it was very disturbing to think of that pretty sandwich—to all appearances a toothsome bit of nutrition—poisoned by the invisible seasoning of my waiter's microbes.

(3) Lastly, it was depressing to think that I had been deprived of a full dose of salmon; it's not good to play around with one's prescriptions.

Well, after putting the sandwich in the fridge, I crawled into bed and took a nap, which, before I heard about salmon, was my old depression cure. So I had about two hours of midday unconsciousness, and then in the late afternoon, I tried to rally and get some work done, but it was useless. The day a complete waste, mostly because my sandwich had been killed, I then opted for socialization and distraction: in the early evening, I went to see *Cast Away* with a lady friend. It was playing at Union Square and the theater was very crowded and we sat in the balcony.

As soon as the movie started, the young waifish woman next to me, who was dressed like a college undergraduate—jeans, T-shirt, unwashed hair—convulsed three times in a row with sneezes. I scrunched myself into the far corner of my seat, hoping this was just a start-of-the-movie sneezing fit, and I felt slightly cursed, recalling of course the salmon incident just a few hours before, but I had no idea the extent of what I was about to go through. The young woman should have been on a croup ward in a hospital in a Dickens novel. Throughout the whole two-hour-and-twenty-minute movie, she coughed, sneezed, sniffled, choked, wheezed, and noisily reinhaled whatever it was her nose was trying to expel. Like most people of her generation (and my generation, too) she had come unequipped of handkerchief or Kleenex.

I kept trying to shame her into submission and good health by turning my neck violently at her, but she continued to infect me and everyone within miles, all the way down to the Angelika theater. It was maddening. She also had some kind of obsessive-compulsive disorder. She kept rearranging her hair nuttily and three times she took out a jar of moisturizer and rubbed down her face and hands. I looked around for two other seats, but there weren't any nearby, and again I was a bit of a closet neurotic—I didn't want my friend to think I was insane, so I didn't tell her what I was going through and suggest that we find seats somewhere else in the large theater.

Now *Cast Away* has this long quiet stretch in the middle, about forty-five minutes, and thus the horror of sitting next to someone creating such a tubercular racket was compounded.

So I was outraged by this young coed, but I also felt somewhat guilty for all my neck-craning in her direction. Just a week ago, I went by myself to see *Crouching Tiger, Hidden Dragon*, and found the movie's opening action scenes so stimulating that these high-pitched joyful squeals came out of me, which caused this fellow in front of me to whip his head around twice to show me that my reactions were immature and uncalled for. But I didn't agree—the whole audience was moaning with pleasure. It's just that I, being a little more permeable to the effects of cinema, happened to be making extra-loud yelps of rapture. When he did it a third time, trying to wither me with his dead eyes, and then returned his gaze to the screen, I let him have it. I spoke hotly into the back of his head: "Listen," I said, leaning forward with virile intent, "let me enjoy this film. What's the big deal if I make a little noise? So just cool it!"

The action element of the movie had me feeling manly and aggressive, which accounts for my verbal assault, and he didn't turn around the rest of the film. I had put him in his place. But I also became self-conscious and didn't squeal quite as much, though I did give myself credit for a moral victory and tried to fake a few loud squeals to show that I was undaunted. Then after the film, I stood up and stared at his back, ready to give him more verbal karate chops—I wanted to accuse him of being a pencil-necked bourgeois—but he pointedly didn't turn to face me. The coward!

So my numerous attempts to shame the flu-ridden pestilence seated next to me at *Cast Away* did give me some pause as I thought of that snobby fool I had encountered and destroyed, but she really did deserve my craning neck. She should have stayed home and overdosed on some cold remedy. And as a result of her lack of respect for the human community around her, I have no idea if *Cast Away* is any good. I was trying to watch Tom Hanks survive on an island, but my own survival—and this wasn't Hollywood fiction—seemed much more precarious.

When the movie ended, I was sorely tempted to cut her in half with this line: "You really shouldn't have come out tonight!" But I held my tongue and raced out of the theater and into the bathroom to wash my face and hands of her damn splattering. I was as riddled with microbes as Bonnie and Clyde with bullet holes.

So there you have it. My whole depressing report. Now I'm a bit hungry, having worked hard to type this to you, and it occurs to me that I still have that smoked salmon sandwich, and I have this mad compulsion to go eat it. But that must be the suicidal ideation rearing its head again, which, if I look at it is the start of all this anyway: the depression and suicidal ideation led me to salmon, which led to the Cafe Melange episode, which sort of led me to feeling the need to go to the movies. But I still believe in salmon, so I'll go out now, return to Cafe Melange, and get a fresh sandwich to go. The I'll come back here and eat it. Alone. In safety.

Feeling a cough developing in the chest, oh, no . . . but sending my love, and not microbes, though perhaps you should handle this letter with rubber gloves . . . though mentioning this at the end is not fair warning, so I'll jot a note on the envelope, well, big kiss and lots of love, Jonathan

My Body Is Like a House
FEED, 2001

There's always been a lot of talk about writing under the influence of drugs and alcohol. I've never gone in for that myself. When I'm high or intoxicated, I don't have the discipline to sit down at a desk and type something—I'll happily ramble and monologize and be a terrible bore, but I can't sit down and write.

But one time in college I came back to my dorm room around 2 A.M. very stoned and I briefly sat at my desk and penned one line in my journal. It was this: "My body is like a house and I can hear different doors slamming."

Well, because I was stoned, I'd had the munchies about twenty minutes before and so on my way back to my dorm, I had sought out the local twenty-four-hour deli, where I ate a noxious hoagie. This foul sandwich then produced quite a lot of wind and rumbling, and it was because of this gastric turbulence that I jotted down the above line.

Now writers should always peruse their old journals, and so it was several years later that I came across that sentence in my journal and I liked it very much. I put it in my first novel at a crucial, heartbreaking moment to help describe how my character felt after a terrible incident.

When the book came out many people remarked to me that it was a beautiful line. And I have to say that very few other sentences were singled out in this way. Not wanting to spoil people's enjoyment of my art, I never told them that I came up with the line to describe marijuana-munchies-induced flatulence. Better to let them think it was inspired by a higher muse than the lower intestine. But that line does stand out to me—and will always be sort of special—as the one sentence in my small body of writing that I can say was written under the influence.

The Eleventh Commandment
Cabinet, 2001

It is a well-known secret among biblical scholars that there is a missing commandment. The Famous Eleventh. But biblical scholars don't like to talk about this mistake because they don't want people to get upset.

Luckily, though, the Eleventh has been preserved orally for thousands and thousands of years. You'll recognize it immediately. "Wear a Hat!" God commanded Moses on that fateful night in the desert, and then He added, "It's chilly up here on this mountain. Are you looking to get sick?" The reason why this crucial commandment got left off was because Moses, like most people back then and continuing to the present, only had ten fingers. So as God rattled off His Laws, Moses jotted them down on his digits with a leaking desert berry. Taking notes this way was a common practice at the time and is the original source for the term "shorthand."

Well, after all ten fingers were used up, he cribbed on his wrist, "Wear a Hat!" I should point out that most commandments originally had exclamatory remarks, but for some reason stiff-necked grammar teachers have had an unusual prejudice against "!"s and they are practically extinct in literature, though they are trying to make a comeback in comic books. If you think about it, there probably would be a lot less breaking of commandments if "!"s were reinstated. There's a big difference between, "Thou shall not commit adultery" and "Thou shall not commit adultery!" Hear the emphasis? Much more intimidating.

Anyway, after getting everything down with his leaking berry, Moses figured that after God left he would put the Laws on stone tablets for his presentation to the group.

The problem is that Moses forgot about the Eleventh Commandment on his wrist because his baggy robe covered it up. The tablets were done by the time he remembered, and it was too arduous a task to start over. You'll notice that there are a lot of misspellings on stone tablets and in Egyptian tombs for this very reason.

Well, Moses let the people know about the Eleventh, and so the Word spread, but it lacked official weight, having been left off the tablets, and people didn't refer to it as a Commandment. But it did become an underground hit, if you know what I mean. And it's the reason to this day why the Pope, religious Jews, country and western singers, sea captains, and people in cold and warm climates—in essence, all people—wear headgear.

Historically, the most strident oral preservers of this commandment were the females of the Hebrews (genus: "The Jewish Mother"), and the explanation for this is clearly scientific. Females talk more than males because males are too embarrassed in mixed company to say most of what they're thinking, for example: "She's gorgeous. Oh, what I could do to her. I wonder what her boobs look like. I'd love to get my mouth on them. Her ass is a little big, but I like it that way. I just wish I could smell her hair and then mount her."

Thus, the women of Moses' tribe—the more biologically prolix of the two sexes—became oral, walking Torahs, especially when it came to the Missing Eleventh. So for thousands of years, Jewish men, like myself, have listened to their Jewish women—that is to say, wives and mothers, who are essentially the same person according to the latest polls—and we always wear a hat, most noticeably when it's cold out and during Yom Kippur.

Now we've come to the point in the article where I segue from this heady scholarly discussion into what is known as a "personal essay." How one makes such a transition is never easy, and that's why it's best to simply announce it, as I have just done.

So my mother and other females in my family—an intrusive great-aunt named Pearl comes strongly to mind—were always urging me as I grew up to cover my head. Like God when He was scolding Moses, they believed that a chill in the area above the neck will cause infections in the whole system. For example, a sub-commandment to the Eleventh, pointed out by radical Talmudists, is "Don't Go Out with a Wet Head!" And I heard this sub-proclamation from my mother, aunts, great-aunts, and grandmothers almost as much as the Oral Eleventh.

But health- and weather-oriented warnings were not confined solely to the women of my clan. My father had a tremendous respect and terror for all things meteorological. He was a traveling salesman of textile chemicals and his livelihood depended on his ability to navigate, like a sailor but in a car, the roadways of the Eastern Corridor. Naturally, weather conditions were very important to him. So each night before retiring and then first thing in the morning upon awakening, he would listen to his special mustard-colored weather radio. The thing was the size of a paperback novel and it possessed a twelve-inch antenna. It had no dials, you simply pressed a button and out came this staticy, nonsensical ticker tape of weather conditions, read most likely by some rotating shift of prisoners at the white-collar federal penitentiary in Lewisburg, Pennsylvania.

I make this conjecture because no person of their own volition could possibly want to read a weather report non-stop for hours at a time. Clearly, it was a depressing job— one could hardly understand what the announcer was saying, the voice was always so deadpan and defeated, though my father was enraptured by these broadcasts and would sit on the edge of his bed in an attentive stupor. I can tell you it wasn't healthy for the young me to see my father like that all the time—children of alcoholics will appreciate, I believe, this kind of early wounding.

So because of his brainwashing at the hands of this weather radio, my father, with great foreboding in his voice, would make announcements to the family, like, "It's going to rain on Thursday!" This kind of thing would usually be stated on a Monday, and I—a mere child of four or five—would be frightfully agitated until that rainfall occurred four days later, by which time, I would have learned from my father that "temperatures are going to drop on Sunday!" There was never a calm moment. I grew up in a constant state of atmospheric peril. The women were telling me to cover my head and my father was telling me that the sky was falling. It did make for a nice synergy, though. It's called anxiety.

So mine was clearly a sheltered upbringing. I didn't know until I was in college that people drove in the rain. And even in snow! To me, this was a revelation, and I became rather rebellious. My freshman year at Princeton, I purposely would go motoring at night during snow flurries.

"I am not my father's son!" I would think triumphantly, as the snowflakes were like white stars in the black sky.

One night, though, during some heavy flurries (I wasn't so rebellious that I'd go out in an actual storm), I did skid and damaged a parked car. I tried to escape, but was spotted by a man walking his dog. In snow flurries! He was obviously a hardy gentile. Police were involved. It cost me a lot of money in fines and reparations. So it just goes to show you that the sins of the father are visited on the sons. If I hadn't been trying so hard not to be fearful like my dad, I wouldn't have scratched that poor innocent parked car.

And I am still in a state of rebellion against my father. Whenever I go home for a visit (traveling by train from New York to New Jersey), I'll call a few days beforehand, and I will say to my dad, "I'll be home on Friday and head back Sunday."

"They're calling for freezing rain on Saturday," he'll say, with the utmost gravity, even though my travel days— by train!—are Friday and Sunday. But in his mind, damaged by that radio of his, any bad weather within twenty-four hours of travel is to be feared.

"Well, let's start worrying about it now," I'll say snidely, rebelliously, and things will be bad between us before I'm even home.

This rebel side of my personality may sound healthy to you—declaring my independence and all that—and perhaps it is, but I have an unhealthy side when it comes to the way I was raised around the issue of weather. Every January and February, because of repressed childhood worry about storms or even humidity, I have Seasonal Affect Disorder (what's known, curiously enough, as SAD) These repressed feelings, usually kept under control ten months out of the year, are let out when I am weakened by a lack of sunlight. Every year I do say I'm going to buy one of those special UV lamps, but I'm always too depressed to go shopping. And then when the depression lifts, I forget about it until next January and by then it's too late to get a lamp because the depression is back. Life can be difficult this way.

So during these depressing months of January and February, I suffer from suicidal ideation and too much sex with self. I spend a lot of time in bed thinking about how different writers have committed suicide and I go over which method I might try—Hart Crane's steamship, Hemingway's shotgun, Plath's oven, Kosinski's plastic bag. But after indulging for a while in these morbid fantasies a surge of life force announces itself. One can only spend so much time in bed before the old hand sneaks down and starts to fondle.

The fondling then completely overtakes the suicidal ideation and I feel pretty good. I have company! It's hard to be depressed when there are others around—my mind is peopled with a variety of Hollywood starlets and local waitresses. A bottle of champagne is presented. There's lots of kissing and bouncing on knees and cries of endearment, like, "Put it in me!" That sort of thing. And this wonderful grand party lasts all of forty-five seconds. The old blasted hand knows too well what it's doing. "Don't go, girls!" I want to cry out, but they vanish, fleeing my mind, no longer interested in me. The champagne is spilled.

After that there's about five seconds of a sort of brain death. I feel quiet. Pax, as if I had taken too much Paxil. But then consciousness returns and demands that somebody clean up the party's mess. "Oh, God," I then think, searching for a towel. "This has been going on for twenty years. I'm pathetic. A lifetime of masturbation. I should just kill myself."

Depression, they say, is cyclical. And this is an obvious example of it. I start out wanting to die, then I want to live—the starlets! the waitresses!—and then I want to die again. I find this very annoying. Luckily, I only have to endure this every January and February.

But there is something that threatens my well-being for all twelve months. Far worse than Seasonal Affect Disorder is having Bush as President. I think he's more damaging than sun-muting winter skies. He's like an eclipse. Every time I think of him in office I lose serotonin. I will dub this syndrome: Bush Affect Disorder. And it's going to last, I'm afraid, for four years, and maybe eight. This is very, very BAD. No wonder he's so into prescription drugs. I'm sure he's in the pocket of the pharmaceutical companies. Antidepressant profits during his administration are going to skyrocket! I'm very angry about this, but my anger has no outlet, and they say that swallowed anger becomes depression, like the way beans become trapped gas. So I'm bloated with anger. Bloated with depression.

Well, we're at the point now in the essay where I tie this all together. Of course, just as with the transition I mentioned several paragraphs ago, this can be difficult. In fact, it's so difficult, I'm not sure I can pull it off. I will tell you that it's mid-February and it's freezing out, and because I'm depressed and sad I'm going to the movies in half an hour. To get to the movies, I have to walk. So I'm going to bundle myself up and I'm going to wear a hat. Rather, I should say, I'm going to wear a hat! And I'll say the same to you—and please pass it on, you'll be doing God's work—WEAR A HAT!

A Boy's Guide to Drinking and Dreaming

Post Road, 2001. Post Road, each
issue, asks writers to recommend a
book or books.

*Below are the books and the authors who shaped me into the man
I am today. So this is actually an anti-recommendation list, and
best aimed at the parents of young boys. Keep these books out of
your sons' hands! That is unless you want them to end up like
me: Thirty-six years old (well, at least they won't die too young,
but it is risky) with a deteriorating, patchy hairline, no savings
or financial security, and suffering from sporadic, destructive
tippling. There are other complaints, too, like constricted bowels,
religious agnosticism (which gives a person absolutely no solace),
and emotional immaturity. I hope I have scared you sufficiently.
These books should come with a Physician's Warning and a
sticker: Keep Out of the Reach of Children.*

This list of books will follow the chronological order
with which I read these dangerous texts and I will make
brief descriptive comments. I should mention there won't
be a single female author, which is not good or politically
correct, but I am being honest when I say that the books
which have truly shaped me have all been written by
men, which is probably why I'm such a mess, but this is
not to say that I haven't enjoyed the work of women—I
have; it's just that no woman writer has presented me with

a role model, and that's what this list is about, the books from which I've tried, over the years, to cull a misshapen identity.

(You have to understand, I would study author photographs to try to figure out how to dress; see I was looking for a father figure; I had one in my own house, but, like many people, I was stupidly looking for another one, and as you'll see I did find Papa . . . So all this to say that I love many women writers, but I never wanted *to be*—despite rumors to the contrary—a woman writer or one of their female or male protagonists.)

Here's the list:

1) In the seventh grade, I was given the first in the series of the *Tarzan* books by my seventh-grade teacher. I went on to read about twenty of them, though I believe Edgar Rice Burroughs produced thirty or more novels chronicling the adventures of the "Lord of the jungle." These books inspired me to be fit and alert: to be like an animal, to be like Tarzan. When my mother would wake me in the morning, I would try to leap out of bed, because there was a description how Tarzan would immediately gain complete consciousness upon awakening. And I wanted to have muscles like the ones he had in the incredible drawings on the front covers—sinews of iron was how they were always described. And I wanted to be able to fly through trees and I wanted to love one woman, like Jane, forever.

2) In the seventh grade, I also devoured all of J. R. R. Tolkien, and I often fantasized that I was Aragorn son of Arathorn, who was the greatest swordsman in Middle Earth and destined to be King. I ran around the woods

near my house, brandishing long sticks, like they were sabres, and then at dinner with my parents, I would keep on pretending that I was Aragorn—at a Tolkienesque Elfin feast, and this made my mother's cooking, which was pretty good, even better. And later, in high school, when I was on the fencing team, I still pretended that I was Aragorn.

3) Sophomore year in high school, I read all of Kurt Vonnegut's work. This opened my innocent eyes to the fact that the world was an imperfect and nutty place, and I found out that other people had strange sexual thoughts, which was comforting.

4) Junior year, I read Hunter S. Thompson's *Fear and Loathing in Las Vegas* and became editor of my school paper. I drove drunk a lot, filled my tires with too much air to make them too fast, which was what Thompson's alter ego did, and I would wear a dark cap and sunglasses while doing research for my newspaper articles—I was aspiring to a Thompsonish costume. My friends called me Hunter.

5) Senior year, I read Jack Kerouac's *On the Road* and this began a many-year obsession with searching for "it" and hitchhiking. I sometimes would tell strangers that my name was Jack and would sign hotel registers, Jack Kerouac. One time, in the summer of 1986 when I was twenty-two and naive and living in New York for the summer and very much in my Kerouac-wannabe mode, I went to an Asian spa, believing the ad I saw in the *Village Voice*, which said that you could get a steam bath and a massage for twenty dollars. The spa was in an old walk-up building on

Twenty-third Street, across from Madison Park, and I climbed three narrow flights of stairs. In the front room of the spa, I paid my twenty dollars, which was all the money I had with me, to an old gray-haired Chinese woman. There was one young, beautiful frail girl in that front room and she led me down a hall to a room with a bed. There was no steam bath, which sort of annoyed me, but I was expecting to at least get my massage, but the girl told me I had to give her one hundred dollars for sex. She spoke English with a thick, slow accent and I told her I didn't want sex, just a massage. She started to cry, saying she would get in trouble; it was her first week working there. There was nothing I could do, I showed her my empty wallet, and then for some reason she stopped crying, had me lie down and she curled up behind me and held me. I kept my clothes on and she stayed in her skimpy dress. She asked me my name. I told her it was Jack. We lay there for about ten minutes, with her kissing my neck; then she had us reverse and I held her for several minutes, kissing her sweet neck. Then there was a knock on the door and she said I had to go. She walked me to the front door and came out to the top of the stairs with me. Away from her boss, the old lady, she kissed me on the lips. It was the oddest thing. I didn't know why she was being so tender with me; I could only guess that she was relieved at not having to have sex. I started to walk down the long, steep staircase. She stayed at the top, watching me, very beautiful and very young. I turned around and waved and she said, in her thick accent, "Goodbye, Jack. Please come back." She seemed unaware of the rhyme she had just made and I waved again and left. As I walked home, I felt bad that I had lied to her about my name, and that was the last time I impersonated Jack Kerouac.

6) Amid the long-running love affair with Kerouac—though I only read *On the Road* and *Dharma Bums*, but I was always looking at pictures of him in biographies and feeling heartbroken that he had been so beautiful and drank himself to death—I had flirtations with Hemingway and Fitzgerald. *The Sun Also Rises* inspired me, when I was twenty, to leave school for a year and to go live in Paris and get in a bar fight with a large Frenchman and have my nose broken. That book also compelled me to travel to Spain to watch a bullfight, which I didn't enjoy at all—it seemed so unfair, the bull didn't have a chance. Fitzgerald's *This Side of Paradise*, which I absorbed my senior year in college, drove me to buy a used white dinner jacket, which I wore to many parties, until I vomited on it and destroyed it.

7) So those three, Kerouac, Hemingway, and Fitzgerald, carried me through my early twenties, and then in my mid-twenties, I read Thomas Mann's *The Magic Mountain* and tried to major in Germanic—despite being Jewish—neurasthenia, like Mann's hero, Hans Castorp. So I went around in sport coats, morbid, but well dressed, like a proper young Hamburg gentleman. And I would take many naps and go for long restorative walks, which I thought were good for my tissues. I was always trying to make my life and my world quiet like I was living in a sanitarium and I was there for a cure. My friends called me Hans.

8) Then in my late twenties and early thirties, returning to my more predictable, American college-campus, cult role-model choices, I ate up the work of Charles Bukowski and like him, got a newspaper column, where I tried to be as

honest and as dirty as he had been. He talked about liking women's legs and asses and so I did the same thing. I did this because I knew his column and all his writings with their sexual frankness brought him a good deal of attention from women, despite his ravaged face, and so I hoped that my column, despite my ravaged bald head, might have the same effect. I think it was a better formula for Bukowski than for myself. I repelled more than I attracted. Also, it occurs to me that by the time he started writing his column he was in his fifties and had already destroyed his life from years of the bottle and working at the post office, so it didn't matter what he wrote. He was freed up to be as honest as he liked. To hell with the world. But I was only in my early thirties when I started my column and hadn't yet earned the right to be honest, hadn't yet destroyed myself, but what I was writing, by defaming my name, was very likely to.

9) In my mid-thirties, just about the present, I became obsessed with the novels of Graham Greene and whilst traveling, which seems a very Greeneish thing to do, I sometimes privately refer to myself as Graham Greenberg, trying to meld my Jewish faith with yet another love affair with a Gentile writer. Quite recently, though, the Greene phase has begun to wane, and I'm not sure who I am these days. I wonder if I read my own books, which I have never done, if I might start to model myself after myself. It may be, as they used to say in Hollywood, the role I've been waiting for.